THE ROLE of GOVERNMENT
in MONITORING and REGULATING
RELIGION in PUBLIC LIFE

THE ROLE of GOVERNMENT in MONITORING and REGULATING RELIGION in PUBLIC LIFE

JAMES E. WOOD, JR.
& DEREK DAVIS, Editors

J.M. DAWSON INSTITUTE OF CHURCH-STATE STUDIES

Baylor University • Waco, Texas 76798-7308

Published by the J.M. Dawson Institute of Church-State Studies
Baylor University
Waco, Texas 76798-7308
USA

THE ROLE OF GOVERNMENT
IN MONITORING AND REGULATING
RELIGION IN PUBLIC LIFE

Address correspondence to
J.M. Dawson Institute of Church-State Studies
P.O. Box 97308, Baylor University, Waco, Texas 76798 USA

FIRST EDITION 1993

Library of Congress Cataloging-in-Publication Data
Preassigned Catalog Card Number: 92-74168

International Standard Book Numbers:
ISBN 0-929182-17-0(CLOTH)   ISBN 0-929182-18-9(PAPER)

Prepared camera ready by the publications staff of J.M. Dawson Institute of
Church-State Studies using Mass-11 TM Version 8.0 © Microsystems
Engineering Corporation on Vax 8700 minicomputer by Digital
Equipment Corporation printing to Varityper VT600W using Palatino
typeface. The latter is trademarked by Allied Corporation. Software
licensed to Baylor University.

Contents

PREFACE

The role of government in monitoring and regulating religion in public life is a subject that deserves serious and thoughtful analysis, both because of its increasing pattern in American church-state relations in which government jurisdiction is extended over religious affairs and because of the threat that government intervention brings to the free exercise of religion. While there are those who may be inclined to argue against any form of government intervention in religious affairs, the reality is otherwise. No matter what one's personal view(s) may be on the matter, the fact is that government is involved, and increasingly so, in monitoring and regulating the role of religion in American public life, an involvement that is inexorably linked with the growth of government into almost all areas of human endeavor, and, ironically, with the growth of religion in public life.

Among the many varied questions that inevitably arise concerning the role of government in monitoring and regulating religion are the following: Should organized religion generally be subject to government monitoring and regulation? What boundaries or guidelines are to be drawn in determining the extent of government monitoring and regulating of religion? Wherein does government's monitoring and regulating religion threaten the constitutional guarantee of the free exercise of religion? Should government have the right to deny, or even to limit, the advocacy role of religious bodies in public affairs in order to maintian their statutory privilege of tax exemption? These are among the many questions addressed in this volume.

This volume, as in the case of its companion volume, *The Role of Religion in the Making of Public Policy*, includes essays expressly prepared for a symposium held at Baylor University under the auspices of the J. M. Dawson Institute of Church-State Studies. The essays in the present volume were prepared for presentation at the symposium on "The Role of Government in Monitoring and Regulating Religion in Public Life," 13-14 April 1992. The symposium was held at a time of increasing concern over the intervention of government in religious affairs, the virtual elimination of the "compelling interest" test in adjudicating the Free Exercise Clause, and the presumed right of government to monitor and regulate religion in its institutional and public life.

While the essays in this volume were originally prepared for presentation at a symposium under the theme of the volume's title, they have been revised and expanded for publication in this volume and, therefore, are original essays that have not been published elsewhere.

The symposium at which these essays were presented was highlighted by a keynote address delivered by United States Supreme Court Justice Antonin Scalia. His stimulating and thoughtful address, "The Supreme Court's Perspective on the Free Exercise of Religion," was attended by approximately 500 persons. Registrants for the symposium included Catholics, Jews, a wide variety of Protestants, and representatives of the National Council of Churches, the Christian Science Church, the General Conference of Seventh-Day Adventists, the Church of Scientology, the Church of Jesus Christ of Latter-day Saints, the Lutheran Institute for Religious Studies, Americans United for Separation of Church and State, the National Association of Independent Colleges and Universities, the Association of Southern Baptist Colleges, and the Association of Catholic Colleges and Universities. Also attending were educators from approximately thirty colleges and universities, as well as a number of attorneys, judges, and nonaffiliated scholars.

Special acknowledgment is made here to the authors for their thoughtful presentations at the symposium and for their special preparation of the insightful essays for inclusion in this volume. In addition, appreciation is expressed to Robert M. Baird, Rosalie Beck, James A. Curry, David M. Guinn, David W. Hendon, Glenn O. Hilburn, David L. Longfellow, Robert T. Miller, Harold W. Osborne, Bob E. Patterson, Stuart Rosenbaum, and Charles M. Tolbert for assisting in various ways in the planning and convening of the symposium; to Wanda Gilbert and Janice Losak for their contributions in the promotion of and registration for the symposium; to Carol Crawford for research assistance; and to Brandon S. Mann for preparation of the index for this volume. A very special word of gratitude is expressed here to Patricia Cornett for her editorial assistance and for creating the camera-ready copy for publication of this volume.

The editors are particularly grateful to The Pew Charitable Trusts for their grant to assist the J. M. Dawson Institute of Church-State Studies of Baylor University in convening the symposium and publishing this volume; their generous support is deeply appreciated and gladly acknowledged.

James E. Wood, Jr.
Derek Davis

Baylor University
Winter 1993

1

Government Intervention in Religious Affairs: An Introduction

JAMES E. WOOD, JR.

The theme of this volume revolves around the question of the role of government in monitoring and regulating religion in public life. Indeed, many would argue that a more fundamental question is whether government should have any role whatsoever in monitoring and regulating religion in public life. No matter what one's personal view may be on this matter, the fact is that government is involved in monitoring and regulating the role of religion in American public life and this role is one that is ever increasing with the growth of government in almost all areas of human endeavor.

I

For more than two decades, government intervention in religious affairs has been a recurring pattern in American church-state relations. For many, it has become the dominant trend and the most crucial single issue facing the churches in their involvement in public affairs and in their relationship to government. Unfortunately, the problem is one which is not only far from resolution but one which must be described as a growing trend in American church-state relations. The trend is one which was characterized at the beginning of the last decade as a "mounting crisis in American church-state relations."[1]

Fifteen years ago, the Governing Board of the National Council of Churches authorized a study of the increasing "governmental intervention in the internal affairs of the churches." Similarly, a year later the National Conference of Catholic Bishops created a committee to be known as "The Bishops' Ad Hoc Committee on Church-Government Issues." Further recognition of the problem of government intervention in religious affairs was dramatically expressed in the convening of a conference in Washington, D.C. in February 1981 on the theme, "Government Intervention in Religious Affairs," under the joint sponsorship of the National Council of Churches, the United States Catholic Conference, the Synagogue Council of America, the National Association of Evangelicals, the Lutheran Council in the United States, and the Southern Baptist Convention. Representatives of over 90 percent of America's religious denominations participated in the conference, characterized as "possibly the most inclusive gathering of religious groups ever assembled [in the United States] and emphasizing the importance of this issue."[2] Several years later, a second conference was held with the same theme, again with the same joint sponsorship. It was characterized as "one of the most comprehensively ecumenical assemblies in the history of the United States."[3] The very inclusiveness of the sponsorship and the wide range of representatives of religious groups in these two conferences bear clear witness to the seriousness with which America's religious bodies have come to view the role of government in religious affairs.

Government intervention in religious affairs continues to constitute a serious threat to both the prophetic role of religion and the constitutional guarantee of "the free exercise of religion." The problem is particularly acute to those religious groups which throughout their history have espoused and sought to maintain an institutional separation of church and state and an advocacy role in public affairs— without accountability to government or the threat of governmental reprisal for being faithful to their religious mission.

This is not to suggest that government should maintain a hands-off posture toward religion, or that the relationship of religious bodies toward government should be one of complete independence from the jurisdiction of government, or one primarily of conflict and confrontation. Indeed, few would deny that there is a legitimate role to be played by government in monitoring and regulating religion, but one would hope that it be an extremely limited one and not without probable cause. In the modern nation-state, except for perhaps a few religious communities which maintain a life of almost complete withdrawal from society and the emergence in the twentieth century of nation-states that expressly prohibit the involvement of religion in society, the affairs of church and state are admittedly never mutually exclusive. While there is meaning and significance to be found in the phrase "separation of church and state" in the American experience and in American jurisprudence, the history of American church-state relations is one of interaction between the institutions of religion and government. The tremendous growth of the institutions of religion and the institutions of government have, however, profoundly changed the patterns of church-state relations in American life. Never before have so many of the functions of the institutions of church and state converged and overlapped as they do today.

The emergence of the growing trend of government intervention in religious affairs may be readily explained as the result of several factors. As alluded to earlier, there is the unprecedented growth of organized religion, with membership in religious denominations reaching the highest proportion of the population, since 1940 in excess of 50 percent, in the history of the Republic. Beyond the growth in membership in proportion to the population, there is also the vast network of agencies and educational and welfare institutions maintained throughout the nation by a wide variety of religious bodies. These agencies and institutions have become increasingly subject to governmental regulations and statutory requirements mandated by established public policy. In addition, the present century has seen the development of denominational offices on public affairs, with broad agendas and maintained by professional staffs, that seek to influence legislation and the formulation of public policy on a wide variety of public issues. This activity, however, is always subject to the potential loss of a religious group's tax exemption should the activity in public affairs fail to meet the test of "substantiality." All of this occurs at a time when there has been the enormous growth of government in education, medical care, and welfare services in which religion has historically played a pioneering and substantial role.

The phenomenal growth of institutional religion and institutional government has inevitably brought new problems and tensions, often resulting in open conflicts between the organs of religion and the organs of government. Just as the Founding Fathers could not possibly have envisioned the extraordinary growth of government with its vast network of social and welfare services and regulatory agencies, so the founders of America's religious denominations in colonial America and during the early history of the republic could not possibly have envisioned the unprecedented growth of organized religion with its manifold agencies and institutions engaged in educational and welfare ministries throughout American society. That problems of the relationship between church and state have been both exacerbated and multiplied during this century should come as no surprise, even if one were virtually to ignore the unmistakable impact of the growth of America's religious pluralism on church-state relations in the United States. The role of religion in public affairs and the role of government in religious affairs have inevitably been matters of intense and heated debates, with many interpretations and ramifications.

II

The problem of government intervention in religious affairs is of particular concern in the United States in view of the religion clauses of the First Amendment. It has long been widely held that the purpose of the Establishment Clause is "to prevent the domination of the state by the church or domination of the church by the state."[4] While the concern of the Founding Fathers was primarily over the possible domination of the state by the church, today there is increasing concern not so much over the domination of the state by the church as over the domination of the church by the state. In recent decades, the ever-expanding role of government has been inevitably accompanied by a marked pattern of increased government intervention in religious affairs.

In the United States, concerns in church-state relations arise out of particular concepts of the church and the state; namely the concept of a religious body as a voluntary association enjoying institutional independence from the state. By institutional independence Americans have meant voluntary associations of religion— free of government control, supervision, and financial support, comprised of persons affiliated with the religious denomination of their choice. Americans' particular understanding of the state is that of a free state, secular in that government is limited to the world of the temporal, of the *seculum*, one in which the state maintains a neutrality, albeit a benevolent one, toward religion and irreligion and the people have excluded civil authority from religious affairs. This view was well enunicated by the United States Supreme Court one hundred and twenty years ago in its first church-state decision based upon the First Amendment, in *Watson v. Jones*:

In this country the full and free right to entertain any religious belief, to practice any religious principle, and to teach any religious doctrine which does not violate the laws of morality and property, and which does not infringe personal rights, is conceded to all. The law knows no heresy, and is committed to the support of no dogma, the establishment of no sect. The right to organize voluntary religious associations to assist in the expression and dissemination of any religious doctrine, and to create tribunals for the decision of controverted questions of faith within the association, and for the ecclesiastical government of all the individual members, congregations and officers within the general association, is unquestioned.[5]

With the phenomenal growth of government in this century, both federal and state, and the ever-expanding role of government in the private sector, a recurring question increasingly arises as to the role of government in monitoring and regulating religion. It is a question which arises particularly in the context of the first sixteen words of the First Amendment, in which two prohibitions are categorically placed on government: "Congress shall make no law respecting an establishment of religion or prohibiting the free exercise thereof." While the language used in reference to the Establishment Clause and the Free Exercise Clause is unequivocal, the interpretations and applications given these clauses are manifestly otherwise. Any presumed institutional independence of religion and government in the United States must take into account the ever increasing role of government in monitoring and regulating religion throughout American society. Unlike Western Europe, where ecclesiastical law is an important part of the body of law, there is the absence of ecclesiastical law in the United States in the light of the First Amendment.

Nonetheless, there is the persistent question of the monitoring and regulating of religion as to compliance with civil and criminal law. While not new to the American scene, government intrusion into religious affairs has become in recent decades one of the most crucial issues facing the churches and synagogues in public affairs and in the relationship of organized religion to government. The problem is one which is far from resolution and one which likely will plague America's religious denominations throughout the final decade of this century.

As noted earlier, the increasing attempts of intrusion on the part of government into religious affairs constitutes a serious threat both to the free exercise of religion and the prophetic role of religion in public affairs. "The free exercise of religion," long regarded in the American experience as essential to the identity and integrity of the churches and synagogues and the cornerstone of their witness in public affairs and in society at large, is increasingly threatened by lobby disclosure legislation, potential loss of tax exemption, discrimination based on one's religion and thereby the denial of equality of all religions under the law, and the increasing enforcement of compliance with government regulations and statutes in the absence of any "compelling interest" test. The increased attempts by government to demand accountability of churches and synagogues to government, both in the way of financial records and disclosures of the nature and degree of the witness of the churches and synagogues in public affairs, add further to the concern of many as to the role of government in monitoring and regulating religion in American society.

III

In recent years, state and federal governmental agencies have repeatedly taken actions that have followed a pattern of government intervention in religious affairs. Whether viewed as inevitable or legitimate, these actions by government agencies to claim jurisdiction over religious organizations and institutions have brought greater intervention in religious affairs and some adjustments, if not conflicts, with the judicial interpretations of the free exercise of religion. Unlike constitutions of authoritarian governments, the American Constitution places limitations on government, and none on religion. Although religion has never enjoyed the right of a carte blanche of non-compliance with American civil and criminal law, many exceptions have been accorded religion in the enactment of federal and state laws based upon the guarantees of the religion clauses of the First Amendment.

In adjudicating the Free Exercise Clause, the United States Supreme Court set forth two judicial standards for regulating actions based upon religious beliefs: the "compelling interest" and the "alternate means" tests. The first specific Supreme Court case to "balance" freedom of religion with compelling public or state interest came in 1944, in *Prince v. Commonwealth of Massachusetts*, in which the Court upheld a state child labor law and denied the right of a Jehovah's Witness to have her nine-year-old niece accompany her in selling religious literature on the street. The Court did so, in the words of Justice Wiley Rutledge, in order to uphold the prior claim of "the interest of society to protect the welfare of the children."[6] In using the "compelling interest" test the Court sought to determine whether or not the state's interest in the application of a particular law was weightier than the individual conscience, as in time of war.

Up until the *Smith* decision of 1990,[7] the Court was inclined to require the state to convince the courts that the "interest" it seeks to protect is greater than the rights that are involved in "the free exercise of religion." Thus, in accord with this reasoning, the Court in the 1972 case of *Wisconsin v. Yoder* held that Amish parents would not be prosecuted for refusing to send their children to school after the age of fourteen. "Only those interests of the highest order," the Court declared, "and those not otherwise served can overbalance the legitimate claim to the free exercise of religion."[8]

Coming almost two decades after the "compelling interest" test, the "alternate means" test was first applied by the Court in 1963, in *Sherbert v. Verner*,[9] to invalidate the denial of unemployment compensation by the State of South Carolina to Adell Sherbert, a Seventh-Day Adventist, because she refused to work on Saturday. The state's unwillingness to find "alternate means" readily available to it, the Court said, imposed a religious burden on the appellant in that it forced her to choose between following her religious convictions and, thus, forefeiting her unemployment compensation or abandoning her religious principles in order to accept employment. "Only the gravest abuses," the Court said, "endangering paramount interest, give occasion for permissible limitation" of the free exercise of religion.[10] The *Sherbert* doctrine was reaffirmed in two similar cases in the 1980s, *Thomas v. Review Board of the Indiana Employment Security Division* and *Hobbie v. Unemployment Appeals Commission of Florida.*[11]

With the United States Supreme Court decision of 17 April 1990, in *Employment Division of Oregon v. Smith*,[12] the Court ruled that a valid law no longer has to demonstrate a compelling interest in order to require its enforcement even if that law is in conflict with a religious practice. No longer, according to the Court's ruling, need a state or government make an exception to the enforcement of such a law on the basis of the free exercise of religion. No longer need a state accommodate its laws to the religious convictions and practices of a particular religion or its adherent. As Professor Angela C. Carmella indicates in her essay in this volume, the *Smith* decision represents the culmination of a trend during the past decade in which "the deference accorded to religious conduct has been drastically narrowed" and it has been made "increasingly easy for the state to show the ascendancy of its interests."[13]

In *Smith*, the Court ruled that compliance with a law may *not* be conditioned upon a person's religious convictions except where there is a compelling state interest. "To make an individual's obligation to obey such a law," the Court said, "contingent upon the law's coincidence with his religious beliefs, except where the State's interest is 'compelling'—permitting him, by virtue of his beliefs, 'to become a law unto himself' . . . contradicts both constitutional tradition and common sense."[14] In a sweeping conclusion in which the "compelling state interest" test is virtually eliminated from the Free Exercise Clause, Justice Antonin Scalia wrote, "Precisely because 'we are a cosmopolitan nation made up of people of almost every conceivable religious preference' [*Braunfeld*] . . . and precisely because we value and protect that religious diversity, we cannot afford the luxury of deeming *presumptively invalid*, as applied to the religious objector, every regulation of conduct that does not protect an interest of the highest order."[15] Protection of the free exercise of religion does not require, the Court said, religious exemptions from "civic obligations."[16] These are permissible, but are not constitutionally required, the Court concluded.

As a result of the Court's decision in *Smith*, exemption of religion from compliance with a valid law is entirely dependent on the will of government or the legislature and need not be concerned with the constraints of the Free Exercise Clause. Without statutory exemption, any free exercise claim of exemption to "valid and neutral laws of general applicability" is automatically denied. Based on the reasoning of *Smith*, such a law may be enforced even when it is in violation of sincerely held religious beliefs and practices without any consideration being given to the compelling interest test.

While the impact of the *Smith* decision still cannot be fully known, it is clear that on the basis of the Court's ruling in this case an increased authority is given to the state and the force of the Free Exercise Clause is diminished. Without any real basis for exemption given to the free exercise of religion, the majority opinion in *Smith* gives to the state the right to force compliance with all its valid laws without any balancing of the claims of the free exercise of religion with a compelling state interest. As a result, the Free Exercise Clause is abridged and the authority of the state over the free exercise of religion is increased.

IV

The prior claim of government authority over a claim of the free exercise of religion in the enforcement of religiously neutral laws extends far beyond the *Smith* decision. As stated at the outset of this essay, government intervention in religious affairs has been a recurring pattern for more than two decades. Nowhere is this trend more evident than in government regulations issued and legislation introduced directly affecting religious agencies and institutions. These rulings and legislation often have profound implications with regard to the relationship of these religious agencies and institutions to government as well as to the religious bodies to which these agencies and institutions are related.

Many examples may be cited of increasing government intervention in religious affairs. In the two volumes cited earlier, *Government Intervention in Religious Affairs* (1982) and *Government Intervention in Religious Affairs, II* (1986), proceedings of two widely representative conferences of national religious bodies in the United States, two dozen examples of government intervention in religious affairs were cited and many of them were critically examined in some detail and made the focus of entire essays in each volume. The well-documented essays in this present volume give ample evidence that the present role of government in monitoring and regulating religion in public life has not diminished. While it is not appropriate or possible to provide a catalogue of examples here, since various essays in this volume focus on a number of these, some additional examples which are not given primary attention in the following essays deserve at least some brief mention.

Perhaps at no point has the church's institutional independence been more seriously threatened than in efforts in the Congress to enact lobby disclosure legislation that would require religious bodies to register with and report to government officials virtually any contacts or efforts undertaken to influence the establishment of any public policy or any proposed legislation. Lobby disclosure legislation introduced in the One Hundred Third Congress, as in the past, includes any oral or written communication to a legislative or executive official aimed at influencing federal legislation, regulation, policy, or executive order. As in previous lobby disclosure legislation, the present legislation includes grassroots lobbying as well as lobbying of federal office holders. Any exclusion of religious bodies is yet to be determined.[17] The question of the inclusion of religious groups in lobby disclosure legislation raised here is quite distinct from the question of the limitations imposed on their advocacy role in public affairs in order to enjoy tax exemption.[18] If ever enacted, the inclusion of religious groups in lobby disclosure legislation would have a seriously inhibiting effect on their work and witness in public affairs. The effect of such legislation would be to require that almost any organized or organizational efforts in public affairs be accountable to and come under the close scrutiny of the federal government.

While the rationale for such legislation has been generally justified as being in the "public interest," the inclusion of churches and synagogues in lobby disclosure legislation would inevitably result in government surveillance of religious bodies engaged in public affairs through what has appropriately been called "an IRS for lobbying."[19] The issue here is one of government monitoring of religious groups in public affairs. Meanwhile, the fact is that the trend toward a demand for government monitoring of all political activity is likely to continue for some years to come. Unfortunately, the trend toward government monitoring of all political activity through lobby disclosure will in all likelihood have little, if any, effect on large well-financed lobby operations, while imposing a substantial burden on small organizations and citizens' advocacy groups and religious bodies.

Although the legislative intent of lobby disclosure legislation per se has not been generally impugned in past years by religious bodies, serious objections have been raised primarily on constitutional grounds, particularly on the basis of the Free Exercise Clause, and the chilling effect such legislation would inevitably have on the work and witness of religious groups in public affairs. If ever enacted into law, it would admittedly impose a substantial burden particularly on small religious bodies and organizations. Of more fundamental importance, however, the effect of such legislation, no matter what its declared intent, would be to inhibit the witness of religious bodies in public affairs and to abridge, at least to some degree, their "free exercise of religion" in public affairs. Here certain questions inevitably come into play. Does government have the right to restrict the work and witness of those religious bodies which are involved in public affairs from speaking out on public policy issues and defending human values according to the insights of their own religious traditions? If the involvement of religious groups in public affairs is regarded by them as integral to their faith and mission, is this role of religion not integral to their "free exercise of religion"? Should not the prophetic role of religion in public affairs be recognized as essential not only to a free church but also to a free society?

V

For many years, questions have been raised concerning government regulations of fund-raising solicitations by religious bodies. It was the subject more than a half century ago in a landmark case, *Cantwell v. Connecticut*, in which the United States Supreme Court unanimously upheld the right of Jehovah's Witnesses to propagate their faith in public and to engage in door-to-door solicitation without a permit or "certificate of approval."[20] Although the Court affirmed that unlike religious belief, religious "conduct remains subject to regulation for the protection of society,"[21] it upheld the right of religious bodies to engage in door-to-door solicitation. A little more than four decades later, however, in *Heffron v. International Society for Krishna Consciousness*, the Court ruled that a state may limit solicitation and the selling of literature at a state fair, even though, as in the case of members of the Hare Krishna, they have a prescribed ritual of Sankirtan that requires them to distribute and to sell their literature publicly.[22]

The following year, however, in response to an amendment to Minnesota's Charitable Solicitation Act, which was directed against new or nonconventional religions, particularly the Unification Church, the Supreme Court in *Larson v. Valente* found the statutory amendment unconstitutional, as violative of both the Establishment Clause and the Free Exercise Clause. Speaking for the majority opinion, Justice William J. Brennan wrote, "The constitutional prohibition of denominational preference is inexorably connected with the continuing vitality of the Free Exercise Clause."[23]

Since 1986, the United States Supreme Court has largely denied the claim of the free exercise of religion as a basis for non-compliance with government regulations involving public benefits. Consequently, religious tests have been a church-state issue for receiving certain public benefits. In *Goldman v. Weinberger*, in a decision of five to four, the Court broadly affirmed the primacy of military uniformity and regulations over the free exercise of religion when it ruled that an Orthodox Jewish officer may be prohibited from wearing his yarmulke (skullcap) while in uniform.[24] In dissent, Justice William J. Brennan wrote that the Court was straining to maintain that discipline and morale will be undermined if exceptions are allowed. Under the "guise of neutrality and evenhandedness," he wrote, "majority religions are favored over distinctive minority faiths." Justice Brennan lamented that the Court had abdicated "its role as principal expositor of the Constitution and protector of individual liberties in favor of credulous deference to unsupported assertions of military necessity."[25] Justice Sandra Day O'Connor, also in dissent, observed, "The Government can present no sufficiently convincing proof in the case to support an assertion that granting an exception of the type requested here would do substantial harm to military discipline and esprit de corps."[26]

In the same year, the Court ruled in another case involving a choice between receiving a governmental benefit and adhering to a religious commitment. In a rather complicated decision, in *Bowen v. Roy*, the Court upheld the requirement of a Social Security number for eligibility for social or medical benefits. Stephen Roy, a Native American, refused to comply with the government's requirement that he provide the Social Security numbers for himself, his wife, and his five-year-old daughter in seeking medical benefits for his two-year-old daughter. Although all other members of his family had their Social Security numbers, afterwards Roy had come to the belief that to obtain a Social Security number for his two-year-old daughter for government use over which she had no control would "rob the spirit" of his daughter. In writing for the majority, Chief Justice Warren Burger set forth the denial of public benefits on the basis of "a uniformly applicable statute neutral on its face" rather than the previously developed test of the "least restrictive means of accomplishing a compelling state interest," as used in *Sherbert*, *Yoder*, and *Thomas*. Justice Burger wrote, "Given the diversity of beliefs in our pluralistic society and the necessity of providing governments with sufficient operating latitude, some incidental neutral restraints on the free exercise of religion are inescapable."[27] While concurring with the majority opinion, Justice O'Connor vigorously dissented from the less restrictive test advanced by Justice Burger, by declaring, "Only an especially important governmental interest pursued by narrowly tailored means can justify exacting a sacrifice of First Amendment freedoms as the price for an equal share of the rights, benefits, and privileges enjoyed by other citizens."[28]

In two other cases, one in 1987 and the other in 1988, the Court continued to advance further the constitutionality of government intervention in ruling on claims of free exercise of religion. In *O'Lone v. Estate of Shabazz*, the Court upheld on the basis of a "reasonableness" test the right of officials at the Leesburg State Prison in New Jersey to issue regulations denying to Black Muslims the right to attend Jumu'ah on Friday afternoons.[29] The following year, in *Lyng v. Northwest Indian Cemetery Association*,[30] in language even more restrictive on the claims of free exercise, the Court ruled that construction of a road through a portion of a National Forest in northwestern California, traditionally used for religious purposes by three American Indian tribes, would not be in violation of the Free Exercise Clause. In writing for the majority, Justice O'Connor rejected the argument that government must show a compelling interest in order to avoid violation of free exercise claims; rather, she argued, government action should be judged on whether it involves coercion or penalties. "However much we might wish it were otherwise," she wrote, "government simply could not operate if it were required to satisfy every citizen's religious needs and desires."[31] Justices Brennan, Thurgood Marshall, and Harry Blackmun strongly dissented with the majority's substitution of the "coercion" test with the earlier established "compelling state interest" test. In writing for the minority, Justice Brennan declared, "Today, the Court holds that a federal land-use decision that promises to destroy an entire religion does not burden the practice of that faith in a manner recognized by the Free Exercise Clause. . . . I find it difficult, however, to imagine conduct more insensitive to religious needs than the Government's determination to build a marginally useful road in the face of uncontradicted evidence that the road will render the practice of respondents' religion impossible."[32]

In any society, the status of religious liberty is most readily discerned by the treatment accorded new and marginal religious groups. Quite appropriately, one entire essay in this volume is devoted to the role of government in monitoring and regulating these groups.[33] Understandably, confrontations with government are more likely to occur, as in the United States, with new or nonconventional religious groups. This has been a recurring pattern in recent decades, as in the distant past, as they have advanced their free exercise claims when in conflict with the laws or public policy. During the past two decades these confrontations have occurred particularly with such groups as the Church of Scientology, the International Society for Krishna Consciousness (ISKCON) or the Hare Krishna movement, and the Unification Church, all of which came to experience considerable disfavor as a result of their winning converts from mainline churches and the Jewish community. Crucial to all confrontations of new and nonconventional religions with the state is the issue of equality under the law, as applied to both religion clauses of the First Amendment. As the Court affirmed in *Everson*, no government, state or federal, "can pass laws which . . . prefer one religion over another."[34]

Admittedly, new and nonconventional religions have often not enjoyed legal rights and equality under the law as have mainline religious groups. One example is to be found in a federal court case of income-tax evasion, *Moon v. United States*, which resulted in the conviction of Rev. Sun Myung Moon, the founder of the Unification Church.[35] The key issue in this case came to light early, namely the selective prosecution of Moon for doing essentially what many other religious leaders of mainline groups have done through the years. Massive support for Moon came from a large number and wide variety of organizations in the forms of amicus curiae briefs, perhaps unprecedented in both number and diversity including: the American Civil Liberties Union; the National Association of Evangelicals; the American Bar Association; the National Council of Churches; the Catholic League for Religion and Civil Rights; the Church of Jesus Christ of Latter-day Saints; the American Association of Christian Schools; the Southern Christian Leadership Conference; the Center for Judicial Studies; and the Institute for the Study of Religion. In addition, amicus curiae briefs were submitted by the States of Hawaii, Oregon, Rhode Island, and Senator Orrin G. Hatch, chair of the Subcommittee on the Constitution of the Senate Committee on the Judiciary.[36] The United States Supreme Court declined to overturn the lower court's conviction and, thus, the conviction was upheld and Moon was sentenced to prison. Unequal government treatment of religious groups is irreconcilable with the guarantees of the First Amendment.

The growing trend of government intervention in religious affairs bears directly upon both of the religion clauses, but even more directly on those guarantees that are associated with the Free Exercise Clause. That there are tensions and conflicts between the role of government in monitoring and regulating religion and the role of government in protecting the right of the free exercise of religion cannot be ignored. Indeed, this apparent oxymoron constitutes an unavoidable dilemma in American church-state relations.

Thus, this volume was planned to address at least some of the crucial questions that inevitably arise in the face of categorical guarantees of the First Amendment and the increasing growth of government and its authority as it affects both individual and corporate expressions of religion in American life. There is no presumption here that there are easy and ready-made answers to the questions raised. At the same time, the essays in this volume have been written on the basis of the presupposition that these major areas of tension between church and state in contemporary American society need careful and critical analysis. In this endeavor, particular attention has been given not only to the judicial interpretations of the meaning of the free exercise of religion, but also to the boundaries to be drawn as to the role of government in monitoring and regulating religion.

NOTES

1. James E. Wood, Jr., "The Church and Public Affairs: Current Trends and Future Prospects," *Search* 9 (Winter 1980):21-31.
2. See Dean M. Kelley, ed., *Government Intervention in Religious Affairs* (New York: The Pilgrim Press, 1982), a collection of sixteen essays expressly prepared for the conference.
3. See Dean Kelley, ed., *Government Intervention in Religious Affairs II* (New York: The Pilgrim Press, 1986), a collection of thirteen essays based on presentations made at the conference.
4. Robert T. Miller and Ronald B. Flowers, *Toward Benevolent Neutrality: Church, State, and the Supreme Court*, 4th ed. (Waco, Texas: Baylor University Press, 1992), 7.
5. *Watson v. Jones*, 13 Wall. 679 (1872) at 729. In this case, the Court ruled that it did not have the power to decide which of two Presbyterian factions contesting for church property represented the true faith or the true Presbyterian Church in the church dispute. The ruling in this case came to be known as the *Watson* doctrine and

to serve as a constitutional rule of law. It was subsequently applied in *Kedroff v. Saint Nicholas Cathedral*, 344 U.S. 94 (1952) and *Jones v. Wolf*, 443 U.S. 595 (1979).

6. *Prince v. Commonwealth of Massachusetts*, 321 U.S. 158 (1944) at 165.
7. *Employment Division of Oregon v. Smith*, 494 U.S. 872 (1990).
8. *Wisconsin v. Yoder*, 406 U.S. 205 (1972) at 215.
9. *Sherbert v. Verner*, 374 U.S. 398 (1963). Although the "alternate means" test was first advanced in *Braunfeld v. Brown* in 1961, it was first used in *Sherbert*.
10. Ibid. at 406.
11. See *Thomas v. Review Board of the Indiana Employment Security Divison*, 450 U.S. 707 (1981) and *Hobbie v. Unemployment Appeals Commission of Florida*, 480 U.S. 136 (1987). The issue being addressed here is not religious discrimination in employment per se, but rather the growing trend of government intervention in religious affairs. For an analysis of the role of government in monitoring and regulating the "free exercise of religion" in the area of employment, see the essay in this volume by David L. Gregory, "Government Regulation of Religion Through Employment and Discrimination Laws," pp. 121-60.
12. *Employment Division of Oregon v. Smith*, 494 U.S. 872 (1990).
13. See the essay in this volume by Angela C. Carmella, "The Religion Clauses and Acculturated Religious Conduct: Boundaries for the Regulation of Religion," pp. 21-49.
14. Ibid. at 885.
15. Ibid. at 888.
16. Ibid.
17. Introduced in the Senate as the "Lobbying Discosure Act of 1933" (S. 349). In the past, numerous bills on lobby disclosure to include religious bodies have been introduced in both Houses of the Congress, with numerous testimonies in opposition submitted by religious bodies.
18. For an analysis of the issue of tax exemption and the involvement of religious groups in public affairs, see the essay in this volume by Stanley S. Weithorn and Douglas F. Allen, "Taxation and the Advocacy Role of Churches in Public Affairs," pp. 51-64.
19. It may be well to remember that lobbying has been a part of the American experience from the beginning of the Republic. Efforts on the part of organized groups of citizens to influence legislation and public policy have been, in fact, a major feature of American political life. As one writer has expressed it, "The history of lobbying comes close to being the history of American legislation"; Edgar Lane, *Lobbying and the Law* (Berkeley: University of California Press, 1964), 18. For a perceptive analysis of lobbying as a constitutional right, i.e., the advocacy of ideas, see Hope Eastman, *Lobbying: A Constitutional Right* (Washington, D.C.: American Enterprise Institute for Public Policy Research, 1977).
20. *Cantwell v. Connecticut*, 310 U.S. 296 (1940). This case is particularly remembered since, for the first time, the Court specifically "incorporated" the Free Exercise Clause into the Fourteenth Amendment, thus making the Clause applicable to the states.
21. Ibid. at 304.
22. *Heffron v. International Society for Krishna Consciousness*, 452 U.S. 640 (1981).

23. *Larson v. Valente,* 456 U.S. 228 (1982) at 245.
24. *Goldman v. Weinberger,* 475 U.S. 503 (1986).
25. Ibid. at 514.
26. Ibid. at 532.
27. Ibid. at 711-12.
28. Ibid. at 728.
29. *O'Lone v. Estate of Shabazz,* 482 U.S. 342 (1987).
30. *Lyng v. Northwest Indian Cemetery Association,* 485 U.S. 439 (1988).
31. Ibid. at 452.
32. Ibid. at 476, 477.
33. See the essay in this volume by David Bromley and Thomas Robbins, "The Role of Government in Regulating New and Nonconventional Religions," pp. 205-40.
34. *Everson v. Board of Education,* 330 U.S. 1 (1947) at 15.
35. *Moon v. United States,* 104 S.Ct. 2344 (1984), denying cert. in 718 F.2d 1210. See Bromley and Robbins, "The Role of Government in Monitoring and Regulating New Religions," pp. 205-40.
36. For complete texts of these briefs, see Herbert Richardson, ed., *Constitutional Issues in the Case of Rev. Moon: Amicus Briefs Presented to the United States Supreme Court* (New York: Edwin Mellen Press, 1984).

2

The Religion Clauses and Acculturated Religious Conduct: Boundaries for the Regulation of Religion

ANGELA C. CARMELLA

Part One of this essay addresses the structure of the American political and constitutional system, which enables religious belief and practice to flourish. Then follows a discussion of current legal trends that distort this structure by justifying increased governmental regulation of religious conduct. In Part Two, the theological concept of acculturated religious conduct is introduced: that is, church activity that is thoroughly engaged with the wider culture or similar to secular conduct.[1] Because acculturated religious conduct is especially vulnerable to government regulation, this essay will argue that increased government oversight threatens to limit and redefine church ministries and missions. It also threatens to affect the ways in which churches relate to the larger culture, thereby influencing and even coercing fundamental theological choices.

The third and final part of this essay proposes a new approach for determining the constitutionality of government regulation of religious conduct. This approach provides for broad religious exemptions from regulation in order to ensure theological breathing room, consistent with historic political and constitutional norms in America.

THE RELIGION CLAUSES: THE BALANCE
BETWEEN DEFERENCE AND LIMITATION

Communities of faith are concerned about governmental regulation and monitoring of religion for two main reasons.[2] Church involvement in all types of activities has grown throughout this century, particularly large-scale efforts at social reform and philanthropy.[3] As a natural outgrowth of traditional religious concerns for the well-being of church members and the larger community, churches now run day-care centers, shelters, foster homes, group homes, rehabilitation centers, hospices, food and clothing programs, low-income housing programs, long-term care facilities, training centers, clinics and hospitals, legal aid centers, counseling programs, retreat centers, radio and television programs, camps, schools, and universities;[4] they offer pension plans and life insurance; and they employ thousands of people nationwide. Churches and synagogues are involved in all sorts of moral-political issues, from the economy to racism, from abortion to global issues.[5] Of course, churches do not have a monopoly on these activities; both secular and religious groups are involved as well in these social, economic, and civic pursuits.

Similarly, the scope of government has grown in this last century, so much so that now "the state" is an expansive and complex web of interconnecting federal, state, and local institutions and laws. The traditional police powers for protecting health, safety, morals, and the general welfare are now expressed in elaborate regulatory schemes governing a tremendous variety of economic and social conduct.[6] The state plays an increasingly normative role[7] as well as an increasingly pervasive role in the building of community.[8] Given the expansion of church activities and the reach of the state, the problem of increased regulation and monitoring of church conduct is inevitable. These trends have led to several major questions: When should church activities be treated like their secular counterparts? When should church activities be regulated, but in less intrusive and less restrictive ways than their secular

counterparts? And, when should church activities be fully
exempted from government regulation?

To begin to answer these questions, one needs to look closely
at America's political and constitutional legacy. Since 1940,[9] the
United States Supreme Court's treatment of the religion clauses
of the First Amendment has gone through several twists and
turns. On some occasions, the Court has adopted a position of
strict separation between church and state,[10] and on others it
has overtly accommodated churches and religious persons.[11]
On yet other occasions the Court has chosen to modify its
contradictory positions with a more "benevolent" neutrality,[12]
and most recently, it has employed an approach of formal
neutrality, which finds laws that are neutral and nondiscrimina -
tory to be constitutional.[13] The Court moves back and forth
among these specific legal categories of separation,
accommodation, and neutrality, often without clear rationales.
The jurisprudential inconsistencies occur not simply because of
changes in court composition or ideological shifts, but because
the Court is attempting to balance two larger political principles:
deference and limitation.[14] "Deference" says the state should
defer on matters of religion to individual conscience and
churches. At an institutional level, this principle recognizes
religious authority and thus permits churches to determine what
is religious and therefore within their competence and
jurisdiction.

Most would agree that the state cannot define the content of
religious beliefs, cannot force anyone to profess a particular faith
or to attend church, and cannot force a church to adopt a
particular doctrine. These are simply outside the competence of
the state. The other political principle— "limitation"— says the
state has the authority to limit the definition of religious
conduct, and to decide what are secular activities and therefore
within its competence to regulate, to monitor, or to prohibit.[15]
Because the state has a monopoly on coercive power and on
lawmaking authority, the use of military force and the protection
of citizens from physical harm are undeniably within its

domain.[16] Obviously, the state can prevent the creation of a church army or ritual sacrifice of children.

The American constitutional system necessarily incorporates both of these principles, balancing deference and limitation.[17] Striking a balance is particularly difficult when such expansive church activities occur within a heavily regulated society. The examples offered— no state-defined beliefs or compelled church attendance, no church army or ritual human sacrifice— illustrate the easy cases. More often, what is within the church's jurisdiction and what is within the state's jurisdiction is not divided by a clear line. For the church-run day-care center, the alcohol and drug rehabilitation program, and the television station, what is religious and what is secular from the perspectives of church and state often differ. Recent legal trends have resolved this tension in favor of the state, strengthening the limitation principle and making it much easier to regulate and monitor churches. The deference principle urgently needs to be revitalized.

Disestablishment, a defining event in our political and constitutional history, gave birth to both deference and limitation. Disestablishment is the institutional separation of church and state that recognizes a separation of powers between religious institutions on the one hand, and government on the other.[18] In rejecting an established church, the founders recognized the centrality of the deference principle. They acknowledged that religion does not need the support of the state (and that such support is indeed harmful to it), and further, that the state is incompetent in religious matters.[19] Thus, individuals and groups have substantive, pre-political rights to possess religious beliefs and engage in religious activity.[20] The founders similarly determined the centrality of the limitation principle when they envisioned a state promoting social order and peace without supporting or taking orders from a church.[21]

Because of its monopoly on lawmaking authority, the state will always have the ultimate authority to define its own jurisdiction and to limit what is within a church's jurisdiction.[22] That is why the state can prohibit human sacrifice; the state could never defer absolutely to churches' definitions of what is religious. Herein lies the paradox: the state is incompetent to act in matters of religion, but the state defines what conduct is religious and therefore outside its jurisdiction, and what conduct is secular and therefore within its jurisdiction. The fact that the state has ultimate definitional authority requires tremendous vigilance on the part of each of the branches of government, and the judiciary in particular, to ensure that the boundaries between church and state are functioning as intended; that is, enabling religion to flourish without frustrating the state's basic ordering role.

Deference and limitation are so fundamental to the nature of the American polity and constitutional scheme that they can readily be seen at work in the Supreme Court's interpretation of each of the religion clauses. Each clause is understood to balance the two principles. The Free Exercise Clause promotes accommodation of religious exercise and autonomy for churches (deference),[23] which is nonetheless limited by the state's ultimate power to compel conformity with general laws (limitation).[24] The Establishment Clause acknowledges autonomy for churches and prohibits excessive entanglement of the state into church affairs (deference),[25] and similarly acknowledges the state's freedom from church control (limitation).[26]

The jurisprudence of the religion clauses as developed by the Supreme Court is currently in a state of serious imbalance, weighted more heavily toward the limitation principle than is appropriate. This is a cumulative effect of legal theories over time, but three examples will illustrate the trend: the church autonomy doctrine, which rests on both religion clauses; the Establishment Clause doctrine; and the Free Exercise Clause doctrine.

In the area of church autonomy, courts were once required to defer to the internal decisions of churches on religious matters, even if those decisions ultimately affected some temporal issues normally within a court's competence to adjudicate. If, for example, a religious dispute led to a schism within the church and the factions were fighting over which group owned church property, the Court would defer to the decisions of the highest

church authority.[27] A shift occurred in 1979, with *Jones v. Wolf,*[28]
when the Court departed from a century of mandatory
deference and gave courts the option of determining that neutral
principles could be applied to internal church disputes.
Deference to the church's highest authority is now required only
if the court decides that its jurisdiction would inevitably involve
it in doctrinal or ecclesiastical matters. Thus, whenever a court
determines that the case before it can be decided without
religious inquiry, it may adjudicate the dispute using neutral,
secular principles. Courts may now review secular documents
such as deeds, and even church documents, using neutral,
secular standards. This option to extend court jurisdiction over
the church when there has been a decision by the highest church
authority and when there is no compelling state interest to do so
is very troubling.[29] The "neutral principles" approach obviously
cuts back on the deference principle by permitting the *courts* to
decide whether the dispute is of a religious or secular nature.[30]

A second example of a weak commitment to deference is
found in the area of Establishment Clause doctrine, particularly
in its prohibition on excessive entanglement of the state into
church affairs. The Supreme Court has never addressed the
specific issue of regulatory jurisdiction over churches and
missed a golden opportunity to do so in *NLRB v. Catholic
Bishop.*[31] In that 1979 case, the National Labor Relations Board
asserted jurisdiction over Catholic high schools to represent lay
teachers in collective bargaining with the school administrations.
The NLRB asserted jurisdiction on the grounds that the
employment of lay teachers was a secular activity. The Court
chose to decide the case on statutory grounds, holding that
Congress did not intend for church schools to be under the
jurisdiction of the National Labor Relations Act. The Court
thought that the exercise of the Board's jurisdiction presented a
risk of entanglement, but refused to develop the entanglement
prohibition (or the church autonomy doctrine, for that matter) to
protect churches generally from intrusive regulations.[32] The
"excessive entanglement" doctrine has instead come to refer to
situations in which the state engages in ongoing, day-to-day
administrative surveillance of church activity, and as such, has

been used primarily to justify denial of aid to parochial schools on the grounds that government oversight of public funds would entangle the state in church affairs.[33]

Third, under the Free Exercise Clause, the deference accorded to religious conduct has been drastically narrowed over the last decade. The classic free exercise balancing test (used for nearly thirty years)[34] assesses the constitutionality of a law by weighing the burdens it places on religion against compelling state interests expressed by that law. If the burden is demonstrated and not outweighed by a sufficiently compelling state interest, then the religious claimant enjoys a mandatory exemption from the law. Over time, however, it has become increasingly difficult to demonstrate a burden to the Supreme Court's satisfaction and increasingly easy for the state to show the ascendancy of its interests.

This trend culminated in the spring of 1990, in *Employment Division v. Smith*.[35] In *Smith*, two members of the Native American Church had been fired from their drug-counseling jobs for participating in the church's ritual peyote ceremony. They were denied unemployment compensation. They sued, challenging the denial of their unemployment compensation on the grounds that their unemployment resulted from constitutionally protected religious practice. The Supreme Court could have used the existing balancing test, which would weigh the religious exercise (the ritual peyote use) against the state's interest in discouraging drug use. The Court instead employed a new test for determining the propriety of government regulation of religious activity. It held that any generally applicable, facially neutral law is valid regardless of burdens it may cause to religious belief and practice. After *Smith*, the state bears no burden to justify its regulation or monitoring of religious conduct (except in several categories of cases to be discussed below). Thus, a state may prohibit all peyote use, and with such general prohibition sweep ritual use within the prohibition; likewise, a state may prohibit all use of alcohol, and with such general prohibition sweep sacramental use of wine within its scope. This is the ultimate assertion of limitation over deference. The expansive state now radically redefines religious activity as

secular simply by extending civil jurisdiction over a larger
category of conduct in which it falls.

There are some areas in which *Smith* preserves deference:
where the state intentionally and exclusively targets religious
practice for discrimination, prohibition or penalty, and where
the state regulates religious belief directly or compels the
profession of faith.[36]   These examples, however, are so
indisputably outside the bounds of state competence as to make
their mention wholly gratuitous. Beyond these areas, *Smith*
recognizes the force and effect of the Free Exercise Clause only
when coupled with a violation of another constitutional right,
such as rights to speech or association.[37] This "hybrid" concept
radically devalues the substantive pre-political right to engage in
religious conduct that flows to us from the religion clauses. The
Smith formulation cannot fully protect religious conduct in a
legal environment bursting with generally applicable, facially
neutral regulations.

As a result of these trends in the doctrines of church
autonomy, entanglement, and free exercise, the Court now
recognizes enormous latitude for state regulation as applied to
churches. Churches enjoy mandatory judicial deference for their
internal decisions only when those decisions cannot be
understood under any neutral secular principles. Churches enjoy
mandatory exemption in the area of regulation under the
Establishment Clause only when the assertion of the state's
jurisdiction would involve the state in comprehensive and
continuing surveillance. And churches enjoy mandatory
exemption under the Free Exercise Clause in the rarest of cases,
where laws are marked by anti-religious discrimination or
infringe another constitutional right.

Of course, legislation may contain religious exemptions. In
fact, even though the Court in *Smith* cut back on judicially
mandated exemptions, the decision explicitly encouraged
legislative accommodations of religion.[38] Laws frequently
exempt religion either specifically or as part of a larger exempt
class. Religious exemptions have been common in the law,
because of long-standing respect for institutional boundaries in
many areas, and because of active communication between

churches and agencies to fashion those boundaries. An additional reason is that legislatures and agencies have been generally aware that courts could ask them to justify the regulatory burdens imposed on religion and could overturn their laws as applied to churches under a variety of legal theories— church autonomy, entanglement, or free exercise.[39] Despite its encouragement of religious exemptions, *Smith* has altered the situation. Legislatures and agencies may not understand *Smith* to mean that they are free to accommodate churches with exemptions; to the contrary, they may understand *Smith* to mean that they are free to regulate churches through general laws without any threat of judicial intervention.

This apparently inexorable slide toward limitation causes a fundamental redefinition of the nation's political and constitutional identity, as embodied in the religion clauses. The major concern becomes how, in this new jurisprudential environment, may the balance between deference and limitation be redressed and the deference principle be revitalized to strengthen and preserve existing exemptions and to ensure continued accommodation of religion? How are distinctions to be made between reasonable regulations' monitoring religious activity and those that overstep constitutional bounds?

THE FAITH-IN-CULTURE DILEMMA: ACCULTURATED RELIGIOUS CONDUCT

Some forms of religious conduct will be more vulnerable to broad regulatory and monitoring schemes than others. The discipline of theology helps to identify such conduct. The Supreme Court has in the past looked to theology to determine whether behavior is religious or secular, once in particular when it relied on theologian Paul Tillich to assist it in determining what constitutes religion in nontraditional conscientious objections to the Vietnam War.[40] This essay continues in that tradition by suggesting that, as a means of revitalizing the deference principle, theology should inform the judicial

measurement of conduct to be considered within the competence
of the church.

Conscientious objections to the demands of the state are
typically considered to be the primary example of religious
activity subject to government scrutiny and control. When
Amish parents in Wisconsin did not want to send their children
to high school because of the exposure to "worldly" values, the
state argued that the application of the general requirement of
compulsory education for all children until the age of sixteen
must be enforced against the Amish.[41] But the Supreme Court
found, in its balance of deference and limitation, that an
exemption for Amish children would respect their conscientious
objection to the schooling and accommodate their distinct
lifestyle without seriously frustrating the goals of the state.
Obviously, conscientious objection rooted in religious belief and
doctrinal objections to particular laws give rise to dramatic legal
conflicts.

But countercultural behavior like that of the Amish is not the
only type of religious conduct burdened by governmental
regulation and monitoring. In fact, most governmental
oversight, particularly comprehensive regulatory schemes,
involves what might be called acculturated conduct: conduct
that is thoroughly engaged with the wider culture or that shares
similarities with conduct undertaken by nonreligious groups.[42]
In broad terms, acculturated conduct refers to churches and their
role in moral discourse, their provision of human services and
philanthropy, their creation and operation of institutions, and
their efforts at maintenance and reform of civic life. Churches
use the media, own property, raise funds, espouse moral-
political positions, operate all types of programs that address
social and spiritual needs, and establish and operate institutions
such as hospitals and universities. Churches do not function only
to reject and insulate themselves from the wider culture, to live
according to distinctive practices, or to engage in civil
disobedience and challenge existing mores. Churches are in
constant dialogue with the wider culture. They routinely
tolerate, support, appropriate, adapt, and transform— and are

transformed by— the values, institutions, and practices of the culture.

Acculturation

A church's continuous evaluation of and interaction with the culture is a well-documented process. Numerous theologians and sociologists of religion have recognized the constant adjustments that churches make to their surrounding cultural environments. In the nineteenth century, theologians identified two types of religious community: church and sect, the sect being countercultural.[43] But by the middle of the twentieth century, theologians such as H. Richard Niebuhr began to realize that churches engaged in much more nuanced interaction with their surrounding cultures.[44] Niebuhr found that unlike the sectarian response, some churches viewed the culture with suspicion but chose to accept the tension and live as best they could within the culture.[45] Other churches found the culture so virtuous that they considered it possible to live out their faith through the culture's institutions and values.[46] Some churches considered the virtues of culture to provide a good foundation but believed their role was to inspire perfection beyond them.[47] And yet other churches chose to engage the culture in order to transform it.[48] In theological circles, these questions and answers about faith and culture are placed within a field known as ecclesiology.[49]

Many other theologians and sociologists of religion have described the varieties of church-culture interaction. Theologian Avery Dulles found that of the many ways churches define themselves, most involve the particular ways in which a church engages the culture.[50] When a church considers itself to be a *herald* proclaiming God's Word, it speaks to the culture.[51] When a church considers itself to be a *sacrament*, it makes "visible signs of grace" through its social actions like charity, community service, and worship.[52] When a church understands itself to be a *servant*, it "seeks to serve the world by fostering the brotherhood of all."[53] The servant church considers itself in dialogue with culture, placed between the culture and its own tradition and beliefs.[54] Similarly, theologian Walter Kasper's typology of modes of being in the modern world reflect a split between countercultural and more acculturated postures, sharing with Niebuhr and Dulles the observation that many churches have adopted a method of theological discourse with the secular world, even a "theology of secularization."[55]

Like these theologians, sociologist Peter Berger has found that there are those who choose to be apart from culture, those who accept culture, and those who seek to engage the culture and transform it through dialogue.[56] Moreover, a group of sociologists studying churches in the Hartford, Connecticut area found a great variety of degrees of acculturation. Those churches with primarily "this-worldly" (as opposed to other-worldly) orientations behaved as *citizen* or *activist*.[57] Given such ecclesiologies, these churches focus heavily on temporal concerns, are more engaged in the larger culture, and often engage in many of the same types of activities in which non-religious groups engage; they are focused on, as Harvey Cox put it, "nourish[ing] the secularization process. . . ."[58]

The notion of transformation occurs repeatedly within these typologies. In fact, the theological method of discourse with the secular culture is widely understood to encourage the transformation of the culture.[59] Religious communities of all types try to meet people "where they find them," to make religion accessible and relevant, in order to lay the foundation for transformative religious experience.[60]

Many authors choose to criticize the most acculturated responses to the faith-in-culture dilemma, referring to extreme acculturation as "culturalism," wherein religion has no meaningful tension with culture and has lost all distinctive characteristics.[61] Rather than playing a transformative role, these religious communities have been overpowered by culture.[62] Interestingly, however, while considering such "cultural religion" theologically bankrupt, even the most ardent critics of extreme acculturation do not suggest withdrawal from culture into insular, countercultural communities.[63] Withdrawal is not an option. As theologian Stanley Hauerwas writes, the question is not *whether* to be in the world but only "*how* to be in the world. . . ."[64] And even those who have chosen a more separatist response use the tools of the culture, such as the media, and often use them quite effectively.[65] Thus, virtually all churches, not just majoritarian faiths or theologically liberal communities, engage in acculturated religious conduct. We have come a long way from thinking that the only ecclesiological choice is between sect and church, countercultural and cultural.

Implications of Acculturation

A church's ecclesiology will manifest itself in the types of acculturated conduct (if any) in which it engages. When a church understands itself as herald, servant, citizen, activist, or transformer, such self-definitions will have a decisive impact on the conduct of that community vis-à-vis the culture. These self-definitions, which focus on the temporal world as the locus of religious and moral action, will compel the church to broad engagement with the culture through moral discourse, human services, charitable works, the creation and operation of institutions, and efforts at reform of civic life. The acculturation process is fluid and dynamic because culture and churches change; the social context, theology, tradition, and social worlds of members will contribute to each generation's church-culture dialogue.[66]

The balance of deference and limitation is hardest with respect to acculturated conduct. The religion clauses recognize the separation of church from state and the substantive pre-political right to associate for religious activities. Yet, because acculturated conduct is, by definition, similar to secular conduct or is widely engaged with culture, it may properly come within the state's jurisdiction. This may be particularly true whenever the state's jurisdiction is justified by its role in protecting the public (when a church runs a hospital, for instance).

On the other hand, however, acculturated conduct flows from, and is an expression of, a church's ecclesiology. Just as the Supreme Court has acknowledged the need to preserve space for the doctrinal development of churches,[67] it is here asserted that churches need space for their ecclesiological development.

Churches must be free to live out their chosen mode of interaction with the culture. Often, acculturated conduct is the way in which they do so. The mode of interaction with culture is inextricably tied to a church's ecclesiological identity and thus deserves broad deference. Even churches that can be criticized for excessive cultural accommodation deserve broad protection: first, because their ecclesiology may change; and second, and more fundamentally, because the degree of acculturation is a theological question not within the state's competence.

Because churches have an interest in defining their interaction with the culture and because the state may consider that interaction to be within its jurisdiction, church and state will often have overlapping, or shared, jurisdictions in cases of acculturated conduct, and tension between these two sovereigns will be inevitable. Some rule is needed to determine how the conflict will be resolved. At present, in the post-*Smith* environment, a statist rule is employed: acculturated conduct will be treated as any secular counterpart. If day-care centers are subject to generally applicable, facially neutral regulations, church-affiliated and secular centers will be treated identically. Preferable would be the opposite presumption: that the state's jurisdiction over church activities be legitimate only after examination and with proof of sufficiently compelling justification.

The most important point to keep in mind is that acculturated religious conduct is religious conduct, not secular conduct. This is the mistake that the Court makes in *Smith*. There the Court presumes that any activity that falls within the scope of a generally applicable, facially neutral law is properly within that scope, regardless of its religious nature or its role in the life of the church or religious tradition. It therefore regards any religious activity that has a secular counterpart to be secular—t o be within the competence of the state.

Undoubtedly, the fundamental question concerns the need to treat acculturated religious conduct differently from its secular counterpart. Why not say that if a church chooses to engage the culture broadly, beyond belief and ritual and beyond its distinctive practices, it impliedly agrees to be subject to whatever laws govern the activity? Why not employ exemptions only to accommodate specific doctrinal objections, if at all? First, because it is patently unfair to determine substantive religious rights by asking whether nonreligious groups engage in the same behavior.[68] And second, because regulation and monitoring threaten the independent ecclesiological and theological development of churches and their religious traditions.

Once churches are locked into a regulatory relationship with the state, the state defines the proper scope of behavior for the church.[69] The church, by complying, accepts the governance by the state over the church's mission and ministries. This affects the way in which the churches define themselves and may stultify creative, theologically-informed ways of meeting human needs and engaging in moral discourse. In essence, it impairs the ability of religious groups to define and carry out their ministries independently. In fact, a common complaint within theological circles is that many churches now see themselves primarily as part of the helping professions;[70] they may start out with theologically-informed community service, but the imposition of government regulation may influence or compel churches to conform to their secular counterparts, encouraging a "domestication" of religion, a loss of independent theological vision.[71] Certainly this has happened where governmental monies are available for social services; churches have characterized their operations as "secular" in order to qualify for monies when, in reality, they were engaging in acculturated religious conduct.

Regulation and monitoring of acculturated conduct have a chilling effect on independent ecclesiological development, freezing the level and scope and method of ministry because the government defines many of the terms of a church's conversation with the wider culture. As Professor Douglas Laycock has written, there are four types of government regulations: "those that merely increase the cost of operations, those that interfere directly with the way an activity is conducted, those that interfere with selection of those who will conduct the activity, and those that forbid an activity entirely or create incentives to abandon it."[72] Regulation inevitably frustrates the fluid and dynamic process of acculturation— the independent choices of whether and how to adapt to the wider culture.

Treating acculturated religious conduct like its secular counterpart does not strike the proper constitutional balance of the principles of deference and limitation. Moreover, narrow exemptions that address specific theological objections are insufficient to ensure constitutional protection of religion. To accommodate churches only when their beliefs include a specific tenet that runs contrary to the government regulation presumes that religion must be countercultural before its adherents can suffer a burden.[73] But the state can affect the church's self-definition and ecclesiology simply by extending its jurisdiction over church activities. One need not find a point of conflict between a particular tenet and the applicable government regulation in order to find burdens on religion. When churches submit to state jurisdiction in the course of operating their ministries, the state affects their theological decisions regarding the use of cultural tools, the methods of engaging the wider culture, and the nature of the dialogue with the culture. These are all central to the ecclesiological freedom of churches.

Consider the example of a church-affiliated day-care center.[74] Assume, as is the case in some states, that when the state regulates day-care centers, it provides not only health and safety standards but also requires that the programs of the center promote a "positive self-concept" and that particular types of training be required for day-care personnel.[75] Some churches, perceiving themselves at odds with the prevailing humanistic value system, would resist the normative aspects of the regulation (complying with health and safety requirements but not more). Here the church would accuse the state of usurping the norm-generating role of the church.

However, the church-affiliated day-care center may have, like its secular counterpart, programs that are intended to promote a positive self-image, and the day-care workers may in fact meet the required training. The church may have, given its theology and ecclesiology, an understanding of childhood development quite consistent with that embodied in the legislation. There is no conflict, but that does not mean that the regulations are not burdensome. The regulations are inherently intrusive. They interfere with the conduct of religious activity and with the selection of religious personnel.[76] Most significantly, the regulations influence the implementation of religious programs, discourage further theological discourse within the affected church on the topic of pre-school education, and prevent an independent evolution of normative understanding no longer coextensive with the values of the wider culture.

PROTECTING ACCULTURATED RELIGION UNDER THE RELIGION CLAUSES: BALANCING DEFERENCE AND LIMITATION PRINCIPLES

Because this author concludes that regulation and monitoring of acculturated activity is harmful to the ecclesiological development of churches, a new judicial approach for determining the constitutionality of regulations as applied to churches in their non-profit work in human services, in their creation and operation of institutions, in their civic involvements, and in their moral discourse, is suggested. A new test will help to strike a new balance between deference and limitation.

Statutes and ordinances often provide generous accommoda - tions for religious exercise.[77] Why the need for a new judicial test? Some would argue that the *Smith* Court's explicit encouragement of legislative exemption will result in sufficient protection to churches. Why not then simply direct their efforts to the political process, not the Court, to obtain religious exemptions? Because only in the pre-*Smith* world did legislative and administrative bodies know that their laws and actions could be reviewed and overturned by courts under church autonomy, establishment, or free exercise doctrine if those laws and actions involved the state in internal church matters, entangled it in church operations, or burdened religious practice without sufficient justification. After the trends of the last decade, and especially after *Smith*, no incentives remain to exempt religious conduct from generally applicable, facially neutral laws (other than, perhaps, the desire to avoid public embarrassment or loss of votes where denial of exemptions might be perceived as anti-religious). On what grounds does a church argue for accommodation, other than as a supplicant to the state or as a special interest group?

Legislative and administrative restraint will not necessarily be internally generated. In seeking to carry out their statutory responsibilities, administrative personnel will not "balance" competing interests unless they are directed to do so by statute or constitutional mandate.[78] And even in those cases, they will still try to balance in favor of their regulatory goals. The state might see a strong case for deference to religious conduct when the church's objections to regulation involve central tenets or beliefs; but since acculturated religious conduct "looks" secular, governmental bodies will not hesitate to extend state jurisdiction over such conduct. Even if a religious exemption exists, agencies may interpret it narrowly to deny eligibility to activities with secular counterparts.[79] Thus, without an active judicial commitment to police the legislative and executive branches, the state has ample opportunity to overreach in enthusiastic pursuit of its various mandates.

This author's proposal to correct this imbalance of limitation over deference is founded upon broad, presumptive autonomy for religious conduct under the religion clauses. This presumption would capture the entire process of acculturation and protect the ecclesiological judgments of churches. Churches and their theologians may argue over the proper degree of acculturation. But this much is clear: religion is not only the tenets and beliefs of a tradition, the rituals associated with it, and those behaviors that distinguish or separate an adherent from the surrounding culture. Sincere religious exercise involves the dialogue between faith and culture, together with the cultural conduct and choice of cultural tools that flow from those ecclesiological judgments. This broad presumptive autonomy for all types of religious conduct respects the institutional separation created by the founders' disestablishment decision, and permits religious exercise to flourish independently, preserving in particular the fluidity and dynamism of the continuous conversation between church and culture.

Churches should enjoy this presumptively broad definition of activities within their competence for three reasons. First, the state has already indirectly shaped the church-culture dialogue by thoroughly penetrating virtually all aspects of culture. Second, the entire process of ecclesiological determination, regardless of the resulting degree of acculturation, is religious exercise. And finally, the state has the ultimate authority to override a church's definition of religious conduct pursuant to the limitation principle, and therefore must exercise this tremendous power with great care.

Given a broad definition of religious conduct that should enjoy presumptive deference, how does one strike the balance with the limitation principle? This author proposes that the state exempt religious conduct (or fashion comparable accommodation) from regulation unless the state can demonstrate that the exemption will (1) frustrate a compelling governmental interest; (2) threaten to breach the institutional separation of church and state; or (3) "coerce, compromise, or influence the religious beliefs" of those who do not benefit from the exemption.[80]

Religious exemptions should be required unless the state can show that a compelling governmental interest of the highest magnitude is implicated (such as public health, safety, or national interest) *and* that it "has a compelling interest in *not* having an alternative arrangement."[81] As Professor Marc Galanter has pointed out, the state can easily meet the first half of this test because it can characterize its interest at the highest level of generality: the state's interests in education, taxation, and national defense are always compelling, but its interest in a particular school program or tax or bomb may not be.[82] Thus, the state must also show that a full exemption for the religious conduct would frustrate the state's ability to further its interest and that there are no less restrictive or less intrusive alternatives, no acceptable accommodations whatsoever. If there are any alternatives, then partial exemptions or reduced governmental oversight must be fashioned to accommodate the church activity as much as possible, with the least degree of entanglement.

If the state can show that deference to churches will cause, as Professor Galanter explains, "tangible harm to specifiable others without their consent,"[83] then it has surely demonstrated a compelling interest: thus, the more widely engaged a church is with the culture, providing large-scale services to non-adherents (such as running a hospital), the easier it will be to regulate to prevent harm to the public.[84] But note how finely tailored this must be: such a rationale would not justify regulation of all large, religiously affiliated institutions, such as universities, where students voluntarily seek admission and where health care is not the primary purpose of the institution.

The compelling governmental interest standard ensures that the state retains its integrity of governance over interests that are undeniably within its sovereign sphere, consistent with disestablishment principles, while at the same time giving sufficient space to churches for their ecclesiological decisions. This solution mirrors not only the disestablishment principle and the resultant notion of "two spheres of competence" but also reflects the classic pre-*Smith* balancing test used under the Free Exercise Clause.

Even if a compelling governmental interest is not present to override deference to churches, a religious accommodation may not be constitutionally permitted if such deference to religious conduct threatens to breach institutional separation. In this second part of the proposal, the Establishment Clause provides further justification for the limitation principle. Exemptions rarely have this result, because they usually protect the separation of the spheres.[85] Occasionally, however, the particu - lar accommodation to the church is too great, and results in a delegation of state authority to a church. This occurred in *Larkin v. Grendel's Den*, decided in 1982.[86] In that case, a state statute gave churches and schools the power to veto applications for liquor licenses within a five hundred-foot radius of the church or school. Such veto power was considered a standardless delegation of governmental decision-making authority to a church, and is obviously impermissible.

The third part of this author's proposed test holds any deference improper under the Establishment Clause if, as Professor Jesse Choper has stated, it is likely to coerce, compromise, or influence the religious beliefs of organizations not within the exemption.[87] A religious exemption that imposes a direct transfer of money from those who do not enjoy the exemption to those who do constitutes a clear violation of the Establishment Clause. But, Professor Choper continues,

> Indirect social costs of religious accommodation. . . do not themselves threaten the values undergirding the Establishment Clause. They do not tend to coerce, compromise, or influence the nonbeliever's religious beliefs. . . . . If accommodations for religion impose religious costs on nonbelievers, then. . . they are forbidden. But if such accommodations impose only non-religious costs, then the Establishment Clause should be held to permit— or, indeed the Free Exercise Clause may be interpreted to demand— that these costs of religious tolerance be paid.[88]

Secular counterparts subject to regulation and monitoring are typically not affected in their religious beliefs when a church engaged in similar activity is exempt. The organization denied permission to build its day-care center in a residential zone is not affected in its religious beliefs because a church is granted permission to build a day-care center in such a zone. Even if the secular group is placed at a competitive disadvantage because of a religious exemption, that still does not influence or coerce beliefs of the secular group: it is a non-religious cost. The disadvantage is an unavoidable consequence of protecting substantive rights to religious exercise under the religion clauses.[89] Under Professor Choper's formulation, only if it can be demonstrated that the availability of the exemption has influenced secular organizations to affiliate sincerely with churches or to take on a religious identity would the exemption be suspect, because that would indicate that the exemption had affected the secular group in its beliefs.[90] But such influences are highly unlikely.

The disparate treatment of secular and religious groups, by itself, would not be enough to violate the Establishment Clause. The Supreme Court confirmed this when it stated that "it has never indicated that statutes that give special consideration to religious groups are *per se* invalid."[91] For the Court, religious exemptions "alleviate significant governmental interference with the ability of religious organizations to define and carry out their religious missions."[92] Where government "lift[s] a regulation that burdens the exercise of religion, [the Court] see[s] no reason to require that the exemption comes packaged with benefits to secular entities."[93]

This maximally deferential approach places the burden on the state to justify the extension of its regulations to religious conduct rather than on the church to demonstrate the need for an exemption before a court, legislature, or agency. With a free exercise case set for argument in the fall of 1992, the Court has the opportunity to redress the imbalance between deference and limitation and to revitalize the deference principle.[94] It would best be accomplished by judicial action that overruled or drastically narrowed *Smith*. It would also be most significant for the jurisprudential development of the religion clauses if the Court analyzed the clauses together.

Typically the clauses are treated separately, and often inconsistently. They are often assumed to be antagonistic. This comes from an unfortunate emphasis on "neutrality" as between religion and non-religion, and a required "secular purpose" under the Establishment Clause, which have made suspect any free exercise deference to religion— because deference to religion can always be recast as non-neutral, non-secular preference of religion over non-religion.[95] Such reasoning not only creates an unnecessary tension between the clauses but threatens to remove the deference principle entirely from constitutional considerations, paving the way for application of all laws against religion, without exemption, just as *Smith* does. It is this author's hope that the Court would squarely acknowledge that religion must be aided by exemptions and other forms of accommodations, so long as the exemptions do not violate the state's basic integrity as protector of the public and so long as the exemptions do not influence or coerce religious belief of nonbeneficiaries.

The statutory protection proposed by the Religious Freedom Restoration Act may also help revitalize the deference principle.[96] This bill provides a statutory cause of action for religious claimants burdened by state action, and requires the state to show a compelling interest to justify the burden. This would certainly provide a judicial check on the political branches and therefore tame the assertions of jurisdiction by agencies. It would also provide churches with leverage in their dealings with government.[97] But to the extent that the interpretation of "burden" might remain limited to protecting countercultural behavior, such interpretation will continue to frustrate efforts at obtaining mandatory exemption from regulation for acculturated religious conduct.

The state should treat acculturated conduct as religious conduct, not simply as equivalent to secular counterparts; it should not regulate or monitor acculturated religious conduct without articulating compelling reasons for doing so. This does not mean that churches will always be immune from governmental regulation. It means only that the state bears the burden to explain why it must extend its jurisdiction over them. In the creative tension between deference and limitation, a swing of the pendulum back toward deference will help the government respect the boundaries that the Constitution creates.

NOTES

1. "Church" refers generally to any religious community or religiously-affiliated organization.
2. This essay does not address the issue of governmental regulation or monitoring of publicly-funded church activities.
3. Robert T. Handy, *Undermined Establishment: Church-State Relations in America, 1880-1920* (Princeton: Princeton University Press, 1991), 97-125; Robert Wuthnow, Virginia A. Hodgkinson and Associates, eds., *Faith and Philanthropy in America: Exploring the Role of Religion in America's Voluntary Sector* (San Francisco: Jossey-Bass, 1990).
4. This list is shortened from one found in Carl H. Esbeck, "Government Regulation of Religiously Based Social Services: The First Amendment Considerations," *Hastings Constitutional Law Quarterly* 19 (Winter 1992): 344-45. See also Virginia A. Hodgkinson,

Murray S. Weitzman, and Arthur D. Kirsch, "From Commitment to Action: How Religious Involvement Affects Giving and Volunteering," in *Faith and Philanthropy*, 93-114.

5. For example, the American Catholic Bishops have been particularly active in moral-political discourse through their pastoral letters on the economy and nuclear war.

6. Handy, *Undermined Establishment*, 98, 102. At the turn of the century many churches encouraged the state to assume a more positive role in order to alleviate the human suffering which had been caused by unfettered industrialization and urbanization.

7. Richard A. Baer, Jr., "The Supreme Court's Discriminatory Use of the Term 'Sectarian,'" *Journal of Law and Politics* 6 (1990): 463-66.

8. Traditionally, private associations (e.g., families, churches, workplaces, unions, ethnic clubs) have provided meaningful communal and social life for people and have mediated between the individual and the state. Now the state itself is concerned with the fostering of community. For a focus on building a sense of community through land use regulation, see Carol M. Rose, "Preservation and Community: New Directions in the Law of Historic Preservation," *Stanford Law Review* 33 (February 1981): 495-533. Through such regulation, the state provides a variety of mechanisms for dispersal and redistribution of power, enabling, for instance, neighborhood self-government even as against a municipal government.

9. *Cantwell v. Connecticut*, 310 U.S. 296 (1940).

10. *McCollum v. Board of Education*, 333 U.S. 203 (1948); *Aguilar v. Felton*, 473 U.S. 402 (1985).

11. *Sherbert v. Verner*, 374 U.S. 398 (1963); *Wisconsin v. Yoder*, 406 U.S. 205 (1972).

12. *Walz v. Tax Commissioner*, 397 U.S. 664 (1970); *Corporation of the Presiding Bishop of the Church of Jesus Christ of the Latter-Day Saints v. Amos*, 483 U.S. 327 (1987).

13. *Employment Division v. Smith*, 494 U.S. 872, 110 S.Ct. 1595 (1990).

14. This is an adaptation (not an application) of a typology developed by Professor Marc Galanter and discussed in Clark D. Cunningham, "Why American Lawyers Should Go to India," *Law and Social Inquiry* 16 (Fall 1991): 800-01. Galanter's typology includes, *inter alia*, models of separation of powers between church and state and of limitation.

15. *Cunningham*, "Why American Lawyers Should Go to India," 800-01. See also, Robert M. Cover, "The Supreme Court 1982 Term-Foreword: Nomos and Narrative," *Harvard Law Review* 97 (1983): 4-68.

16. Sovereignty is defined as "a political organization having the ability to maintain a practical monopoly in the use of force to effect sanctions in a defined geographic area." John J. Gibbons, "Intentionalism, History, and Legitimacy," *University of Pennsylvania Law Review* 140 (December 1991): n. 19. With sovereignty comes exclusive lawmaking capacity, even though other "communities of interpretation"— like churches— have their own "law" relating to their "narratives, experiences, and visions." Cover, "Nomos and Narrative," 42-43. This is the case because, as Cover continues, "The state's claims over legal meaning are, at bottom. . . closely tied to the state's imperfect monopoly over the domain of violence," 52.

17. A balance is constitutionally necessary because absolute limitation could force churches to serve as arms of the state, or could outlaw religion altogether; total deference to churches could weaken the state's police powers, could threaten the establishment of one or more dominant churches, or could permit the usurpation of the machinery of the state for the goals of a church.

18. For excellent discussions of the disestablishment decision, see Carl H. Esbeck, "Establishment Clause Limits on Governmental Interference with Religious Organizations," *Washington and Lee Law Review* 41 (Spring 1984): 347; and Steven D. Smith, "Separation and the 'Secular': Reconstructing the Disestablishment Decision," *Texas Law Review* 67 (April 1989): 959-75.

19. James Madison, "Memorial and Remonstrance Against Religious Assessments, 1785," in Arlin M. Adams and Charles J. Emmerich, *A Nation Dedicated to Religious Liberty: The Constitutional Heritage of the Religion Clauses* (Philadelphia: University of Pennsylvania Press, 1990), 104-10. The founders rejected the Hobbesian model of an omnipotent state and adopted a decidedly Lockean perspective of limited government.

20. "The religion clauses of the Constitution seem to me unique in the clarity with which they presuppose a collective, norm-generating community whose status as a community and whose relationship with the individuals subject to its norms are entitled to constitutional recognition and protection." Cover, "Nomos and Narrative," n. 94.

21. James Madison, "Memorial and Remonstrance," 104-10.

22. "Although the U.S. constitutional scheme is often described as if the relationship [between church and state] is that of separation of powers, Galanter suggested that the mode is more that of limitation. In the limitation mode legal authorities shape religion indirectly by limiting religious authority to fields defined by law as religious and overruling religious claims of authority over fields defined by the law as secular. This very power to define what is secular and what is religious gives law superiority over religion, thus distinguishing the limitation mode from true separation of powers, where legal authorities would presumably defer to a religion's own definition of what was religious and what was secular." Cunningham, "Why American Lawyers Should Go to India," 800-01.

23. *Wisconsin v. Yoder*, 406 U.S. 205 (1972); *Kedroff v. Saint Nicholas Cathedral*, 344 U.S. 94 (1952).

24. *United States v. Lee*, 455 U.S. 252 (1982); *Employment Division v. Smith*, 494 U.S. 872 (1990).

25. *Lemon v. Kurtzman*, 403 U.S. 602 (1971); *Walz v. Tax Commission*, 397 U.S. 664 (1970).

26. *Larkin v. Grendel's Den*, 459 U.S. 116 (1982); *County of Allegheny v. ACLU*, 492 U.S. 573 (1989).

27. *Watson v. Jones*, 13 Wall. 679 (1872). The federal common law holding in this case was later constitutionalized in *Kedroff v. Saint Nicholas Cathedral*, 344 U.S. 94 (1952).

28. *Jones v. Wolf*, 443 U.S. 595 (1979).

29. See generally, Douglas Laycock, "Towards a General Theory of the Religion Clauses: The Case of Church Labor Relations and the Right to Church Autonomy," *Columbia Law Review* 81 (November 1981): 1373.

30. For a criticism of this case, see Douglas Laycock, "The Remnants of Free Exercise," *The Supreme Court Review* (1990): 10-11.

31. *NLRB v. Catholic Bishop,* 440 U.S. 490 (1979).
32. *Jimmy Swaggart Ministries v. Board of Equalization,* 493 U.S. 378 (1990).
33. *Lemon v. Kurtzman,* 403 U.S. 602 (1971).
34. The test was enunciated in *Sherbert v. Verner,* 374 U.S. 398 (1963).
35. *Employment Division v. Smith,* 494 U.S. 872 (1990).
36. *Smith,* 110 S.Ct. at 1599. Additionally, *Smith* provides, at 1603, that the state cannot treat religious reasons worse than other reasons when it engages in individualized assessment of persons under statutes that permit exemptions.
37. Ibid. at 1601.
38. Ibid. at 1606.
39. Mary Ann Glendon and Raul F. Yanes, "Structural Free Exercise," *Michigan Law Review* 90 (December 1991): 532.
40. *United States v. Seeger,* 380 U.S. 163 (1965).
41. *Wisconsin v. Yoder,* 406 U.S. 205 (1972).
42. For another discussion of this topic, see, Angela C. Carmella, "A Theological Critique of Free Exercise Jurisprudence," *The George Washington Law Review* 60 (March 1992): 782.
43. Ernst Troeltsch noted the church-sect distinction, which is discussed in H. Richard Niebuhr, *Christ and Culture* (New York: Harper and Row, 1951), 45-82 (chapter entitled "Christ Against Culture").
44. Niebuhr, *Christ and Culture,* identifies five "types" of religious response to the problem of faith and culture, and only one of them is sectarian.
45. Ibid., 149-89 (chapter entitled "Christ and Culture in Paradox).
46. Ibid., 83-115 (chapter entitled "The Christ of Culture").
47. Ibid., 116-48 (chapter entitled "Christ Above Culture").
48. Ibid., 190-229 (chapter entitled "Christ The Transformer of Culture").
49. While the term "ecclesiology" has developed in Christian circles, its underlying concept seems more generally applicable to other traditions. The Orthodox, Conservative, and Reform branches of Judaism, for instance, take different approaches to the wider culture. The term is used here as shorthand for the faith-in-culture dilemma that faces most religious traditions. Ecclesiology focuses on the church's relation to society, and is not to be confused with a church's polity (i.e., its internal governance structure, such as hierarchical or congregational polity), or with a church's position on the proper relationship between church and state (i.e., a state church or strict separation), although these are usually significantly related to the ecclesiology. For an historical example of the complex interplay of these concepts, see C.M.A. McCauliff, "Law as a Principle of Reform: Reflections from Sixteenth-Century England," *Rutgers Law Review* 40 (Winter 1988): 457-63.
50. Avery Dulles, S.J., *Models of the Church* (New York: Doubleday, 1974).
51. Ibid., 71.
52. Ibid., 66.
53. Ibid., 85.
54. Ibid., 85-86.
55. Walter Kasper, *Theology and Church* (New York: Crossroads, 1989), 47. Kasper discusses at 45-46 the restoration model (critical of the modern era) and the progressive model (under which "the modern era has ceased to be viewed as an apostacy. It is now seen as the

realized form of Christianity in the world."), 55. He rejects the theology of secularization of the progressive model and offers an alternative model of correlation and analogy, 49.

56. Berger's analysis is discussed in Aylward Shorter, *Toward a Theology of Inculturation* (Maryknoll, N.Y.: Orbis Books, 1988), 48.

57. David A. Roozen, William McKinney, and Jackson W. Carroll, *Varieties of Religious Presence: Mission in Public Life* (New York: Pilgrim Press, 1984).

58. Harvey Cox, *The Secular City* (New York: Macmillan, 1965), 36.

59. See, for instance, Shorter, *Toward a Theology of Inculturation.*

60. Tex Sample, *U.S. Lifestyles and Mainline Churches: A Key to Reaching People in the 90s* (Louisville: Westminster/John Knox, 1990); Mark Ellingsen, *The Evangelical Movement: Growth, Impact, Controversy, Dialog* (Minneapolis: Augsburg, 1988).

61. Shorter, *Toward a Theology of Inculturation*, 42-45. See also, Stanley Hauerwas and William H. Willimon, *Resident Aliens: Life in the Christian Colony* (Nashville: Abingdon Press, 1989); John Howard Yoder, "A People in the World : Theological Interpretation," *The Concept of the Believer's Church*, ed. James Leo Garrett, Jr. (Scottdale, Penn.: Herald Press, 1969), 252-83.

62. Shorter, *Toward a Theology of Inculturation*, 42-45.

63. Hauerwas and Willimon, *Resident Aliens*, 41-43; Yoder, "A People in the World."

64. Hauerwas and Willimon, *Resident Aliens*, 43.

65. "Fundamentalism is a series of parallel socio-religious movements in the modern world that accept the *instrumental benefits of modernity* but not its value reorientations." Bruce B. Lawrence, *Defenders of God: The Fundamentalist Revolt Against the Modern Age* (San Francisco: Harper and Row, 1989), 6 (emphasis added).

66. Roozen et.al., *Varieties of Religious Presence*, 260-63.

67. The Court has been particularly vigilant in permitting churches to define their own doctrine and to preserve breathing room for "the free development of doctrine." *Presbyterian Church in the United States v. Mary Elizabeth Blue Hull Memorial Presbyterian Church*, 393 U.S. 440 (1969) at 449.

68. For a discussion of regulations which serve "to subsume religiously motivated conduct into the category of similar activities carried on by 'secular counterparts,' and thus to deny it the protection to which it is entitled as the 'free exercise' of religion," see Philip E. Draheim, "Concordia College Challenges the IRS," *Government Intervention in Religious Affairs*, ed. Dean M. Kelley (New York: Pilgrim Press, 1982), 90. For support of a presumptively broad understanding of religion when churches engage in activities also undertaken by secular counterparts, see James A. Serritella, "Tangling With Entanglement: Toward a Constitutional Evaluation of Church-State Contacts," *Law and Contemporary Problems* 44 (Spring 1981): 155-57.

69. "Regulation by the state . . . inevitably influences and alters churches' performance of their religious functions, sometimes in dramatic ways. . . . Governmental regulation typically reflects the dominant values of the community. Although regulation may alter churches, the change would likely be (at least from a majoritarian perspective) for the better. A secularist viewpoint may in any event attach slight value to the religious functions performed by churches and may therefore see little or no harm in regulations

that interfere with churches' performance of these functions."
Smith, "Separation and the 'Secular'," 1016-17.

70. Hauerwas and Willimon, *Resident Aliens*, 58-59, 116-124.
71. Laycock, "Remnants of Free Exercise," 56.
72. Laycock, "Towards a General Theory," 1412.
73. See this author's discussion of this point regarding *Jimmy Swaggart Ministries v. Board of Equalization*, 493 U.S. 378 (1990) in Carmella, "A Theological Critique," 798-99.
74. Professor Carl Esbeck has an excellent discussion of child-care licensing schemes in "Government Regulation of Religiously Based Social Services," 385-97.
75. Some facts for this hypothetical have been extracted from *Michigan Department of Social Services v. Emmanuel Baptist Pre-School*, 455 N.W. 2d 1 (Mich. 1990) discussed in Esbeck, "Governmental Regulation," 392-93.
76. Laycock, "Towards a General Theory," 1412.
77. See, e.g., *Corporation of the Presiding Bishop of the Church of Jesus Christ of the Latter-Day Saints v. Amos*, 483 U.S. 327 (1987).
78. Laycock, "Remnants of Free Exercise," 57.
79. Draheim, "Concordia College Challenges the IRS," 84-96.
80. Jesse Choper, "The Religion Clauses of the First Amendment: Reconciling the Conflict," *University of Pittsburgh Law Review* 41 (1980): 686.
81. Marc Galanter, "Religious Freedom in the United States: A Turning Point?" *Wisconsin Law Review* (1966): 280.
82. Ibid.
83. Ibid., 282.
84. Laycock, "Towards a General Theory," 1403-09.
85. *Walz v. Tax Commissioner*, 397 U.S. 664 (1970); *Corporation of the Presiding Bishop of the Church of Jesus Christ of the Latter-Day Saints v. Amos*, 483 U.S. 327 (1987).
86. *Larkin v. Grendel's Den*, 459 U.S. 116 (1982).
87. Choper, "Reconciling the Conflict," 686.
88. Ibid. 694-95.
89. Cf. this formulation with that set forth in *Texas Monthly, Inc. v. Bullock*, 489 U.S. 1 (1989), at n. 8, which focuses on the substantiality of the burden imposed on nonbeneficiaries and on the type of religious burden alleviated.
90. Choper, "Reconciling the Conflict," 696-98.
91. *Corporation of the Presiding Bishop of the Church of Jesus Christ of the Latter-Day Saints v. Amos*, 107 S.Ct. 2862 (1987) at 2869.
92. Ibid. at 2868.
93. Ibid. at 2869.
94. *Church of the Lukumi Babalu Aye v. City of Hialeah*, 723 F. Supp. 1467 (S.D. Fla. 1989), aff'd, 936 F.2d 586 (11th Cir. 1991).
95. Choper, "Reconciling the Conflict," 685.
96. Religious Freedom Restoration Act, H.R. 2797 (1991).
97. The Religious Freedom Restoration Act "would make a real difference, at least with respect to practices that judges and bureaucrats can recognize as religious. However the courts interpret it, RFRA would give churches and believers a legal theory and bargaining leverage in disputes with government agencies. The experience of lawyers representing religious communities is that officials often grant exemptions rather than go to the trouble of providing a compelling interest." W. Cole

Durham, Jr., Edward McGlynn Gaffney, Douglas Laycock, and Michael W. McConnell, "How to Restore Religious Freedom: A Debate," *First Things* 22 (April 1992): 51.

3

Taxation and the Advocacy Role of the Churches in Public Affairs

STANLEY S. WEITHORN and DOUGLAS F. ALLEN

When playing an advocacy role in public affairs, churches face the vexing possibility of losing their federal income tax exemptions by violating statutory limitations imposed upon their lobbying and campaign activities. There is, of course, a special irony about the imposition of these limitations on churches, since most of the matters about which churches might be stimulated to become politically active involve moral issues that go to the very core of their religious mission. This essay deals with the dilemma faced by churches as a consequence of this contradictory circumstance and argues that these limitations imposed upon churches by Congress, even if not constitutionally suspect, are in many respects not only extremely vague but often both unnecessary and undesirable.

CHURCHES AND TAX EXEMPTION

Before considering the nature and scope of the lobbying and campaign limitations placed upon churches, it is appropriate to consider the fundamental question of whether the federal government, because of the wording of the religion clauses, has the right to grant to, or withhold from, churches exemption from federal taxation. This is a crucial question because if the government cannot constitutionally grant tax exemptions to churches, then the lobbying and campaign limitations, which apply only to exempt organizations, would be inapplicable to churches.

The religion clauses provide that "Congress shall make no law respecting an establishment of religion, or prohibiting the free exercise thereof." An inherent conflict exists between these two clauses that fundamentally calls into question the ability of the federal government to regulate churches. This conflict can be observed by considering a series of questions. Does the prohibition on free exercise mean that the federal government cannot limit the tax-related activities of churches? If the prohibition does not mean this, then at what point does accommodation of the state to free exercise create so preferred a position for churches — first, in contrast to taxable entities and, second, in contrast to secular nonprofits — as to become the forbidden establishment of religion? If exemptions for churches were eliminated, would more substantial federal regulation including, at the extreme, federal taxation constitute impermissible interference with the free exercise of religion? Should the state even be involved in a dichotomy incapable of satisfactory resolution?

The United States Supreme Court has recognized the tension that exists between the two clauses and therefore has warned against "excessive administrative entanglement" with religion.[1] The opinion of the Court in the case of *Walz v. City of New York Tax Commission*, in which an individual contended that, as a property taxpayer, he was being forced by New York City to contribute indirectly to organized religion because of the exemption of churches from taxation, concluded that neither the Free Exercise Clause nor the Establishment Clause is violated by the existence of a state statute exempting religious organizations from real property taxes. In *dicta*, Chief Justice Warren Burger stated that the question of whether taxation, or exemption, of religious organizations violates either clause of the First Amendment depends on the degree of governmental entanglement. Entanglement itself is a vague concept. In one sense it connotes unnecessary involvement, but in a broader sense it suggests the taking of positions on issues that often arouse strong passions. While the Court's opinion in *Walz* dealt with city property tax exemptions, not federal income tax exemptions, the Court's decision was a strong affirmation of a government's right to tax churches or to refrain from taxing churches. The religion clauses are violated only if the taxation of a church or its receipt of a grant of tax exemption creates an excessive entanglement between government and religion.

Notwithstanding the significance of the *Walz* decision in respect to the issue of the constitutionality of granting tax exemption to churches, federal tax exemption for churches has long been recognized in the United States, dating back to the early stages of federal income taxation, as set forth in the Corporation Excise Tax of 1909.[2] The present tax statute, the Internal Revenue Code of 1986, continues the policy of granting tax exemptions, but with certain limitations. Section 501(c)(3) of the Internal Revenue Code sets forth an affirmative requirement — that the "church," in whatever format, be organized and operated exclusively for religious purposes. The same section also imposes three limitations. No part of the "church's" net earnings may inure to the benefit of any private shareholder or individual; no *substantial* part of the "church's" activities may consist of carrying on propaganda or otherwise attempting to influence legislation; and the "church" may not participate in, or intervene in (including the publishing or distribution of statements), any political campaign on behalf of (or in opposition to) any candidate for public office.

The Internal Revenue Service has a serious problem regarding the definition of terms such as "church" and "religious purposes."[3] A satisfactory definition is essential because of the privileges associated with exempt classification. Obvious privileges are exemption from income taxation and the deductibility of contributions by individuals to such organizations. Not so obvious, but of great significance, are other less publicized benefits. For instance, "churches" are exempt from federal financial reporting and tax audit provisions applicable to secular nonprofit organizations. In addition, "churches, their integrated auxiliaries, and conventions or associations of churches" are not required to file an application for determination of tax-exempt status as a precondition to exemption and eligibility to receive tax deductible contributions.[4]

"Churches, their integrated auxiliaries, conventions or associations of churches and the exclusively religious activities of any religious order" are not required to file annual returns[5] unless they have certain business income unrelated to their religious functions.[6]   Additionally, the Church Audit Procedures Act of 1984 repealed then existing church audit provisions and established certain new procedures.[7]   These new procedures apply to "churches, any convention or association of churches and any organization claiming to be a church." The procedures do not apply to integrated auxiliaries, church-supported schools, or other organizations incorporated separately from the church. It is disturbing to many that the Church Audit Procedures Act has added the concept of "any organization claiming to be a church," but has provided no definition for this term. While it is clear that a category, relating to exemption or deductibility, has been established that is broader than found elsewhere in the Code, its extent is unknown. The Act has attempted to establish some balance by providing that the audit limitation rules do not apply to fraudulent tax evasion schemes that utilize the form of a church in an effort to avoid taxes.[8]   Of course, there is no workable definition of such schemes. The "Catch-22" of the fraudulent schemes rule is that the Internal Revenue Service may not commence a church audit unless the regional commissioner reasonably believes, on the basis of facts and circumstances recorded in writing, that the organization may not be qualified, may be carrying on an unrelated trade or business or be otherwise engaged in profit-making activity. A notice, specifying grounds for the audit must be given at least fifteen days in advance and a pre-examination meeting must be offered. Other notice requirements apply as well.

Obviously, there are definitional problems with the word "church." "Church" does not appear in the United States Constitution; "religion" is used in the First Amendment, but it is not necessary for an individual to belong to a church in order to be considered religious. For instance, in *Torcaso v. Watkins*,[9] the United States Supreme Court held that a person otherwise qualifying cannot be barred from services as a notary public because he refused to take an oath invoking God, since this would otherwise prefer religion over irreligion or theistic religions over nontheistic religions. The tax law distinguishes between "churches" and nonchurch religious organizations. A Treasury Regulation to the Internal Revenue Code provides, in part, as follows:

The term 'church' incudes a religious order or a religious organization if such order or organization (a) is an integral part of a church, and (b) is engaged in carrying out the functions of a church, whether as a civil law corporation or otherwise. . . . A religious order or organization shall be considered to be engaged in carrying out the functions of a church if its duties include the ministration of sacerdotal functions and the conduct of religious worship. What constitutes the conduct of religious worship or the ministration of sacerdotal functions depends on the tenets and practices of a particular religious body constituting a church.[10]

This purported definition in fact proves to be no definition at all and merely indicates the problem of definition. As long as American society is characterized by extreme religious pluralism, there will always be an insurmountable definitional problem, leaving open the door to abuse or, at the least, intimidation by governmental agencies such as the Internal Revenue Service.

Once an individual's or organization's activities meet the "religious" standard, some level of governmental oversight is still warranted. Religious beliefs of course should be protected, but legitimate governmental responsibilities, including reasonable oversight of religious activities, also should be permitted. Moreover, religious activities should be required to meet reasonable standards established by the government pertaining to both civil and criminal conduct. Religious activities such as those that might constitute a breach of the peace, that endanger public morals, or that violate laws aimed at protecting the public welfare should be, and usually are, prohibited by law. Use of the mails to perpetuate a fraud, or to endanger public safety, for instance, also can be regulated by law.

The Internal Revenue Service, however, is restricted in its regulatory efforts by the lack of information required to be supplied by churches, in contrast to the extensive reporting required of nonreligious organizations. Other enforcement routes are utilized by the Internal Revenue Service against, for instance, perceived abuses by mail-order ministries, where audits have been conducted not of the ministries themselves, but rather of the individual members seeking to evade the payment of taxes.[11] In other cases, nontax statutes at the local level have been utilized in oversight and enforcement efforts. In America's diverse society, the activities, as distinguished from the beliefs, of an ever-increasing number of nonconventional groups will raise, for tax purposes, troublesome questions about how to distinguish genuine religious activity from fraudulent tax evasion.

Unfortunately, the current exemptions for churches do not distinguish between activities and beliefs. Lack of adequate definition in creating the special church reporting and audit rules allows too much governmental subjectivity in enforcement, creating the opportunity for governmental suppression of beliefs, often expressed in positions on controversial public moral issues. Additionally, granting preferences to churches creates for them a privileged position as compared with secular organizations that may be performing substantially the same functions, thereby restricting secular advocacy. Thus, by statutorily classifying "churches" in a preferred position over secular nonprofit organizations, Congress has given the Internal Revenue Service the opportunity to enforce, or not to enforce, the preference under ill-defined standards, raising the possibility that unpopular beliefs or positions on current social and moral issues may be repressed, and the possibility that certain beliefs, in addition to activities, may be preferred.

The issue of governmental oversight of religious organizations has been distorted because of the administrative entanglement concept expressed by the United States Supreme

Court in the *Walz* case. In essence, the Supreme Court said that tax exemption is beneficial to all concerned, because it avoids excessive governmental entanglement with religion. However, contrary to this assertion, it may be argued that, with regard to federal income taxation, the forgiving nature of the Internal Revenue Code's reporting and audit rules constitutes an interference with the federal government's legitimate interest in maintaining the integrity of its tax system.

MORAL ISSUES AND THE ADVOCACY ROLE OF CHURCHES

The federal government's involvement in the resolution of moral issues necessarily invokes the Establishment and Free Exercise Clauses of the First Amendment. The First Amendment precludes the government from establishing, or disestablishing, a religious institution. The First Amendment is designed to separate the bureaucracy of the state from the bureaucracy of the church. Throughout American history, churches and the federal government have been involved in attempts to resolve such moral issues as slavery, women's suffrage, temperance, and civil rights, to name just a few. Thus, religious and political beliefs are invariably intertwined, leading, of course, to conflicts between the two.

In considering the role of churches and government in resolving moral issues, one must start with two premises. First, the advocacy role of churches on moral issues is a proven and necessary function. Second, Congress has a legitimate interest in maintaining the integrity of the federal income tax system. To the extent that the temporal activities of churches (as opposed to their beliefs on moral issues) impact the tax system, the federal government has an overriding interest in supervising such activity. However, to the extent that the government, through its tax policy, chills the advocacy role of churches on moral issues, that tax policy should and must yield to the right of churches to engage freely in their religious mission.

It also is important to examine the role of tax policy and its
impact on the advocacy role of churches in public affairs in two
areas: first, the role of tax policy in the Internal Revenue
Service's validation or revocation of exempt status in the case of
"nonconventional" church groups and, second, the role of tax
policy in the participation of "mainstream" churches in public
advocacy concerning various moral issues.

The nature of churches in the United States has been one of
constant evolution. Many nonconventional church groups
operate throughout the United States, from the most marginal of
church groups to some of the most active churches in the
country such as the Church of Jesus Christ of Latter-day Saints,
Jehovah's Witnesses, and the Church of Scientology. These
churches advocate lifestyles and moral values in many cases
substantially different from those of mainline churches.
However, as noted earlier, there is no accepted definition of the
word "church." An organization labeling itself a "church" is, in
contrast to the secular nonprofit organization, largely insulated
from financial scrutiny by the Internal Revenue Service. These
groups, many with only a marginal relationship to "mainstream"
churches, initially, at least, enjoy a constitutionally created
freedom of organization and action that does not exist for
secular, nonprofit groups— a special benefit that results in the
growth of tax evasion schemes under the umbrella of the
"church."

The provisions of section 501(c)(3) require that a church, in
order to be tax-exempt, must be organized and operated
exclusively for "religious purposes." Yet there are no universally
accepted definitions of either "church" or "religious purposes."
Useful guidance for, and control of, the Internal Revenue Service
in its enforcement program for this aspect of tax exemption is
lacking.

Section 501(c)(3) requires that no part of a church's net
earnings may inure to the benefit of any private shareholder or
individual. This provision provides a weapon to be used by the
Internal Revenue Service to unmask fraudulent new religious
organizations such as "mail order ministries," small
nondenominational churches, and television evangelists who

solicit funds from the general public primarily for the benefit of the church founders. Examples of fraud are provided by cases such as *Basic Bible Church v. Commissioner*,[12] describing an obvious scheme to benefit the "church" founder, and *Riker v. Commissioner*,[13] involving the operation of a restaurant with the intent of evading tax on a secular, business activity.[14]

It is recognized, however, that the provision of special religious services such as baptism, marriages, and funerals, which are for the exclusive benefit of church members, do not constitute private inurement. The "religious purpose" of these kinds of services outweighs any element of private benefit. Along the same lines, the Internal Revenue Service has ruled that payment for pew rentals is a deductible religious contribution notwithstanding its exclusive consumption characteristic.[15]

When private inurement is an issue, the Internal Revenue Service often focuses on audits of the benefited individuals, particularly because there are no auditing restrictions for individuals. When the organization itself is examined, resort has been had on occasion to the proposition that a private benefit may result when "public policy" has been violated. For instance, in *Bob Jones University v. United States*,[16] the United States Supreme Court held that a religious college dedicated to the teaching and propagation of fundamentalist religious beliefs and not affiliated with any religious denomination, was not a tax-exempt organization because it practiced racial discrimination (it believed that the Bible forbids miscegenation), which constituted a violation of public policy. The *Bob Jones* decision highlighted the question as to whether a religious organization is subject per se to public policy limitations.

With a lack of workable guidelines, especially in dealing with the marginal church, the Internal Revenue Service is permitted to attack as the political pressures of the majority view of society may dictate. "Public policy" standards could be utilized as a weapon by mainline churches, through the political process, to suppress diversity, involving the state in the "excessive administrative entanglement" warned against in the *Walz* case. Because it holds the power to revoke the tax-exempt status of churches, the Internal Revenue Service is given an opportunity to control, through intimidation, those ideas it deems socially or politically unacceptable. While the federal government has a legitimate purpose in protecting its tax system from the perpetration of fraudulent activities, enforcement of tax policies always should be secondary to protecting the legitimate expression of ideas. This is especially true where, as here, tax policy guidelines are not clearly defined.

The lobbying and political activity limitations of section 501(c)(3) may limit the advocacy role even of mainline churches in the public debate of moral ideas. The rule to which churches are subject provides that no "substantial" part of their activities may consist of carrying on propaganda, or otherwise attempting to influence legislation. Thus, religious organizations are allowed to engage in an "insubstantial" amount of lobbying, whatever that may mean. There is an election under section 501(h) which allows as much as 20 percent of the expenditures of certain section 501(c)(3) organizations to be made for lobbying activities. But the section 501(h) election is not available to "churches," ironically, as the result of lobbying on this very issue by an important mainline church, although it is available to nonchurch religious organizations. The result is, once again, that a church advocating a minority position may be subject to enforcement action by the Internal Revenue Service because of its expression of ideas.

Unlike the lobbying limitation, the election campaign intervention prohibition, to which all section 501(c)(3) organizations are subject, is absolute. A violation can, under the literal language of the Internal Revenue Code, lead to Internal Revenue Service revocation of tax-exempt status and virtual destruction of the entity. For purposes of this prohibition, there is no distinction drawn among "churches," religious organizations, and other exempt organizations. This prohibition evolved from a Senate floor amendment offered by then-Senator Lyndon Johnson in 1954, apparently as a reaction to the provision of financial support to his 1954 primary opponent by an exempt organization. It represents questionable tax policy with no prior common law or statutory basis, and was enacted without hearings or debate.

The prohibition contains four elements. First, it prohibits participation or intervention, whether by oral and written statements, or other forms of speech. Even issue advocacy, rather than direct candidate advocacy, such as pro-choice or anti-abortion advocacy, may be prohibited. The Internal Revenue Service's rulings on issue advocacy have provided little meaningful guidance and only illustrate the capriciousness of that agency's enforcement actions. For instance, in one recent technical advice memorandum, the Internal Revenue Service found no intervention when an organization ran a series of issue advertisements which could be viewed as supporting one presidential candidate over another.[17] Shortly thereafter, on almost the same facts, the IRS ruled that the circulation of voter registration materials supporting "conservative" legislation was an impermissible intervention.[18]

Second, there must be a "campaign," but there is no definition of what constitutes a campaign, or when it begins or ends. For example, on the one hand, helping a governor-elect select his appointees and develop his legislation program has been held to be participation in a campaign, even though it took place after the election.[19] On the other hand, primaries, as opposed to general elections, have been held not to be campaigns.[20]

Third, there must be a candidate, which raises issues such as who is a "candidate" and when does an individual becomes a candidate. The only guidance is a Treasury Regulation which provides that a candidate is "an individual who offers himself or is proposed by others, as a contestant for an elective public office, whether such office be national, state or local."[21] This definition provides very little guidance, especially when contrasted with definitions that have been promulgated by other governmental agencies such as the Federal Election Commission[22] and the Federal Communications Commission.[23]

Fourth, there must be a "public office" involved. Once again, no clear definition is provided under section 501(c)(3). A definition drawn from an analogous area (private foundations) may, however, be of some use in this regard: "Whether a public employee holds a public office depends on the facts and circumstances of the case, the essential element is whether a significant part of the activities of a public employee is the independent performance of policy making functions."[24] In one case, an organization lost its tax exemption by urging its members to seek election as Democratic or Republican precinct committeemen.[25] Presumably, if a precinct committeeman is deemed to hold a "public office," virtually any civil officeholder would as well.

These Draconian results, based on ill-defined concepts, lead to the perception of abuse, particularly in the case of churches and other religious organizations which have a long history of public advocacy with respect to moral issues. There have been a number of recent occurrences of nonuniform enforcement of these rules by the Internal Revenue Service. For example:

Jesse Jackson's 1988 run for the presidential nomination was frequently endorsed by black churches, but that action was not followed by any significant Internal Revenue Service enforcement activity.

Jimmy Swaggert Ministries, which endorsed Pat Buchanan's presidential bid, was the subject of a recent "press release" which indicated that enforcement action not only had fallen short of revocation but was no more than a slap on the wrist and the extraction of a promise, in effect, "not to do it again." The press release, issued by the Swaggart organization, represented a most unusual procedure.[26]

John Cardinal O'Connor's threat to excommunicate pro-choice Catholic politicians running for reelection evoked no Internal Revenue Service sanctions.

Third party actions were commenced (but were dismissed by the Court on procedural "standing to sue" grounds) where the Internal Revenue Service was perceived to fail in its enforcement duties.[27]

The belief held by most churches that there is an obligation to speak out on moral issues that are irreversibly implicated in a political campaign will inevitably lead to conflict. The statutory restrictions described above create a serious chilling effect on churches, especially marginal churches, regarding their participation in public advocacy. Even so, there are widespread compliance problems. At the very least, there is a need to establish effective definitions. Viable definitions would allow churches to establish awareness education with respect to matters such as political campaign activity in contrast to political activity in general, the distinction between political campaign activity and lobbying activity, and individual as opposed to organizational campaign activity.

CONCLUSION

There is no valid historical reason for restricting the advocacy role of churches in public affairs. The present system of tax exemption, while necessary to protect the federal system of taxation from abuse, creates a chilling effect on issue advocacy. The Internal Revenue Service has shown itself not particularly well suited to an enforcement role in the area of church exemption. By establishing better definitions, Congress could control sporadic enforcement measures and encourage self-regulation, reducing the risk of excessive administrative entanglement. These improvements would enable America's churches (both mainline and "marginal") to engage in public advocacy on moral issues without the risk of unwarranted intervention by the federal government.

NOTES

1. *Walz v. Tax Commission of the City of New York*, 377 U.S. 664 (1970).
2. Chapter 6, Section 38, 36 Stat. 11.
3. See the essay in this volume by Derek Davis, "The Courts and the Constitutional Meaning of Religion: A History and Critique," pp. 89-119.
4. I.R.C. § 508(a)(c)(1)(A).
5. I.R.C. § 6033(a)(2)(A).
6. I.R.C. § 511.
7. I.R.C. § 7611.
8. I.R.C. § 7611(i).
9. *Torcaso v. Watkins*, 367 U.S. 488 (1961).
10. Treasury Regulation § 1.511-2(a)(3)(ii).
11. In early 1992 the Bush Administration considered placing in the 1993 federal budget a proposal requiring churches to disclose the names of all donors contributing over $500. Churches heretofore had not been subject to any reporting requirements as to donors. The proposal was not acted upon.
12. *Basic Bible Church v. Commissioner*, 74 T.C. 846 (1980).

13. *Riker v. Commissioner*, 244 F.2d 220 (9th Cir. 1957).
14. See, however, *C.E. Hobbs Foundation for Religious Training and Education, Inc. v. U.S.*, 91-2 USTC ¶50,444(8 October 1991), in which a menu that could have been for an annual church banquet was insufficient evidence to establish that a church was in the restaurant business.
15. See, as an illustration, Revenue Ruling 70-47, 1970-1 C.B. 49, but see also *Hernandez v. Commissioner*, 490 U.S. 680 (1989), in which the Supreme Court found that contributions to the Church of Scientology for participation in religious training and auditing sessions were quid pro quo transactions in which the church member received a tangible benefit, resulting in denial of a charitable deduction. In a dissenting opinion in *Hernandez*, Justices Sandra Day O'Connor and Antonin Scalia noted that the Internal Revenue Service has not acted in a consistent manner in the allowance of charitable deductions for gifts to churches.
16. *Bob Jones University v. United States*, 461 U.S. 574 (1983).
17. Technical Advice Memorandum 8936002 (24 May 1989).
18. Technical Advice Memorandum 9117001 (5 September 1990).
19. Revenue Ruling 74-117, 1974-1 C.B. 128.
20. *Fulani v. League of Women Voters Educational Fund*, 882 F.2d 621 (2d Cir. 1989).
21. Treasury Regulation § 501(c)(3)-1(c)(3)(iii).
22. The Federal Election Campaign Act of 1988, United States Code §431(2), defines a candidate as one who has either received or expended $5,000 or more seeking election to a federal office.
23. Regulations defining "candidate" for equal opportunity with respect to broadcasting are found in 47 Code of Federal Regulations §73.1940(a).
24. Treasury Regulation § 53.4946(1)(g)(2).
25. General Counsel's Memorandum 39811.
26. Jimmy Swaggert Ministries Press Release dated 17 December 1991; reprinted in The Exempt Organization Tax Review, Vol. 5, No. 2, p.205 (February 1992).
27. See *Abortion Rights Mobilization* cases: 487 U.S. 72 (1988); 885 F.2d 1020; 824 F.2d 156.

4

Government Monitoring of Religious Organizations

SHARON WORTHING VAINO

American society is one with a superabundance of information. Data collection is a $1 billion-a-year industry;[1] when last computed in 1982, it was found that the federal government maintained more than 3.5 billion files on individual Americans — averaging fifteen per person.[2] The Federal Bureau of Investigation is creating a data base on the 25 million Americans who have ever been arrested, even if not convicted.[3]

In 1991, a sixteen-member Information Reporting Program Advisory Committee was created as a forum to discuss information reporting to the Internal Revenue Service. The IRS currently processes a total of over 1 billion Form 1099s and Form W-2s annually,[4] as well as a myriad of other forms. This information does not sit idly; federal, state, and local employees administering various entitlement programs may follow procedures to obtain return information from the Wage and Information Returns File, which includes Form 1099s filed by payors of interest and dividends.[5] Is there too much investment income? The would-be recipient of benefits is found out and barred by this efficient use of reported information.

Churches and their affiliated institutions are not exempt from inclusion in the many centers of information processing found at the federal and state levels. Although a number of exemptions have been created to limit the information reporting required of churches and their related institutions, to the extent that they

fulfill "secular functions" (which very many do), they may be
subject to much the same reporting obligations as are imposed
on their "secular counterparts."

For example, the Internal Revenue Code requires that annual
information returns be filed with the IRS by all tax-exempt
organizations, with certain exceptions.[6] The statutory exceptions
are "churches, their integrated auxiliaries, and conventions or
associations of churches,"[7] certain small organizations,[8] and "the
exclusively religious activities of any religious order."[9] In
defining the most mysterious phrase in this exemption,
"integrated auxiliary of a church," Treasury Regulations state
that such an organization is one "whose principal activity is
exclusively religious."[10] The regulations add that this
requirement will not be met if the organization's principal
activity is "educational, literary, charitable, or of another nature
(other than religious) that would serve as a basis for exemption
under section 501(c)(3)" (the section pursuant to which churches
and their related organizations, as well as various other types of
organizations, are recognized as federally tax-exempt).[11]
Accordingly, unless church-related organizations not deemed to
be exclusively religious are the subject of a discretionary
exemption, they must file information returns with the IRS just
like similar secular organizations.

Supporters of enhanced reporting and disclosure
requirements can usually identify some examples of breaches of
trust by charitable or religious organizations which seem to
mandate more supervision by government. Unfortunately,
despite increasing levels of supervision, there will still be found
individuals who manage to maintain the appearance of
compliance until their actions are revealed in other ways.
Recently the United Way of America has appeared in the
headlines following the retirement of William Aramony, its
president since 1970, amid charges of financial misdealing. In a
report prepared for the United Way, hundreds of thousands of
dollars are described as having been diverted to improper uses.
Mr. Aramony reportedly denies the charges. The IRS, the Justice
Department, and the Congressional General Accounting Office
are said to have requested a copy of the report.[12] One would

expect that if any organization was in compliance with governmental reporting and disclosure requirements, the United Way of America would be. Such requirements apparently did not succeed in deterring the conduct which apparently occurred.

Compelled disclosure is often seen as the mildest means of government regulation available. In *Buckley v. Valeo*,[13] a case dealing with federal election reporting and disclosure requirements, the Supreme Court stated, "We note and agree with appellants' concession that disclosure requirements, certainly in most applications, appear to be the least restrictive means of curbing the evils of campaign ignorance and corruption that Congress found to exist."[14] The Court quoted a famous statement of Justice Louis Brandeis: "Publicity is justly commended as a remedy for social and industrial diseases. Sunlight is said to be the best of disinfectants; electric light the most efficient policeman."[15]

Opposing these commendations applied to mandatory submission of information to government are portions of the Bill of Rights constraining compelled disclosure. Compelled disclosure has been found to violate the Establishment Clause[16] and the Free Exercise Clause[17] of the First Amendment to the United States Constitution. The Third Amendment provides a certain protection against government intrusion. The Fourth Amendment provides protection from unreasonable searches and seizures. The Fifth Amendment limits the ability of government to compel testimony against oneself. A general "right to privacy" has been found to result from such guarantees. Accordingly, protection from the compelled submission of information is a significant aspect of a number of freedoms enumerated in the Bill of Rights.

THE INTERNAL REVENUE SERVICE
AS AN INFORMATION REPOSITORY

The largest, most effective national repository of information on churches and affiliated institutions is the IRS.[18] Much of this information is contained in the Exempt Organization section of

the Business Master File maintained by the IRS.[19] Prior to 1
January 1981, there was a separate Exempt Organization Master
File; it was then merged into the Business Master File, but as a
separate section.[20] The term "Master File" will be used here to
refer to both the earlier Exempt Organization Master File and the
Exempt Organization section of the Business Master File,
without distinction.

The Master File was commenced after a mailing of
questionnaires in the summer of 1964 to about five hundred
thousand organizations shown in the records of the IRS to be
tax-exempt. Since that time, the IRS has added organizations to
the Master File when it issued letters to them or received forms
from them.[21] Some churches have what are known as group
exemption letters — letters recognizing the exemption of a
central organization and those organizations it identifies as
affiliates. The central organization holding such a letter is
included in the Master File, but its subordinates generally are
not unless the subordinates are required to file returns with the
IRS. Churches or synagogues that have received individual
determinations from the IRS are listed unless "affiliated with
well-known religious denominations." [22]

Each record on an exempt organization included in the
Master File is divided into two parts. One is an "entity module"
with data that describes the organization and its exemption; the
other is a "return section" with information from returns filed by
the organization and examinations of it.[23] The Internal Revenue
Manual lists thirty data elements from the Master File that apply
to an included organization.[24] Some of these elements are: a
status code that indicates any actual or potential deficiencies in
the organization's tax exemption, a code indicating the amount
of the organization's assets, a code for the organization's gross
receipts as shown on its most recent return, and the year the
most recent audit was conducted. One of the status codes
indicates an intention by the IRS to conduct a pre-examination of
a church that has never received a determination regarding its
exempt status from the IRS.[25]

Another data element consists of the organization's "activity
codes." These codes are maintained on a current basis primarily

through the submission of applications for tax-exempt status and annual information returns. Organizations that submit applications to the IRS for recognition of their tax-exempt status are required to list up to three activity codes that best describe the organization.[26] Churches and their integrated auxiliaries are not required to file applications for tax-exempt status, but may wish to do so to assure their contributors of deductible contributions and to obtain special mailing rates more easily.

As described above, an annual information return filed with the IRS is also required of various tax-exempt organizations, but not churches and their integrated auxiliaries.[27] In 1969 the U.S. Senate continued the exemption of churches from filing information returns "in view of the traditional separation of church and state."[28] The information return formerly contained space for an organization to list up to three activity codes. The current version of the return does not require these codes to be listed, but does state that the organization must describe any activities not previously reported to the IRS.[29] Accordingly, the IRS would continue to receive information necessary for the activity codes to be kept current.

The list of activity codes in the Internal Revenue Manual[30] shows nine categories of religious activities, including "mission" as one category and "missionary activities" as another. There are four kinds of civil rights activities, and there are thirty-five codes under the heading of "Advocacy: Attempt to influence public opinion concerning" the Selective Service System, pacifism and peace, anticommunism, separation of church and state, and racial integration, among other issues. The Master File does not only record an organization's type, but also a very exact description of its issues of concern.

The National Computer Center is the source of individual output tapes which are then forwarded to various other divisions within the IRS. A wide range of outputs is regularly issued from the Master File. One of these outputs is a computerized national report produced quarterly showing all organizations with the various activity codes.[31] Another standard output is a register of certain churches and governmental instrumentalities not required to file pursuant to their exemption. This register is sequenced by district and then by year of latest examination; it is distributed to each key district.[32]

In addition to the outputs regularly issued from the Master File, other outputs are available upon request through the Exempt Organizations Standard Extract Program.[33] These outputs may be requested by IRS personnel and, to the extent permitted by the Internal Revenue Code, to members of the general public on a cost reimbursement basis. The Program can be used to identify all organizations exempt under a particular subsection of the Internal Revenue Code; such a criterion could be combined with a request for organizations identifying themselves with particular activity codes. One to three activity codes may be selected per request.

Thus, a list could readily be produced containing organizations exempt under section 501(c)(3) of the Internal Revenue Code that engaged in missionary activities and attempted to influence public opinion on the use of tobacco. As mentioned earlier, section 501(c)(3) is the section exempting what is generally regarded as the charitable sector — charitable, religious, educational, scientific, and certain other organizations. Listings produced under the Exempt Organizations Standard Extract Program include the name and address of each organization listed, its employer identification number, the applicable subsection under the Internal Revenue Code, a private foundation indicator, and other information depending on the nature of the request.[34]

Thus, there exists a highly sophisticated system capable of keeping track of all tax-exempt organizations in the country with a particular ideological persuasion. Furthermore, tax-exempt organizations' applications for exemption and annual information returns are open to public inspection, except for the schedule of contributors and information relating to trade secrets or similar matters.[35] The annual information return includes the names and addresses of directors and officers, the time they spend on their positions, and their compensation.[36] An interested person, having learned of the existence of a particular organization through this amazing indexing system, could then contact the individuals responsible for the organization or take certain actions with respect to them.

A proposal advanced early in 1992 by the Bush Administra-tion would have significantly increased the reach of the IRS tracking system. Organizations eligible to receive tax-deductible contributions with annual gross receipts of $25,000 or more, *including* churches and their affiliated organizations, would be required to file new information returns with the IRS and with certain donors. These information returns would report total charitable contributions of more than $500 by any individual donor during the calendar year.[37] Although the vice president stated that this proposal did not have his support or the support of President Bush, the White House chief of staff subsequently said that the proposal was not dead.[38] At present, the legislation containing this proposal appears unlikely to be adopted; however, the advancement of the proposal is significant.

If such a proposal were enacted, a computerized data base similar to the Wage and Information Returns File, discussed above, could easily be created.[39] One would expect that from this new file a printout could be produced listing the name, address, and Social Security number of each person contributing more than $500 in a year to a specified church. In addition, printouts could be produced listing other organizations to which donors to a particular church had made tax-deductible contributions of over $500. In this way, advocacy positions being forwarded by church members could be identified. Persons or organizations, including churches, found to support causes opposed by those with access to this information could conceivably be selected for some form of retribution.

STATE GOVERNMENTS
AS INFORMATION REPOSITORIES

State governments also collect information on charitable organizations, the broad category in which churches and their affiliated institutions are generally included, through regulation of charitable fundraising (or solicitation). A recent survey of the

fifty states and the District of Columbia found that only in
Alaska, Delaware, Idaho, Mississippi, Montana, and Wyoming is
charitable solicitation unregulated.[40] Idaho statutes nevertheless
give the attorney general the authority to supervise charitable
organizations.[41] In states where charitable solicitation is
regulated, the initial registration and ongoing reporting
requirements which are often a cornerstone of such regulation
may be imposed through laws giving the attorney general
power to supervise charitable organizations, rather than through
the solicitation provisions.[42] Again, reporting and disclosure
may be perceived as the least restrictive means of imposing
government regulation.

In the states which regulate charitable solicitation, religious
exemptions from registration and reporting requirements are
evident in the statutes of all states but Nevada.[43] This fact
illustrates the legislative approach, expressed in the Senate
report quoted above, of minimizing the regulation and
monitoring of churches by government. The types of
exemptions provided by the various state statutes vary, based
upon such characteristics as solicitation by professional
fundraisers, paid organizational staff, volunteers, and within or
outside one's membership; the purpose, manner, and
geographical scope of solicitation; and federal tax exemption and
purpose of the soliciting organization. Exemptions are generally
provided for small organizations. The range of exemptions
applicable to religious institutions from registration and
reporting is indicated in the following brief summaries of several
of these exemptions:

Indiana: All charitable organizations are exempt.[44]

New Hampshire: Religious organizations and their integrated
auxiliaries, conventional educational institutions, and hospitals
are exempt.[45]

Rhode Island: Religious organizations and affiliated integral
groups which have received a declaration of current tax-exempt
status from the IRS are exempt.[46]

Florida: "Bona fide" religious institutions and educational
institutions are exempt.[47]

Of course, the actual nature of the exemption will depend on how a statute is administered in a particular state. Some states have rather narrow wording governing their religious exemptions. For example, in Kentucky the statutory religious exemption applies to "solicitations by a religious organization for funds for religious purposes such as maintenance of a house of worship, conduct of services and propagation of its faith and tenets as distinguished from other charitable and civic purposes employed by nonreligious organizations."[48] Other exemptions in the Kentucky statutes apply to certain solicitations by educational institutions and by organizations from their own membership.[49] In Marylanstatutory religious exemption is somewhat broader, and applies only if a professional solicitor is not employed to "a bona fide religious organization, its parent, or a school affiliated with it, if the religious organization, its parent, or the affiliated school has received a declaration of current tax-exempt status from the government of the United States."[50] An exemption also applies to an organization soliciting within its membership, if no professional solicitor is employed.[51]

The Illinois statutory religious exemption applies, if the requirements discussed below are met, to a broad range of organizations: "a corporation sole or other religious corporation, trust or organization incorporated or established for religious purposes";[52] "any agency or organization incorporated or established for charitable, hospital or educational purposes and engaged in effectuating one or more of such purposes, that is affiliated with, operated by, or supervised or controlled by a corporation sole or other religious corporation, trust or organization incorporated or established for religious purposes";[53] and "other religious agencies or organizations which serve religion by the preservation of religious rights and freedom from persecution or prejudice or by fostering religion, including the moral and ethical aspects of a particular religious faith."[54]

Although the Illinois statutory religious exemption is broad in terms of the organizations covered, it is narrow in that, unlike almost all other states, the exempted religious organization must still file a registration statement and receive notice from the attorney general that the claimed basis of exemption is genuine.[55] As stated above, the actual administration of this provision determines the effective scope of the exemption.

Under statutory provisions enacted in 1991, Nevada requires that all federally tax-exempt organizations operating in Nevada and receiving their major support from public donations file an annual report showing all receipts and expenditures realized through operating in the state. There is no stated exemption for churches.[56] This is the only state that regulates charitable solicitation in which an express exemption covering churches was not found.

It is apparent from the above summary that there is almost universal consensus among the states that religious organizations ought not to be subject to the reporting and disclosure requirements applicable to charitable organizations generally. Is this because religious organizations have higher standards and are less in need of supervision? Probably not; the more likely explanation seems to be that the state governments feel religion is not a proper subject of regulation under constitutional principles and the concept of church-state separation. Given the increasing importance of the legislature in today's environment of judicial interpretation, these attitudes expressed in state statutes are quite significant.

There have been occasional efforts by localities to use regulation of fundraising in an effort to deter religious organizations not to their liking. An example is a charitable solicitation ordinance passed by the City of Clearwater, Florida, later amended, which was aimed at the Church of Scientology in Clearwater. The constitutionality of the amended ordinance is currently being litigated.[57]

COMPELLED DISCLOSURE AND THE COURTS

As mentioned above, compelled disclosure of information to governmental authorities has been found to implicate a number of rights set forth in the Bill of Rights. Churches and their related institutions have periodically challenged various forms of compelled disclosure, generally as part of a larger regulatory scheme. Such challenges have at times met with success, depending to a significant degree on a particular court's perception of equity.

One of the most pronounced victories for a church-related institution challenging compelled disclosure occurred in the 1979 case of *Surinach v. Pesquera de Busquets*,[58] a first circuit decision. At issue was an order of the secretary of Consumer Affairs of Puerto Rico for production of documents regarding the cost of parochial school education. The order was contested by the president of the Inter-Diocesan Secretariat for Catholic Education of Puerto Rico and by various superintendents of Roman Catholic schools in Puerto Rico. The court found the order to be unconstitutional, resting its decision "solely on the free exercise clause,"[59] and citing the "palpable threat of state interference with the internal policies and beliefs of these church related schools."[60] A review of circuit court decisions citing *Surinach*, however, indicates a tendency towards enforcing mandated disclosure and other regulatory efforts.

Of nine circuit court decisions citing *Surinach*, discussed below, three decisions found a constitutional or statutory violation; of the two finding constitutional violations, one was reversed by the Supreme Court on procedural grounds and the other was contrary to the decision of the Supreme Court in an appeal taken in another case with very similar issues. In a fourth decision, the court was evenly divided. The other five decisions found no church-state violation.

A constitutional violation was found by the circuit court in *Dayton Christian Schools, Inc. v. Ohio Civil Rights Commission*, reversed by the Supreme Court on procedural grounds.[61] The Supreme Court, with Justice William H. Rehnquist writing for the majority, held that because of the nature and stage of state proceedings at issue in the case, under the abstention doctrine the case should not have been adjudicated in federal court.[62] The Ohio Civil Rights Commission would not necessarily violate federal constitutional principles if its proceedings were continued; if it did so, such claims could be raised in judicial review of these proceedings in state court.[63] The Supreme Court also stated that constitutional rights were not violated by a mere investigation of the facts by the Commission.[64]

The circuit court in this case had held that to permit the application of the Ohio Civil Rights Act against a pervasively religious school[65] under the facts presented "impermissibly entangles the state in issues of faith in violation of the Establishment Clause of the First Amendment."[66] The school had terminated a married teacher for consulting an attorney after being told that her contract would not be renewed because she was pregnant; the school believed that mothers should stay home with their young children. The school claimed that in consulting an attorney, the teacher had not followed the "Chain of Command" described in her employment contract, a procedure the school believed to be biblically based.

The court cited *Surinach* in this case for the principle that if a regulatory scheme promises to lead to "serious constitutional problems," the courts should invalidate the scheme without waiting for these problems to run their full course.[67] The disclosure of information was not a matter of dispute in the *Dayton Christian Schools* case; however, in pursuing its investigation of the employment discrimination issue, the Ohio Civil Rights Commission had requested employee personnel files, information about employee pregnancies, blank employment applications, job descriptions, model contracts, employee handbooks, and employee rules and regulations.[68] In reaching its conclusion that impermissible entanglement was created by the Ohio Civil Rights Commission's evaluation of the teacher employment decisions by Dayton Christian Schools, the court stated that the continuing exercise of jurisdiction over employment disputes by the Ohio Civil Rights Commission, "along with the types of records the [Commission] seeks and the Commission's subpoena power, create the likelihood that allowing the Commission to exercise jurisdiction will result in the 'comprehensive, discriminating, and continuing state surveillance' of which the Court disapproved in *Lemon I*."[69] Accordingly, the element of compelled disclosure was a factor in the circuit court's finding of impermissible entanglement.

Another circuit court decision citing *Surinach* and finding a constitutional violation was *Rhode Island Federation of Teachers v. Norberg.*[70] The issues in this case were very similar to those in *Mueller v. Allen;*[71] the latter case, affirmed by the Supreme Court, found no constitutional violation. The *Norberg* court referred generally to *Surinach* when stating that excessive entanglement of church and state would result from the involvement necessary to guarantee that instructional materials for which tax deductions were taken were secular.[72]

Compelled disclosure of information was the central issue in *United States v. Holmes,*[73] in which the IRS sought to enforce a summons against David Holmes, bishop and director of the Miletus Church, Inc., in an investigation of the church's entitlement to tax-exempt status. This case was decided on statutory grounds. The court noted that in 1969 Congress had limited the power of the IRS to audit churches by adding subsection (c) to section 7605 of the Internal Revenue Code, restricting audits as follows: "No examination of the religious activities of [a church or convention or association of churches] shall be made except to the extent necessary to determine whether such organization is a church or a convention or association of churches, and no examination of the books of account of such an organization shall be made other than to the extent necessary to determine the amount of tax imposed by this title."[74] The court stated that the "extent necessary" wording was narrower than the "may be relevant" standard that might otherwise apply. The court found that the summons, which requested all minutes of meetings of officers, directors, trustees, or ministers and all correspondence for almost three years, as well as a sample of every piece of literature relating to the Miletus Church and all documents regarding church organization, was too far-reaching under this statutory standard.[75]

Although constitutional interpretation was not necessary in addressing the problem at hand, the *Holmes* court reviewed constitutional considerations and concluded that if the summons were properly narrowed, it would be enforceable.[76] It cited *Surinach* when stating that the "excessive entanglement" argument being made by Holmes was "conceptually . . . grounded in the free exercise clause and not the establishment clause."[77] The "excessive entanglement" test was developed, of course, in the context of Establishment Clause interpretation.[78]

The last of these circuit decisions citing *Surinach* in which a religious objection was accommodated was *Universidad Central de Bayamon v. National Labor Relations Board*.[79] An equally divided circuit court, sitting en banc, did not grant the National Labor Relations Board's request to compel the University to bargain with a faculty union.[80] The original circuit decision[81] had ordered enforcement of the National Labor Relations Board's order.[82] In his dissenting opinion in the original decision, Judge Juan Torruella cited the same passage from *Surinach* as was cited in *Dayton*. The University at issue had been founded by the Dominican Order of the Roman Catholic Church, which maintained administrative control and provided a "'basically' secular education."[83]

Various other circuit decisions citing *Surinach* found that excessive entanglement did not result from the particular practice at issue. In the circuit court decision in *Mueller v. Allen*,[84] later affirmed by the Supreme Court as stated above, the court dealt with a tax statute very similar to that challenged in *Rhode Island Federation of Teachers v. Norberg*.[85] The court excerpted the treatment of *Surinach* in *Norberg*, described above, in its discussion,[86] but preferred the reasoning of Judge Robert Renner of the lower court. Judge Renner had stated that the entanglement resulting from review of questionable textbook purchases would be minimal, and that the deduction would be policed by means of the individual audit, which would not necessarily result in excessive entanglement of the state in church affairs.[87]

In *New Life Baptist Church Academy v. Town of East Longmeadow*,[88] a school operated by an independent congregation challenged the approval procedure sought to be applied to it by the School Committee of the Town of East Longmeadow.[89] The Academy stated that it did not object to supplying certain information to the School Committee and permitting its officials to visit the school and observe classes, but did object if these activities were conducted as part of an approval procedure. The Academy did not believe it should submit to an approval process, and suggested standardized testing as part of an alternative approach.[90] In reversing the lower court and finding the School Committee's approach acceptable, the Court of the First Circuit reviewed both free exercise and establishment arguments.

In reasoning not reflecting the Supreme Court's decision in *Employment Division v. Smith*,[91] the circuit court found that any burden placed on religious free exercise by the School Committee's intended procedures was constitutional.[92] The court then examined whether excessive entanglement would be created between government and religion in violation of the Establishment Clause. Although the court found it possible that the School Committee might implement its procedures "in ways that would unreasonably and unnecessarily entangle it with the religious aspect of teaching,"[93] it did not find a "'reasonable likelihood' of excessive entanglements" (quoting *Surinach*),[94] and thus did not find an Establishment Clause violation.

The Department of Consumer Affairs of Puerto Rico, defeated in *Surinach*, made another appearance in *Cuesnongle v. Ramos*.[95] This case also involved the Universidad Central de Bayamon, whose confrontation with the National Labor Relations Board was discussed above.[96] Following disruption of the University's activities by a strike by some non-teaching employees, some students alleged that their contract was breached by the University. The Department of Consumer Affairs ordered the University to return the registration fee to one of the students for breach of contract.[97] In summarizing the issues, the initial circuit court decision stated: "In *Surinach* the matter of religion was conceded; the issue was the degree of interference, which we found excessive. Here there is no question that there was interference; the issue is religion."[98] Because the University gave degrees in many disciplines, the court concluded that it was not "primarily carrying on a religious activity in the First Amendment sense."[99] Because it did not believe that religion was an element of the controversy, the court determined that there was no free exercise violation,[100] but remanded the case to permit amendment of the complaint to assert other First Amendment objections.[101]

When the remanded case was later appealed, the circuit court found that First Amendment rights had not been abridged.[102] It cited the lower court's statement that the order to return the registration fee was not a "governmental surveillance, control, and regulation over the internal affairs" of the University that would violate the University's academic freedom.[103] It stated that the University "was not compelled to disclose any matters which would harm associational or speech rights."[104] Once again, the matter of compelled disclosure was considered significant, although a violation was not found.

Other parties attempting to use *Surinach* as a shield from compelled disclosure have been even less successful. In *United States v. Gering*,[105] *United States v. Freedom Church*,[106] and *Ambassador College v. Geotzke*,[107] *Surinach* was used in an effort to strike down a mail cover on a minister, a church, and its related enterprises;[108] the enforcement of an IRS summons directing production of books and records, including lists of substantial contributors and members who had taken vows of poverty;[109] and a court order compelling discovery of information, including names of persons in Georgia who conveyed or devised property to Ambassador College, and the compensation of officers, directors, and trustees.[110] In each case, the circuit court indicated less than full confidence in the bona fides of the party seeking protection, and in each case, the *Surinach* protection was denied.[111]

STATUTORY RESTRICTIONS ON CHURCH AUDITS

Clashes between churches and the IRS over the IRS audit process led to the repeal of section 7605(c) of the Code governing IRS examination of churches, quoted above in the discussion of *United States v. Holmes*,[112] and the adoption of a new section 7611.[113] Section 7611 contains very detailed provisions as to required notifications that the IRS must provide to a church under investigation, stages of inquiry, the level of the IRS official's authorizing the investigation, time limits, and protections applicable to church records. It is evident that much care was taken in drafting these provisions and the "Questions and Answers" issued by the IRS's interpreting them.[114] The "Questions and Answers" express an awareness of constitutional issues in the examination of churches.[115]

For the purposes of section 7611, "church" includes any organization claiming to be a church, as well as any convention or association of churches.[116] The "Questions and Answers" add that separately incorporated church-supported schools and other separately incorporated organizations are not considered churches for purposes of section 7611.[117] Certain types of inquiries are outside the scope of section 7611, as interpreted by the "Questions and Answers." These are so-called routine requests to a church;[118] requests to a church for information enabling the IRS to locate records held by a third party, such as bank records, and the acquisition of such records by the IRS;[119] inquiries relating to the tax liability of a person other than a church (such as a pastor, as in the examination of possible inurement); special assessments under other enumerated sections of the Code; knowing failure to file a return; willful efforts to evade tax; and any criminal investigations.[120] Consequently, a great deal of information relating to a church may be obtained without application of the limiting provisions of section 7611. The "Questions and Answers" provide, however, that third party bank records and examinations of individuals' and other organizations' tax liabilities will not be used in a manner inconsistent with the procedures of section 7611.[121] In addition, before the IRS may determine that a church is not entitled to tax exemption or make an assessment of unrelated business income tax against a church, requirements of section 7611 must be followed.[122] Contributor and membership lists held by a church are to be examined in accordance with the procedures of section 7611.[123]

The "Questions and Answers" issued under section 7611 contain interesting provisions relating to informants. The "Questions and Answers" state that when notice is provided to a church pursuant to section 7611 upon commencement of a church tax inquiry, the concerns giving rise to the inquiry should be explained, but that the IRS "would not be required to reveal the existence or identity of any so-called 'informers' within a church (including present or former employees)."[124] In a subsequently written notice of a proposed examination of a church, also governed by section 7611, the "Questions and Answers" provide, "Disclosure to the church will be subject to restrictions regarding the disclosure of the existence or identity of informants."[125] The latter notice must offer the church an opportunity for a conference with the IRS; at such a conference, the identity of third-party witnesses and information regarding evidence provided by them "will not be revealed."[126] Clearly the IRS contemplates the receipt of information from informants as a component of its church audit program. (Of course, the role of "informant" in church life has well-known historical precedent.)

Similar to its predecessor statutory section, section 7611 states that the IRS may examine church records only "to the extent necessary to determine the liability for, and the amount of, any tax imposed by this title."[127] This restriction was interpreted in *United States v. Church of Scientology of Boston, Inc.*[128] In that case, the IRS asserted that in order to obtain the church records it sought, it need only prove that the records "may be relevant" to the inquiry.[129] The court stated that according to the reading of the statute advanced by the IRS in that case, the "necessary" restriction of the statute would "forbid the IRS to look at church books for purposes of determining liability for some other tax, or for purposes of determining whether the church was breaking some totally different law, or perhaps just for fun."[130] As long as the examination was intended to determine the right type of liability, however, it would be considered "necessary," according to the IRS.[131] The court rejected this creative reading and stated that because the IRS had not shown the church records it sought to be "necessary" to its investigation, the refusal of the district court to enforce the summons was affirmed.[132]

The enforcement of IRS summonses for information was again at issue in *United States v. Church Universal and Triumphant, Inc.,* a decision of the United States District Court for the District of Montana.[133] In this case, however, the court held that the IRS had properly followed the procedures of section 7611 of the Internal Revenue Code, that the information being sought by the two summonses at issue was necessary to the IRS investigation, and that the summonses should be enforced.

CONCLUSION

Federal and state statutory provisions, as well as case law based on constitutional restrictions, show concern for the effect compelled disclosure by religious organizations may have upon religious and other freedoms. The continuation of statutory and regulatory protections indicates a reluctance by governmental authorities to invade what are felt to be constitutionally protected areas of church autonomy. There is scant judicial precedent for denying a governmental attempt at compelled disclosure on solely constitutional grounds, however, when nothing further is immediately at stake. The increasingly ready use of information that may be achieved through computer data bases has amazing potential for monitoring and surveillance of religious organizations, and should inspire to vigilance those who cherish religious freedom.

NOTES

1. Richard Lacayo, "Nowhere to Hide," *Time*, 11 November 1991, 34.
2. Ibid., 39.
3. Ibid., 40.
4. "New IRS Advisory Panel to Address Information Reporting," CCH Standard Federal Tax Reports, Taxes on Parade, no. 49, 30 October 1991, 3-4.
5. "Return Information Available to Government Agencies," CCH Standard Federal Tax Reports, Taxes on Parade, no. 34, 31 July 1991, 4-5.
6. Internal Revenue Code, § 6033(a)(2)(A).
7. Ibid., § 6033(a)(2)(A)(i).
8. Ibid., § 6033(a)(2)(A)(ii).
9. Ibid., § 6033(a)(2)(A)(iii).
10. Treasury Regulations, § 1.6033-2(g)(5)(i)(c).
11. Ibid., § 1.6033-2(g)(5)(ii).
12. "United Way Finds Pattern of Abuse by Former Chief," *New York Times*, 4 April 1992, 1.
13. *Buckley v. Valeo*, 424 U.S. 1 (1976) (*per curiam*).

14. Ibid. at 68 [footnotes omitted].
15. Ibid. at 67.
16. *Lemon v. Kurtzman*, 403 U.S. 602 (1971).
17. *Surinach v. Pesquera de Busquets*, 604 F.2d 73 (1st Cir. 1979).
18. For an extensive discussion of the IRS role in overseeing tax-exempt organizations and churches in the 1970s, see Sharon Worthing, "The Internal Revenue Service as a Monitor of Church Institutions: The Excessive Entanglement Problem," *Fordham Law Review* 45 (March 1977): 929-48.
19. See Internal Revenue Manual 4 (CCH), Exempt Organization/Business Master File Handbook, § 410.
20. Ibid., § 410(1).
21. Ibid.
22. Ibid., § 220(2)(a).
23. Ibid., § 220(1).
24. Ibid., Exh. 15.
25. Ibid., § 440(6).
26. IRS Form 1023, Application for Recognition of Exemption Under section 501(c)(3) of the Internal Revenue Code, Part I, line 6; see also IRS Form 1024, Application for Recognition of Exemption Under section 501(a) or for Determination Under section 120, Part I, line 6.
27. Internal Revenue Code, § 6033(a).
28. Senate Committee on Finance, 91st Cong., 1st Sess., Tax Reform Act of 1969, Compilation of Decisions Reached in Executive Session 53 (Comm. Print 1969).
29. IRS Form 990, Return of Organization Exempt From Income Tax, Part VI, line 76.
30. Internal Revenue Manual 4 (CCH), Exempt Organization/Business Master File Handbook, Exh. 24.
31. Ibid., § 636.
32. Ibid., § 622(7).
33. Ibid., Chapter (10)00.
34. Ibid., Exh. 19.
35. IRS Instructions for Form 990, Return of Organization Exempt From Income Tax, General Instruction L.
36. IRS Form 990, Return of Organization Exempt From Income Tax, Part V.
37. H.R. 4150, *Economic Growth Acceleration Act of 1992*, 102d Congress, 2d Sess., 4 February 1992, § 363; Joint Committee on Taxation, *Summary of Revenue Provisions in the President's Budget Proposal for Fiscal Year 1993* (JCX-1-92), 3 February 1992, 40-41.
38. "I.R.S. Still Asks To See Church Records," *New York Times*, 6 March 1992, A17 .
39. See "New IRS Advisory Panel to Address Information Reporting," CCH Standard Federal Tax Reports, Taxes on Parade, no. 49, 30 October 1991, 3-4.
40. "State Laws Regulating Charitable Solicitations" in Charitable Giving and Solicitation (P-H), 901-45.
41. Idaho Code § 67-1401(4) (Michie 1989).
42. See, e.g., Ann. California Codes, Business & Professions Code, § 17510-17510.7 (West 1987, Supp. 1992); ibid., Government Code, § 12584-12586 (West 1992).
43. See "State Laws Regulating Charitable Solicitations" in Charitable Giving and Solicitation (P-H) at 901-945; Nevada Revised Statutes Ann. § 82.191 (Michie Supp. 1991).

44.   Burns Indiana Statutes Ann., § 23-7-8-1 (Michie 1989).
45.   New Hampshire Revised Statutes Ann., § 7:19 (Equity 1988).
46.   General Laws of Rhode Island, § 5-53-1(a)(1) (Michie 1987). A
      limited reporting requirement applies to a broader category of
      organizations referred to in the statute as "exempt." Ibid., § 5-53-
      3(b).
47.   Florida Statutes Ann., § 496.403 (West Supp. 1992).
48.   Kentucky Revised Statutes, § 367.660(2) (Michie 1987).
49.   Ibid., § 367.660.
50.   Ann. Code of Maryland, 1957, art. 41, § 3-203(4) (Michie 1990).
51.   Ibid., § 3-203(3).
52.   Smith-Hurd Illinois Ann. Statutes, ch. 23, § 5103, § 3(a)(1) (West
      Supp. 1992).
53.   Ibid.
54.   Ibid.
55.   Ibid., § 3(a).
56.   Nevada Revised Statutes Ann., § 82.021, 82.191 (Michie Supp.
      1991).
57.   See Plaintiffs' Memorandum in Support of Plaintiffs' Final Motion
      for Summary Judgment, *Americans United for Separation of Church
      and State v. City of Clearwater, Florida*, No. 84-699-CIV-T-17 (U.S.
      Dist. Ct., M.D. Fla., 29 Jan. 1992).
58.   *Surinach v. Pesquera de Busquets*, 604 F.2d 73 (1st Cir. 1979).
59.   Ibid. at 79, n.6.
60.   Ibid. at 76-77.
61.   *Dayton Christian Schools, Inc. v. Ohio Civil Rights Commission*, 766
      F.2d 932 (6th Cir. 1985), *reversed on procedural grounds*, 477 U.S. 619
      (1986).
62.   *Dayton Christian Schools* at 625.
63.   Ibid. at 629.
64.   Ibid. at 628.
65.   *Dayton Christian Schools*, 766 F.2d 932, 938 (6th Cir. 1985), *reversed
      on procedural grounds*, 477 U.S. 619 (1986).
66.   *Dayton Christian Schools*, 766 F.2d 932 at 961.
67.   Ibid. at 950, n.31.
68.   Ibid. at 935.
69.   Ibid. at 958-59 (citation omitted), quoting *Lemon v. Kurtzman*, 403
      U.S. 602 (1971) at 619.
70.   *Rhode Island Federation of Teachers v. Norberg*, 630 F.2d 855 (1st Cir.
      1980).
71.   *Mueller v. Allen*, 676 F.2d 1195 (8th Cir. 1982), *aff'd*, 463 U.S. 388
      (1983).
72.   *Rhode Island Federation of Teachers v. Norberg*, 630 F.2d 855 at 862.
73.   *United States v. Holmes*, 614 F.2d 985 (5th Cir. 1980).
74.   Ibid. at 988, n.5.
75.   Ibid. at 988.
76.   Ibid. at 990.
77.   Ibid. at 989.
78.   See discussion of *Dayton* beginning at n. 61.
79.   *Universidad Central de Bayamon v. National Labor Relations Board*,
      793 F.2d 383 (1st Cir. 1985) (citing *Surinach* in dissent), *vacated and
      enforcement denied by evenly divided court en banc*, ibid. (1st Cir.
      1986).
80.   Ibid. at 399.
81.   Ibid. at 397.
82.   Ibid. at 391.

83. Ibid. at 399-400.
84. *Mueller v. Allen,* 676 F.2d 1195 (8th Cir. 1982), *aff'd.* 463 U.S. 388 (1983).
85. *Mueller v. Allen,* 676 F.2d 1195 at 1200.
86. Ibid. at 1200, n.12.
87. Ibid. at 1202.
88. *New Life Baptist Church Academy v. Town of East Longmeadow,* 885 F.2d 940 (1st Cir. 1989), *rehearing and rehearing en banc denied* (1989), *cert. denied,* 494 U.S. 1066 (1990).
89. *New Life Baptist Church Academy v. Town of East Longmeadow* at 941.
90. Ibid. at 943.
91. *Employment Division v. Smith,* 494 U.S. 872 (1990).
92. *Employment Division v. Smith,* 885 F.2d 940 (1st Cir. 1989) at 952, *rehearing and rehearing en banc denied* (1989), *cert. denied,* 494 U.S. 1066 (1990).
93. *Employment Division v. Smith,* 885 F.2d at 953.
94. Ibid. at 954.
95. *Cuesnongle v. Ramos,* 713 F.2d 881 (1st Cir. 1983), *decision on remand aff'd,* 835 F.2d 1486 (1st Cir. 1987).
96. See discussion beginning at n. 79.
97. *Cuesnongle v. Ramos,* 713 F.2d 881 at 882-83.
98. Ibid. at 882.
99. Ibid. at 883.
100. Ibid. at 884.
101. Ibid. at 886.
102. *Cuesnongle v. Ramos,* 835 F.2d 1486 at 1502.
103. Ibid. at 1490.
104. Ibid. at 1502.
105. *United States v. Gering,* 716 F.2d 615 (9th Cir. 1983).
106. *United States v. Freedom Church,* 613 F.2d 316 (lst Cir. 1979).
107. *Ambassador College v. Geotzke,* 675 F.2d 662 (5th Cir. 1982), *rehearing and rehearing en banc denied* (1982), *cert. denied,* 459 U.S. 862 (1982).
108. *United States v. Gering* at 619.
109. *United States v. Freedom Church* at 318, n.4.
110. *Ambassador College v. Geotzke* at 663.
111. *United States v. Gering* at 620; *United States v. Freedom Church* at 320; *Ambassador College v. Goetzke* at 665.
112. *United States v. Holmes,* 614 F.2d 985 (5th Cir. 1980).
113. Internal Revenue Code, § 7611.
114. Treasury Regulations, § 301.7611-1.
115. See, e.g., ibid., Q&A-9, stating that the written notice to be sent upon the commencement of a church tax inquiry should explain "applicable administrative and constitutional provisions with respect to the inquiry."
116. Internal Revenue Code, § 7611(h)(1).
117. Treasury Regulations, § 301.7611-1, Q&A-3.
118. Ibid., Q&A-4.
119. Ibid., Q&A-5.
120. Ibid., Q&A-6.
121. Ibid., Q&A-5, Q&A-8.
122. Ibid., Q&A-5.
123. Ibid., Q&A-8.
124. Ibid., Q&A-9.
125. Ibid., Q&A-10.
126. Ibid.

127. Internal Revenue Code, § 7611(b)(1)(A).
128. *United States v. Church of Scientology of Boston, Inc.*, 933 F.2d 1074 (1st Cir. 1991), *rehearing denied* (1991).
129. Ibid. at 1076.
130. Ibid. at 1077.
131. Ibid.
132. Ibid. at 1075.
133. 92-1 U.S. Tax Cases (CCH), par. 50,015 (D. Mont. 1991).

5

The Courts and the Constitutional Meaning of "Religion": A History and Critique

DEREK DAVIS

Central to any discussion of the role of government in monitoring and regulating religion in public life is the meaning of the term "religion." The outcome of a variety of cases hinges upon the definition of this term as well as related terms such as "religious belief" and "religious organization." Entitlement to federal income tax exemptions and state property or sales tax exemptions are often dependent upon an organization's being classified as "religious." The ability of an organization to receive tax deductible contributions frequently depends upon its "religious" characterization. One's entitlement to an exemption from military service under federal law has usually required conscientious objection on "religious" grounds. And a minister's ability to opt out of the federal social security system requires proof of the "religious" character of his or her work.

All of these entitlements arise from statutory requirements that a recipient's beliefs or activities be adjudged sufficiently religious. Since it is typically government employees who make such determinations, this places in the hands of government officials an awesome power to regulate religion merely by characterizing certain activities or beliefs as nonreligious. The check on this power is ultimately located in the First Amendment's religion clauses, which provide: "Congress shall make no law respecting an establishment of religion or

prohibiting the free exercise thereof." While it may require
judicial action to invoke this check, the religion clauses are an
indispensable safeguard in our free society against protected
religious beliefs or activities being administratively classified,
without warrant, as nonreligious.

Yet the task of distinguishing religion from nonreligion has
proven to be a difficult one for American courts. The operative
word of the religion clauses— religion— was left undefined by
the framers. This omission, however, did not result from
oversight. To define the term would have placed a permanent
imprimatur upon only those forms of faith and belief that
conformed to their definition. The framers instead chose to
leave the term undefined, thereby protecting a diversity of
beliefs, not merely the traditional ones, from undue
advancement or prohibition of expression by government. This
guarantee of freedom of religion, the centerpiece of American
liberties, has served to protect all religions, old and new, against
governmental preference, intrusion, and harassment.

In considering the regulation of religion that occurs in the
definitional task, it has thus far been mentioned only that the
need for distinguishing religion from nonreligion arises in the
interpretation of statutes. Of course, the need arises in the
nonstatutory context as well. Frequently, individuals and
groups seek religious classification for their own beliefs merely
to enjoy the free exercise of those beliefs without governmental
interference. The kinds of examples that could be mentioned
here are infinite, but consider, for instance, the case of a prisoner
of a state correctional facility whose beliefs prohibit him on
religious grounds from cutting his hair. The state, which
requires regular haircuts for health reasons, claims that the
prisoner's beliefs are not religious at all, but emerge only from a
personal philosophy about living "according to nature." Are the
prisoner's beliefs protected under the Free Exercise Clause?
Some definition or description of the term "religion" is obviously
needed to resolve the dispute.

Regardless of whether the need to define religion arises in a
statutory or nonstatutory context, there are two fundamental
constitutional problems that make problematic any attempt to

define religion. First, any definition would arguably have the effect of dictating to religions, past and present, what they must be, and would therefore violate the Free Exercise Clause.[1] Second, because defining religion would approve of or support religions that conform to the definition in preference to those that do not, the Establishment Clause is arguably contravened as well. In deference to these constitutional checks on its power, government— whether legislatures, administrative employees, or judges— might tend to be too lenient, regarding as religious every system of beliefs that seeks to be regarded as such. This would create a chaotic situation, however, because our culture is one in which a great many entitlements attach to a religious determination. Government is therefore compelled to closely scrutinize religious claims to weed out those that are illegitimate. This dilemma in which government finds itself— on the one hand, being compelled by constitutional restraints to avoid defining religion and, on the other hand, being compelled by functional necessity to define or at least give clear description to the term "religion"— reminds us that the definitional task is at once improper and yet essential.

The task of giving meaning to the term "religion" inevitably falls to the judicial branch. By tracing the evolution of the meaning of religion, this essay will show that as religious pluralism in America has expanded, the constitutional meaning of religion has expanded as well. It is argued that the American courts' unwillingness to adhere to any fixed definition of religion prevents, in statutory and nonstatutory contexts alike, an otherwise inevitable erosion of religious liberty and diminution of our free society.

EARLY ATTEMPTS TO DEFINE "RELIGION"

The American judiciary's formal inquiry into the constitutional meaning of religion commenced in 1878 when the United States Supreme Court decided the case of *Reynolds v. United States*.[2] In that case the Court considered a Mormon's argument that his practice of polygamy was a religious duty and therefore protected under the Free Exercise Clause. The Court held that the trial court had not been in error to refuse to charge the jury that if Reynolds believed it was his religious duty to practice polygamy, he must be found not guilty of bigamy. In searching for the scope of protected religious activity in the Constitution, the Court stated: "The word 'religion' is not defined in the Constitution. We must go elsewhere, therefore, to ascertain its meaning, and nowhere more appropriately, we think, than to the history of the times in the midst of which the provision was adopted."[3]

The Court examined statements made by James Madison and Thomas Jefferson for guidance in ascertaining the framers' meaning of the word "religion." For Madison, religion was "the duty we owe to our creator,"[4] and for Jefferson, " a matter which lies solely between man and his God."[5] While these statements are far from being exhaustive definitions, they accord with the common understanding of religion in late eighteenth-century America as a relationship between a person and some Supreme Being. But while Madison, Jefferson, and most of the founders were theists, there is no evidence that the constitutional framers wrote the First Amendment to protect only theism. Some of the founders clearly sought religious freedom for nontheists. Jefferson, for example, wrote that his Virginia Statute for Religious Freedom was to "comprehend within the mantle of its protection the Jew and Gentile, the Christian and Mahometan, the Hindoo, and infidel of every denomination."[6] The Court's inquiry into the founders' understanding of the meaning of religion produced no clear answers. Satisfied that the defendant's polygamous practices were too unconventional to be protected by the First Amendment, the Court found it unnecessary to formulate a definition of religion.

Twelve years later the propriety of polygamy was again the issue before the Supreme Court. In *Davis v. Beason*,[7] the Court upheld an Idaho statute that required individuals registering to vote to swear that they neither practiced polygamy nor belonged to any organization that looked upon polygamy favorably. The defendant, a devout Mormon, asserted that the statute violated the Free Exercise Clause. This time the Court was more specific in stating its understanding of the term "religion": "The term 'religion' has reference to one's views of his relations to his Creator, and to the obligations they impose of reverence for his being and character, and of obedience to his will."[8] But while the defendant's beliefs and practices clearly fit within this definition, the Court held that only his beliefs, and not his practices, were protected under the First Amendment. In finding the statute not to be in violation of the First Amendment, the Court stated: "Whilst legislation for the establishment of a religion is forbidden, and its free exercise permitted, it does not follow that everything which may be so called can be tolerated. Crime is not the less odious because sanctioned by what any particular sect may designate as religion."[9] The First Amendment provides no protection, the Court said, for "acts inimical to the peace, good order and morals of society."[10]

The struggle of the Mormons before the American courts to validate their religious practices mirrored the struggle of many minority faiths in the nineteenth century to find acceptance in a Protestant-dominated society. The immigration of great numbers of Catholics and Jews between the 1830s and 1850s occurred simultaneously with the growth of Mormonism, America's oldest indigenous community of faith. But even with this expansion of religious and cultural pluralism, the liberties of the First Amendment did not, for all practical purposes, extend far beyond the Protestant world. While no Protestant denomination enjoyed the patronage of government in any official sense, traditional Protestants collectively expected, and enjoyed, an unofficial government endorsement. The consequence was the restriction of the full religious liberties of lesser known communities of faith.[11] The Mormon decisions of the late nineteenth century should be read and understood in this context.

The *Davis* Court's substantive definition of religion emphasizing traditional ideas of obedience to and worship of a deity continued to be affirmed by American courts well into the twentieth century.[12] As late as 1931, the Supreme Court seemed to reaffirm this interpretation when Chief Justice Charles Evans Hughes concluded that "the essence of religion is belief in a relation to God involving duties superior to those arising from any human relation."[13] And it was not uncommon to see courts interpreting religion even more narrowly than this. Among the scores of examples that could be cited is an Oklahoma court's conviction of a spiritualist fortune-teller in 1922 for her commercial activities even though she believed in God and claimed merely to be practicing her religion.[14] In another case, a county board of commissioners in Nebraska denied a property tax exemption to a Masonic order, ruling that the order was not religious because it was not sectarian and did not demand the exclusive "religious" allegiance of its members. The board's decision was affirmed on appeal.[15] Such narrow, content-based interpretations of religion, however, were to become much less common as courts were increasingly confronted with pleas by adherents of nontraditional religions for First Amendment protection.

DEVELOPMENT OF THE MODERN
DEFINITION OF RELIGION

Beginning in the 1940s, American courts began to move away from narrow, substantive definitions of religion to broader, functional ones. The shift seems to have come in two significant cases: *United States v. Ballard*,[16] decided by the U.S. Supreme Court in 1944, and *United States v. Kauten*,[17] a federal circuit court case decided a year earlier.

In the *Ballard* case, the founder of the "I Am" movement was prosecuted for using the mails for fraudulently promoting his faith-healing powers. Guy Ballard told his followers that his ministry had been sanctioned by personal encounters with Jesus and Saint Germain. Followers were encouraged to send contributions to the movement, and many did. When many contributors, contrary to Ballard's promises, failed to experience physical healing, a San Francisco district attorney sought prosecution. The United States Supreme Court held that the trial court had ruled properly when it told the jury that it could inquire into the sincerity, but not the truth or falsity, of Ballard's religious beliefs. In his majority opinion, Justice William O. Douglas wrote:

Heresy trials are foreign to our Constitution. Men may believe what they cannot prove. They may not be put to the proof of their religious doctrines or beliefs. Religious experiences which are as real as life to some may be incomprehensible to others. Yet the fact that they may be beyond the ken of mortals does not mean that they can be made suspect before the law. . . . If one could be sent to jail because a jury in a hostile environment found one's teachings false, little indeed would be left of religious freedom. . . . The religious views espoused by respondents might seem incredible, if not preposterous, to most people. But if those doctrines are subject to trial before a jury charged with finding their truth or falsity, then the same can be done with the religious beliefs of any sect. When the triers of fact undertake that task, they enter a forbidden domain.[18]

In *Ballard*, the distinction between sincerity and credibility became an important judicial criterion for assessing what kinds of religious activities are protected under the First Amendment. The credibility of one's beliefs were less important than the sincerity with which those beliefs were held. As repugnant as the religious practices of a particular religion might be to its nonadherents, the price of religious freedom, as Justice Robert H. Jackson put it in his dissenting opinion, "is that we must put up with, and even pay for, a good deal of rubbish."[19] *Ballard* attempted no concrete definition of religion, but the case made it clear that a broad spectrum of religious beliefs, at least those that did not violate the legitimate concerns of the state, might be protected under the First Amendment.

An even greater protection of a wide range of beliefs was granted by the Second Circuit in *United States v. Kauten*. The case marked the beginning of a series of decisions in which the judicial interpretation of congressional statutes on conscription became the vehicle for addressing the legal definition of religion. *Kauten* dealt with a conscientious objector who was convicted under the 1940 Selective Service Act for refusing to submit to induction. He claimed exemption as a conscientious objector, defined by the act as any person "who, by reason of religious training and belief, is conscientiously opposed to participation in war in any form."[20] Kauten, an atheist, was opposed to war, claiming that it solves none of the world's problems and that the draft was President Franklin D. Roosevelt's personal scheme to reduce unemployment. The court held that Kauten's beliefs were strictly philosophical and political and fell outside the statute's requirement of "religious training and belief." The court did, however, propose that something less than a belief in God might qualify as religion. Judge Augustus Hand offered this definition:

Religious belief arises from a sense of the inadequacy of reason as a means of relating the individual to his fellow-men and to this universe. . . . It is a belief finding expression in a conscience which categorically requires the believer to disregard elementary self-interest and to accept martyrdom in preference to transgressing its tenets. . . . [Conscientious objection] may justly be regarded as a response of the individual to an inward mentor, call it conscience or God, that is for many persons at the present time the equivalent of what has always been thought a religious impulse.[21]

Whereas prior cases saw religion in theistic terms, *Kauten* saw religion in psychological terms— as belief that produced effects upon one's life that were similar to the effects produced by traditional religion. *Kauten* remains a landmark case because it was the first to offer a functional definition of religion. The Second Circuit, only months later, indicated its commitment to this approach; relying on *Kauten*, the court in two separate cases exempted from the draft two men whose objections to war were not based on a belief in a deity, but only that war is immoral.[22]

This expanded understanding of religion was not immediately accepted. In *Berman v. United States*, decided in 1946, the Ninth Circuit dismissed Judge Hand's definition of religion in *Kauten* as mere dictum, and affirmed the conviction of a humanist pacifist because the "religious training and belief" required for exemption under the Selective Service Act could not, "without the concept of a deity . . . be said to be religion in the sense of that term as it is used in the statute."[23] Congress agreed with the *Berman* formulation and in the 1948 amendment to the Selective Service Act specifically defined "religious training and belief" to mean "an individual's belief in a relation to a Supreme Being involving duties superior to those arising from any human relation, but [excluding] essentially political, sociological, or philosophical views, or a merely personal moral code."[24]

This amended language was interpreted in 1965 by the U. S. Supreme Court in three cases decided under the style of *United States v. Seeger*.[25] All three of the defendants were conscientious objectors who had been convicted in federal district courts for refusal to submit to induction after Selective Service officials had rejected their claims for exemption. All three men had similar worldviews, and none had a traditional concept of God. Seeger, for example, said that he was uncertain of whether a Supreme Being existed, but that his "skepticism or disbelief in the existence of God" did "not necessarily mean lack of faith in anything whatsoever." His, he stated, was a "belief in and devotion to goodness and virtue for their own sakes, and a religious faith in a purely ethical creed."[26]

Writing for a unanimous Supreme Court, Justice Tom Clark wrote that Congress had not intended to restrict the exemption for conscientious objectors only to those who believe in a traditional God. The expression, "Supreme Being," rather than "God," had been employed by Congress "so as to embrace all religions" while excluding "essentially political, sociological, or philosophical views." The test of belief required by the act, the Court held, is "whether a given belief that is sincere and meaningful occupies a place in the life of its possessor parallel to that filled by the orthodox belief in God of one who clearly qualifies for the exemption."[27] The Court specifically found the beliefs of the three defendants to be "religious" within the meaning of the Selective Service Act.

Congress was not pleased by the Court's expansive interpretation of "religious training and belief." Congress had obviously intended to limit conscientious objector status to those who held a traditional belief in God. The Court, however, rather than ruling that the statute was unconstitutional, grounded its decision in a rather loose reading of congressional intent. Reading between the lines, the Court's tactful approach may have been what led Congress to go along with the Court's ruling by removing the "Supreme Being" clause in the new Military Selective Service Act of 1967, although the new provision retained the restrictive phrase which ruled out inclusion of "essentially political, sociological, or philosophical views, or a merely personal moral code."[28]

Three years later, in *Welsh v. United States*,[29] the Supreme Court considered the case of a conscientious objector who had initially refused to label his objection as "religious" as required under the new Military Service Act. In his written objection, he struck out the word "religious" and wrote that his beliefs had been formed by reading in the fields of history and sociology. Although he had first claimed that his beliefs were nonreligious, he later wrote in a letter to his appeal board that his beliefs were "certainly religious in the ethical sense of the word."[30] If anything, Welsh's beliefs were even more remotely religious than Seeger's. The Court was thus faced with considering whether the Act's requirement of "religious training and belief" would extend protection to a person motivated in his objection to the draft by profound moral conviction. The Court again enlarged the scope of the statute, and held: "If an individual deeply and sincerely holds beliefs which are purely ethical or moral in source and content but that nevertheless impose upon him a duty of conscience to refrain from participating in any war at any time, those beliefs certainly occupy in the life of that individual 'a place parallel to that filled by . . . ' God in traditional religious persons."[31]

With such an expansive statutory interpretation, one might have expected some disagreement among the Court's members. Justice John Harlan wrote a concurring opinion in which he essentially stated that he would vote with the Court only to be consistent with *Seeger*. He acknowledged, however, that he had erred in joining the majority in *Seeger* where the Court had upheld a nontheistic belief. He felt that the Court had gone too far in distorting the legislative intent of the act, and he refused to subscribe to the "lobotomy" now performed in the *Welsh* decision. He found little consolation in the Court's assurances that religion under the statute could not be construed to mean virtually anything. The Court stated that the statute was intended to bar objector status to those whose beliefs rested "solely upon considerations of policy, pragmatism or expediency."[32]

Between *Kauten* and *Berman*, on the one hand, and *Seeger* and *Welsh*, on the other, three additional cases that arose outside the context of the federal conscription laws were a clear sign that the courts had shifted toward a functional definition of religion. These cases are important in tracking the evolution of the constitutional meaning of religion because none of the conscription cases already discussed was decided on constitutional grounds. Instead, the courts merely interpreted congressional statutes in a way that extended the privilege of conscientious objection to those of nontraditional beliefs. Nevertheless, because the conscription cases dealt specifically with the meaning of religion, cases arising outside the conscription context that have been decided on constitutional grounds, such as the three discussed here, have often resorted to the language of the conscription cases as useful precedents. In turn, later conscription cases such as *Seeger* and *Welsh* found these cases to be useful as precedents because of their expanded descriptions of the meaning of religion.

The first of these cases, *Torcaso v. Watkins*,[33] decided in 1961, dealt with a Maryland citizen seeking to become a notary public who was unwilling to make the required statutory declaration of a belief in God. The Court held that the Maryland law violated the Establishment Clause because it put "the power and authority of the State of Maryland . . . on the side of one particular sort of believers— those who are willing to say they believe 'in the existence of God.'"[34] It further maintained that the Establishment Clause forbids government to "aid those religions based on a belief in the existence of God as against those religions founded on different beliefs."[35] The Court footnoted this statement with a seemingly strong confirmation of its belief that religion embraces nontheism. The Court wrote that "among *religions* in this country which do not teach what would generally be considered a belief in the existence of God are Buddhism, Taoism, Ethical Culture, Secular Humanism, and others."[36]

The Court in *Torcaso* supported its holding by referring to two lower court cases in which humanist organizations without theistic beliefs were granted property tax exemptions. In *Washington Ethical Society v. District of Columbia*,[37] the District of Columbia Circuit held that belief in a Supreme Being or supernatural power was not a prerequisite to qualify for the property tax exemption to which religious organizations were entitled. In *Fellowship of Humanity v. County of Alameda*,[38] a California appellate court held that a county statute exempting religious organizations from property taxes must not favor those with theistic systems of belief over those with nontheistic beliefs. The court stated that the content of the belief was irrelevant; instead the focus should be placed on the belief's function in the life of the organization.[39] The court proposed the following two-part test for religious exemption: "Whether or not the belief occupies the same place in the lives of its holders that . . . orthodox beliefs occupy in the lives of believing majorities, and whether the group . . . conducts itself the way groups conceded to be religious conduct themselves."[40] It was this formulation that the Supreme Court seemed most to rely upon in deciding the *Seeger* case eight years later.

The foregoing decisions, especially *Kauten, Ballard, Torcaso, Seeger,* and *Welsh,* expanded the constitutional meaning of religion in a way that paralleled the expanding pluralism of American religion. Their chief effect was to include nontheistic beliefs under the protection provided by the religion clauses. It is doubtful that the framers contemplated the way in which American religion would become so diversified. At the nation's founding, Catholics and Jews together represented less than 1 percent of the population. Catholics now constitute 28 percent of the population, Jews about 1.5 percent. The Church of Jesus Christ, Latter-day Saints, which had its beginning half a century after the founding of the Republic, now has a membership of about 4 million in the United States, a number that exceeds the present total number of American Jews. Much more significant, of course, is the expansion of pluralism beyond the Judeo-Christian traditions. The number of Muslims in America, for example, is about the same as it is for Mormons. The number of Hindus and Buddhists has increased dramatically in recent decades, and they are now numbered among many nontraditional religions which enjoy the protection of the religion clauses.[41]

As the diversity of religions benefiting from First Amendment protection has expanded, the ability of government to regulate religion on definitional grounds has correspondingly diminished. The judicial means by which this development has occurred has been the adoption of functional criteria, in replacement of substantive criteria, for defining religion. The substantive model generally delimits religion to the range of traditional theisms: Christianity, Judaism, Islam, Hinduism, and so on. The functional model, in contrast, allows for a greater range of religions, theistic as well as nontheistic. By defining religion according to its social function, the functional approach treats religion largely as synonymous with such terms as worldview, belief system, moral order, ideology, and cosmology.[42] In *Seeger*, the Supreme Court spoke approvingly of the views of German-American theologian Paul Tillich, who located the essence of religion in the phrase, "ultimate concern." The Court quoted from Tillich for the proposition that the phrase "ultimate concern" may be more definitive than the word "God" in the designation of religious belief: "And if that word [God] has not much meaning for you, translate it, and speak of the depths of your life, of the source of your being, of your ultimate concern, of what you take most seriously without reservation. Perhaps in order to do so, you must forget everything traditional that you have learned about God. . . ."[43] The Court's interpretation of "ultimate concern" as referring to a belief which occupies "the same place in the life of an objector as an orthodox belief in God"[44] was confirmed in *Welsh* where the Court held, Welsh's atheism notwithstanding, that "because his beliefs function as a religion in his life, such an individual is as much entitled to a religious conscientious objector exemption . . . as is someone who derives his conscientious opposition to war from traditional religious convictions."[45]

Seeger and *Welsh* thus served to establish the "parallel position" rule and the "ultimate concern" rule as the twin criteria to judge whether a belief is religious in nature. So long as an "ultimate concern" occupies in the possessor's life a place parallel to traditional ideas of God, and so long as the beliefs are not based on "policy, pragmatism, or expediency," they are constitutionally religious. Under this content-neutral, functional approach, few of the "new" religions are deprived of religious status.[46] The courts have had little difficulty, for example, in concluding that the Unification Church is a religion.[47] The Church of Scientology, which one well-known sociologist of religion has called only a quasi-religion,[48] also has been held by the courts to be a religious organization.[49] Likewise, the religious nature of the International Society for Krishna Consciousness has been firmly established in the courts.[50] Indeed, the *Seeger-Welsh* framework has created an environment making it possible for a wide array of nontraditional or "new" religions to receive protection under the First Amendment.

DEVELOPMENTS SINCE *SEEGER* AND *WELSH*

In recent years, there have been signs that the *Seeger* and *Welsh* formulations might be too broad in describing what should be considered religion. In the case of *Wisconsin v. Yoder*,[51] decided in 1971, the Supreme Court appeared to retreat somewhat from the broad reaches of *Seeger* and *Welsh*. In that case, Amish parents were charged with violations of Wisconsin's compulsory education laws because they failed to send their children to public schools beyond the eighth grade. The Amish argued that to do otherwise would be contrary to their sincerely held religious beliefs. Before weighing the free exercise rights of the Amish with the interest of the state in educating children, the Court considered the fundamental question of whether the Amish lifestyle was rooted in *religious* belief. This inquiry was necessary, Chief Justice Warren E. Burger wrote, because: "Although a determination of what is a 'religious' belief or practice entitled to constitutional protection may present a most delicate question, the very concept of ordered liberty precludes allowing every person to make his own standards on matters of conduct in which society as a whole has important interests."[52] Indeed, as some commentators have observed,[53] this statement can be seen to undercut the implication of *Seeger* and *Welsh* that a claimant's own statement is sufficient to create a presumption that his beliefs are religious. Burger went on to affirm that mere philosophical beliefs are beyond the purview of the First Amendment: "If the Amish asserted their claims because of their subjective evolution and rejection of the contemporary secular values accepted by the majority, much as Thoreau rejected the social values of his time and isolated himself at Walden Pond, their claims would not rest on a religious basis. Thoreau's choice was philosophical and personal rather than religious, and such belief does not rise to the demands of the Religion Clauses."[54] As Justice William O. Douglas noted in dissent, this statement seems clearly to be contrary to *Seeger* and especially to *Welsh*, in which Welsh received the exemption based on his nonreligious, humanistic philosophy.[55] In its holding, the majority justified the right of the Amish children to be exempt from compulsory public school attendance beyond the eighth grade because the Amish position arose from sincere *religious*, not philosophical, convictions. In its ruling, however, the Court made no reference to the *Seeger* and *Welsh* decisions. In contrast, Justice Douglas stated his belief that the content-neutral test of *Seeger* and *Welsh* was more in keeping with the religiously pluralistic society found in America. The significance of the *Yoder* case was that it implied that some examination into the *content* of one's beliefs, not merely the *effect* of one's beliefs, was possible in a determination of whether a system of beliefs is religious.

The Third Circuit Court of Appeals has been the most aggressive in developing this more restrictive approach. In *Malnak v. Yogi*,[56] it was alleged that the instruction in Transcendental Meditation (TM) in the New Jersey public high schools was an unconstitutional establishment of religion, despite the denial of its religious character by representatives of the TM movement. Five high schools during the 1975-76 academic year offered to its students on an elective basis a course called "The Science of Creative Intelligence-Transcenden - tal Meditation." It was taught four or five days a week by teachers specially trained by the World Plan Executive Council-United States, an organization whose objective is to disseminate the teachings of TM throughout the United States. The textbook used was developed by Maharishi Mahesh Yogi, the founder of TM. It teaches that "pure creative intelligence" is the basis of life, and that through the process of TM students can perceive the full potential of their lives.

Central to the practice of TM is the "mantra," a sound aid used by the practitioner while meditating. To acquire his or her mantra, a practitioner must attend a ceremony called a "puja." Every student who enrolled in the TM course was required to attend a puja as part of the course. During the puja, lasting between one and two hours, the student stood or sat in front of a table while the teacher sang a chant and made offerings to a "Guru Dev." During the chant, the Guru Dev might be described as the personification of any of a number of superlatives: "the creative impulse of cosmic life," "the essence of creation," "kindness," "bliss of the Absolute," "transcendental joy," "the Self-Sufficient," "the One," "the Eternal," "the Pure," "the Immovable," "the embodiment of pure knowledge which is beyond and above the universe like the sky," "the Unbounded," "the omnipresent in all creation," and "the true preceptor." The trial court observed that "no one would apply all these epithets to a human being,"[57] and found that the TM course constituted a religious activity under the First Amendment.

On review, the court of appeals affirmed the trial court's holding in a brief per curiam opinion. Judge Arlin Adams's concurring opinion, however, went much further in exploring the constitutional meaning of religion. Drawing from *Seeger* and *Welsh*, Adams noted that "expectations that religious ideas should always address fundamental questions is in some way comparable to the reasoning of the Protestant theologian Paul Tillich, who expressed his view on the essence of religion in the

phrase 'ultimate concern'. . . . Thus, the 'ultimate' nature of the
ideas presented is the most important and convincing evidence
that they should be treated as religious."[58] Adams found that the
textbook for the course taught that the Science of Creative
Intelligence was "the basis for everything" and that TM is the
means for contacting this "impelling force." He added "that the
existence of such a pervasive and fundamental life force is a
matter of 'ultimate concern' can hardly be questioned."[59]
Finally, Judge Adams stated that while TM is not a "theistic
religion," it nevertheless "concerns itself with the same search for
ultimate truth as other religions and seeks to offer a
comprehensive and critically important answer to the questions
and doubts that haunt modern man."[60] Of particular interest in
Adams's concurrence, however, was his attempt to flesh out the
Seeger and *Welsh* cases by identifying three useful indicia to
determine the existence of a religion. The indicia are at once a
refinement and an extension of the "ultimate concern" and
"parallel belief" tests of *Seeger* and *Welsh*.

The first of the three indicia suggested by Judge Adams to
determine the existence of a religion is that the religion must
address fundamental and ultimate questions having to do with
deep and imponderable matters. As Judge Adams saw it,

One's views, be they orthodox or novel, on the deeper and more
imponderable questions— the meaning of life and death, man's role in
the Universe, the proper moral code of right and wrong— are those
likely to be the "most intensely personal" and important to the believer.
They are his ultimate concerns. As such they are to be carefully
guarded from governmental interference, and never converted into
official government doctrine. The first amendment demonstrates a
specific solicitude for religion because religious ideas are in many ways
more important than other ideas. New and different ways of meeting
those concerns are entitled to the same sort of treatment as the
traditional forms.[61]

The second indicia advocated by Judge Adams is that a
religion must be comprehensive in nature; that is, it must consist
of a belief system as opposed to an isolated teaching. In the

court's view, the so-called "Big Bang" theory, an astronomical interpretation of the creation of the universe, may be said to answer an "ultimate" question, but it is not, by itself, a "religious idea." Likewise, moral or patriotic views are not by themselves religions, but if they are pressed as a part of a comprehensive belief system that presents them as "truth," they might well rise to the religious level.

Adams's third element to consider in ascertaining whether a set of ideas should be classified as a religion is any formal or external signs or practices that may be analogized to accepted religions. Such signs might include formal services, ceremonial functions, the existence of clergy, structure and organization, and efforts at propagation. Judge Adams acknowledged that a religion may exist without these signs and are therefore not determinative, at least by their absence, in resolving a question of definition. Applying these three factors, Adams concluded that the Science of Creative Intelligence-Transcendental Meditation constituted a religion under the First Amendment despite the contentions of its leaders to the contrary.

The *Malnak* case, especially in view of the significant contributions of Judge Adams's concurring opinion, indicated that the federal judiciary would follow, but might attempt to fine-tune, the "ultimate concern" and "parallel-belief" tests developed by the Supreme Court to achieve a closer approxima - tion of the constitutional meaning of religion. The three indicia proposed by Judge Adams represent a determined effort to do what the Supreme Court had failed to do— define the meaning of such terms as "ultimate concern" and "parallel belief"— while remaining within the parameters of a functional approach to defining religion.

Africa v. Pennsylvania,[62] decided in 1981, was an occasion for the Third Circuit to consider the three indicia proposed by Judge Adams in *Malnak* for determining whether a set of beliefs constitutes a religion. Frank Africa was a prisoner who requested that the state provide him with a special diet of raw foods. Africa claimed that for him to eat anything else would violate the tenets of the MOVE organization, a body which he claimed to be religious and whose goals were "to bring about absolute peace . . . to stop violence altogether, to put a stop to all that is corrupt."[63] Central to attaining these goals was a "natural" lifestyle, including a diet of uncooked fruits and vegetables. A Pennsylvania federal district court, by applying the three indicia outlined in Adams's *Malnak* opinion, held that MOVE was not a religion. The court of appeals, with Judge Adams writing for the three-judge panel, affirmed, ruling that the district court had correctly applied the three indicia in holding that Africa's beliefs were not religious.

In applying the three-part test, the circuit court found that MOVE's tenets failed to meet the "ultimate" ideas criterion— i t referred to no transcendental or controlling force and did not address matters of morality, mortality, or the meaning of life.[64] The court concluded that Africa's beliefs were a product of a secular philosophy rather than religious conviction, citing Chief Justice Burger's statement in *Yoder* about Henry David Thoreau, whose solution at Walden Pond resulted from philosophical choices, not religious belief.[65] MOVE's tenets also failed to satisfy the second of the indicia, comprehensiveness. The court found that MOVE espoused a single governing idea, best described as a philosophical naturalism, rather than an all-encompassing worldview. Africa's claim that "every act of life is invested with religious meaning and significance"[66] was not sufficient to make Africa's beliefs comprehensive. Finally, the court found that MOVE also failed to show any of the signs which constitute the third of the indicia set forth in *Malnak*. There were no "external signs" of a religion such as holy days, religious services, or a holy scripture. Even though Africa claimed to be a "naturalist minister" of MOVE, the court discovered that all MOVE members held the same position. The absence of these signs, which the court said were not necessarily controlling, strengthed the conclusion that MOVE was not a religion.

The Ninth Circuit seemingly adopted Judge Adams's three-pronged test in *Callahan v. Woods*.[67] Callahan refused on religious grounds to obtain a social security number for his daughter, believing that the number was the "mark of the beast" and all who received it would be damned. Judge Arlin Adams, appointed by a special designation to sit with the Ninth Circuit Court to hear the case, wrote the opinion for a unanimous court.

In finding Callahan's beliefs to be religious, the court concluded that his beliefs were a part of "traditional religious beliefs" which, although entitled to no greater protection than nontraditional beliefs, are "more readily ascertained" to be religious.[68] Therefore, the court had little difficulty in finding that Callahan's beliefs satisfied all three parts of the *Malnak* three-part test. In support of this finding, the court noted that Callahan belonged to a Baptist church, his belief regarding the evil nature of social security numbers was theistic in nature, the belief was derived from his interpretation of the Book of Revelation, and his beliefs were eschatological, relating to end-time events.[69] Moreover, citing *Ballard*, the court found Callahan's beliefs to be sincere while noting that it was not proper to inquire into the truth or falsity of his beliefs.[70]

When taken together, *Yoder*, *Malnak*, *Africa*, and *Callahan* clearly represent a shift toward attempting to balance the early substantive tests for defining religion and the subsequent functional approaches epitomized by *Seeger* and *Welsh*. They might be summarized as holding that although it is improper to assess the truth or falsity of religious claims, it is proper to examine the content of beliefs claimed to be religious to insure that they are more than merely philosophical. These holdings differ from *Seeger* and *Welsh* primarily in their emphasis that "ultimate concerns" must be clearly "religious," not according to a theistic, substantive definition, but according to traditional markings of religion such as those set forth in Judge Adams's rulings. Judge Adams's opinions were the first to attempt to give meaning to terms like "ultimate" and "parallel" which the Supreme Court left undefined. In this respect the opinions are a needed attempt to give direction to other courts in assessing religious claims, but they can be criticized on several grounds as well.

First, while *Malnak*, *Africa*, and *Callahan* attempted to crystallize the inquiries as to what such terms as "ultimate concerns" and "parallel beliefs" mean, since they were all written by a single judge, they might be criticized by some as a one-man crusade to insure that only genuinely "religious" beliefs are protected by the First Amendment. It is uncertain whether the Supreme Court will someday disavow the approach of Judge Adams which is now binding only in two circuits.

Second, as one commentator has noted,[71] Judge Adams's three indicia may be perceived by some judges as the only relevant factors in judging religious claims. While Judge Adams emphasized that his three factors were not exhaustive,[72] some lower courts have already adopted Adams's three-part test without considering other factors that might be equally important in assessing religious claims.[73]

Third, the Adams opinions support a fairly intrusive inquiry by the courts into the beliefs of a claimant as well as the function of those beliefs in the claimant's life.[74] This intrusion would seem to violate the requirement of *Lemon v. Kurtzman*[75] that government not become excessively entangled in religious questions. The same problem is present under the *Seeger* and *Welsh* formulations, but not as obviously because the scope of permissible inquiry into beliefs under those cases is ambiguous.

Finally, and most significantly, the three-part test propounded by Judge Adams, by seeking to demarcate religious from philosophical beliefs, tends to threaten borderline belief systems that seek protection under the religion clauses. The potential harm is the suppression and unfair treatment of some religions, an end the religion clauses were intended to prevent. It is possible to level this charge against the Third Circuit in the *Africa* case. The court concluded that MOVE members were not concerned with ultimate matters, lacked any comprehensive governing ideas, and were uncommitted to any defining structural characteristics of a traditional religion. Yet the all-consuming belief of MOVE members in a "natural" or "generating" way of life very closely resembles, as counsel for Frank Africa argued, the religion of pantheism. The court admitted "that the matter is not wholly free from doubt" but found that MOVE's beliefs were "more the product of a secular philosophy than of a religious orientation."[76] Certainly the court's finding could have gone the other way. Pantheism's essential assertions, that everything that exists constitutes a unity and that this all-inclusive unity is divine, can arguably be located within the tenets of MOVE. Moreover, the court held that MOVE failed the comprehensiveness test because its philosophical naturalism consisted only of a single governing idea. If MOVE's beliefs approximate pantheism, however, its "single governing idea" would correspond to the theme of unity found in pantheism and would be a doctrinal strength rather than a weakness. The same argument, of course, could be made in reference to the court's finding that MOVE lacked formal identifying characteristics. In sum, by using a limiting definition-by-analogy approach, the court in *Africa* may have robbed Frank Africa of the right to the free exercise of his legitimately religious beliefs. A belief system that likely would have been considered religious under a strict application of the *Seeger-Welsh* principles was found wanting under Judge Adams's more restrictive guidelines.

Arguably even more controversial than the outcome in *Africa* was the decision rendered by a New Jersey federal district court in *Jacques v. Hilton*.[77] There, two prison inmates brought an action alleging that Trenton State Prison officials denied them the right to practice their religion under the Free Exercise Clause. The inmates belonged to the Universal Life Church of California, from which they obtained mail order certificates ordaining them as ministers. The inmates regularly met with about a dozen other inmates for worship and study. No rituals occurred at these meetings and "the group did not utilize a Bible or other holy book in its worship."[78] The purpose of the meetings was to integrate the inmates' beliefs with everyday life. Once each year, the group would eat only food from the sea in recognition of the fact that all life originated from the sea. In keeping with the tenets of the Universal Life Church, the inmates recognized the existence of a supernatural force or Supreme Being referred to as the "Spirit of Life." However, each church member was permitted to work out the meaning of the "Spirit of Life" or "God" in keeping with the dictates of his conscience. The Church justified this freedom on the basis that one's "relationship with his maker is a highly personal one."[79]

The court held that the beliefs professed by the inmates did not rise to the level of a religion entitled to the protection of the First Amendment. Relying strictly upon Judge Adams's three indicia for determining the existence of a religion, the court first held that the doctrines of the Universal Life Church did not address the question of human morality or the purpose of life and therefore failed to reach the required standard of a concern for "fundamental and ultimate questions." The court seems to have failed to recognize, however, that the church did not discourage beliefs about morality and life's purpose; the church only declined to take an official stance on these questions, thereby leaving the resolution of such matters to the individual conscience. The court, then, by requiring the church to enunciate its doctrines on fundamental theological points, made the critical error of reducing religion to that embraced within traditional, accepted norms.

The court further found that the church lacked the comprehensiveness, cohesiveness, and commonality of beliefs characteristic of accepted religions, and that the church therefore failed the "comprehensiveness" test advanced by Judge Adams. The court noted that the inmates professed a sincere belief in a naturalistic all-pervasive force uniting all living things as well as a belief in the primacy of individual conscience, but stated that "it is difficult to envision how the church can promulgate 'ultimate and comprehensive truth' or how a 'shared world view' can exist when each individual is made the arbiter of his own truth."[80] Again, the emphasis on shared beliefs is misplaced. If courts are to remain open to religious diversity, they will recognize that American culture overall is becoming less and less insistent on absolute authority of a particular viewpoint. This is, indeed, the basic premise of postmodernism, which holds that there has been a fundamental shift away from certainty and commonality to uncertainty and diversity. As Craig Van Gelder has expressed it, "The search to find and/or state the central thesis, grand narrative, or essential principles of life has given way to an acceptance of pluralistic alternatives and competing viewpoints. Claims to an authoritative perspective or conclusive findings have given way to paradox, diversity, and juxtaposition as new ways of seeing reality. . . ."[81] Postmodern thinking, as an emerging worldview, is certain to influence religion as much as it is already influencing art, architecture, and literature. It therefore becomes increasingly incumbent upon the courts to accommodate, within a functional approach to defining religion, postmodern as well as all other religious perspectives that might not square with more traditional forms of faith and practice.

Finally, the court found that the Universal Life Church lacked the defining structural characteristics of a traditional religion. It is true that the inmates' practices were characterized by few of the formal identifying marks common to most recognized religions. Even if it is granted that groups making religious claims must possess outward signs and ceremonies (which itself is suspect because some religions emphasize private, personal faith over communal, external faith), the inmates did exercise a number of visible signs of traditional religion. They met regularly (the testimony indicated at least weekly), they encouraged one another in their faith, they sought to propagate their faith by bringing other inmates into their circle, they made efforts to put their faith into daily practice, and they enjoyed an annual diet ritual. Why were these not acceptable characteristics analogous to more traditional religions?

The *Jacques* court was far too intent on staying within the three-part test proposed by Judge Adams in *Malnak*. While it might be argued that the practices of the inmates in *Jacques* in fact met the three-part test, the application of facts to guiding principles is an admittedly difficult enterprise for all judges. The failure in *Jacques*, however, was not faulty application, but an unreserved adoption of the *Malnak* three-part test. The test is, in this author's opinion, overly restrictive and threatens to disqualify as religious those ideas and practices that fall too readily outside the trappings of traditional religion. Courts will do well in the future to avoid the unwarranted regulation of religion that sometimes occurs when a too restrictive definition-by-analogy approach, as exemplified by *Jacques*, is employed.

While Judge Adams's three indicia are helpful in ascertaining the religious nature of one's beliefs, other, more probing factors could be considered as well. For example, the inquiry into one's ultimate and fundamental concerns, in the framework of Judge Adams's definition-by-analogy approach, probes for ultimate beliefs that are comparable primarily to known religions. This tends to confine the inquiry to religions in which a deity or some controlling, universal force undergirds the belief system. This is inappropriate because belief in a deity, as the *Welsh* and *Seeger* cases affirm, is not always fundamental to religious belief. A religious belief system can be quite private and personal, and should be measured not by its conformity to traditional religious systems, but rather by the fundamental meaning it gives to any particular individual's life.

The same criticism can be leveled against Judge Adams's required inquiry into comprehensiveness and external signs of a religion; the search tends to look for traditional forms of religion that are all-encompassing in one's life and that bear the marks of established ritual forms. Rather than focusing on the comprehensiveness of a religion in one's life, the more important question is: Does an adherent's system of beliefs constitute the most comprehensive framework by which his or her life is lived? This is a very different inquiry because it recognizes that the belief system may not be as comprehensive in an adherent's life as are most traditional religious systems; it may hold a central place in the adherent's worldview, but there may be other, competing views that are brought into the mix. The real inquiry along these lines is: Does the belief system consistently make an important contribution to giving meaning and direction to the adherent's life? The prisoners' naturalistic beliefs in the *Jacques* case would likely have qualified as religious under this type of inquiry.

Finally, in considering external signs, it must be recognized that some religions have little or no rituals. Pantheism, for example, typically is accompanied by no formal rituals. It is the nature and sincerity of one's beliefs, rather than the external signs fostered by those beliefs, that is most crucial in determining the existence of a religion. Moreover, some of the most standard signs of traditional religions need not be part of a religious system. For example, most religions operate with recognized leaders: ministers, priests, or other recognized authorities. But some religions, the Gnostics in the early Christian era and the Quakers today as examples, have usually operated with an essentially egalitarian polity— all adherents are seen as equals, and none are deemed more authoritative than others.

These are only suggested possible inquiries that could be added to those proposed by Judge Adams. The suggestions are by no means intended to be exhaustive. It is only submitted here that Judge Adams's three-pronged test does not go nearly far enough in probing the kinds of factors that should be considered in determining the existence of a religion.

CONCLUSION

Defining religion for constitutional purposes has proved to be a difficult and controversial task for American courts. Until the mid-twentieth century, courts tended to define religion according to traditional, theistic conceptions of religion. Corresponding with the rise of religious pluralism in the nation, the courts subsequently began to expand the definition of religion, looking less to the content of a claimant's set of beliefs than to whether those beliefs served the traditional function of religion in the claimant's life. More recently, a trend exemplified in the definition-by-analogy approach of the Third Circuit has developed which seeks to balance these two approaches.

The Third Circuit's approach leans dangerously toward a policy that threatens religious freedom. When government constricts the meaning of religion, the result is typically the exclusion of legitimate, although nonconventional, religions and religious ideas. Conversely, when the meaning of religion is enlarged, the result is the expansion of recognized, although sometimes questionably religious, individuals and groups enjoying the protection of the First Amendment's religion clauses. Constriction inevitably leads to regulation of religion, whereas enlargement usually advances religious freedom. The

Third Circuit's approach, in its present form, is an unfortunate move toward constriction.

A governmental policy that favors enlargement over constriction, contrary to what some would argue, does not hold that every central idea or belief system should be regarded as religious. Critics of the Supreme Court's holdings in *Seeger* and *Welsh* have argued that the functional approach to describing religion set forth in those cases is so broad as to obliterate any distinction between religion and nonreligion.[82] But as this author reads *Seeger* and *Welsh*, those cases do not protect *nonreligion*; they merely propose that *religion* embraces ideas and beliefs that go beyond those that have historically been considered religious. *Seeger* and *Welsh* acknowledge that religion cannot be reduced to precise definition or description. Moreover, the expansive approach to describing religion set forth in those cases recognizes that the exercise of one's religion is an inviolable, protected right under the First Amendment, and that only a broad framework for describing various religious forms, in spite of the attendant risks, will protect all religious ideas.

Admittedly, courts must continue to distinguish religion from nonreligion. Not every deeply held conviction that guides an individual should be recognized as religious. Any definition of religion that failed to distinguish religion from nonreligion would empty the religion clauses of their fundamental meaning and elevate to the status of religion every conceivable set of ideas or philosophy that any individual claimed to be central to his or her life. But an expansive approach to defining religion as set forth in *Seeger* and *Welsh* is essential to provide constitutional protection to the endless variety of religions, both old and new, foreseen and unforeseen, that carry transcendent meaning for people.

Seeger and *Welsh*, however, left many cloudy issues that the Supreme Court, now more than two decades after they were decided, has yet to address. Specifically, the Court left open the meaning of terms such as "ultimate concern" and "parallel belief" and failed to address the degree to which inquiries into the content of beliefs arguably falling within the meaning of those terms is appropriate. Judges like Arlin Adams are to be commended for their efforts to resolve some of these problems. Adams's three-pronged test for determining what is a religion is a welcome start towards fleshing out the twin tests of *Seeger* and *Welsh*, although it is, in this author's view, too limited in naming the kinds of factors that courts should consider in making their assessments. In its present form, Adams's test tends too obviously to favor traditional over nontraditional religions. In evaluating the claims of today's nontraditional religions, courts must be ever mindful that many religions now commonplace, including most Protestant groups, were persecuted, misunderstood, and condemned at their inception. Nevertheless, courts should be encouraged to follow Adams's lead by attempting to give clearer meaning to the Supreme Court's functional approach to defining religion as set forth in *Seeger* and *Welsh*. Those cases appropriately focus less on the content of one's beliefs than on the effect those beliefs have upon one's life. The commitment of courts to the essential parameters of the *Seeger-Welsh* formulation will serve to protect individuals and communities of faith in the emerging postmodern world from unwarranted regulation of religion at the hands of government.

NOTES

1. Jonathan Weiss, "Privilege, Posture, and Protection: 'Religion' in the Law," *Yale Law Journal* 73 (1964): 593.
2. *Reynolds v. United States*, 98 U.S. 145 (1878).
3. Ibid. at 162.
4. James Madison, "A Memorial and Remonstrance on the Religious Rights of Man," in *The Papers of James Madison*, William T. Hutchinson and William M.E. Rachal, eds. (Chicago: University of Chicago Press, 1973), 8:293.
5. Thomas Jefferson to Danbury Baptist Association, 1 January 1802, in Philip B. Kurland and Ralph Lerner, eds., *The Founder's Constitution* (Chicago: University of Chicago Press, 1987), 5:96.
6. William A. Blakely, ed., *American State Papers Bearing on Sunday Legislation*, rev. ed. (Washington, D.C.: Review and Herald, 1911), 133 n.l.
7. *Davis v. Beason*, 133 U.S. 333 (1890).
8. Ibid. at 342.
9. Ibid. at 345.
10. Ibid. at 342.

11. James Davison Hunter, "Religious Freedom and the Challenge of Modern Pluralism," in James Davison Hunter, ed., *Articles of Faith, Articles of Peace* (Washington, D.C.: Brookings Institution, 1990), 55.
12. See, for example, *People v. Deutsche Gemeinde*, 249 Ill. 132, 136, 94 N.E. 162, 164 (1911).
13. *United States v. MacIntosh*, 283 U.S. 605, 633-34 (1931) (Holmes, J., dissenting).
14. *McMasters v. State*, 21 Okla. Crim. 318, 207 Pac. 566 (1922).
15. Affirmed in *Scottish Rite Bldg. Co. v. Lancaster County*, 106 Neb. 95, 182 N.W. 572 (1921).
16. *United States v. Ballard*, 322 U.S. 78 (1944).
17. *United States v. Kauten*, 133 F.2d 703 (2d Cir. 1943).
18. *U.S. v. Ballard* at 86-87.
19. Ibid. at 95.
20. Selective Service Act Sec. 5(g), 54 Stat. 887 (1940).
21. Ibid. at 708.
22. *United States ex rel. Reel v. Badt*, 141 F.2d 845 (2d Cir. 1944); *United States ex rel. Phillips v. Downer*, 135 F.2d 521 (2d Cir. 1943).
23. *Berman v. United States*, 156 F.2d 377, 381 (9th Cir. 1946), cert. denied, 329 U.S. 795 (1946).
24. Selective Service Act of 1948, 62 Stat. 604, 613 (1948).
25. *United States v. Seeger*, 380 U.S. 163 (1965).
26. Ibid. at 166.
27. Ibid.
28. Military Selective Service Act of 1967, 81 Stat. 100, 104 (1967).
29. *Welsh v. United States*, 398 U.S. 333 (1970).
30. Ibid. at 341.
31. Ibid. at 340.
32. Ibid. at 343.
33. *Torcaso v. Watkins*, 367 U.S. 488 (1961).
34. Ibid. at 495.
35. Ibid.
36. Ibid. at 495 n.11.
37. *Washington Ethical Society v. District of Columbia*, 249 F.2d 127 (D.C. Cir. 1957).
38. *Fellowship of Humanity v. County of Alameda*, 315 P.2d 394 (1957).
39. Ibid. at 406.
40. Ibid.
41. Hunter, "Religious Freedom," 56, 61.
42. Ibid., 58.
43. *U.S. v. Seeger* at 187.
44. Ibid. at 184.
45. *Welsh v. United States* at 340. For an insightful discussion of the Court's reliance upon Tillich, see James McBride, "Paul Tillich and the Supreme Court: Tillich's 'Ultimate Concern' as a Standard in Judicial Interpretation," *Journal of Church and State* 30 (Spring 1988): 245.
46. William C. Shepherd, *To Secure the Blessings of Liberty: American Constitutional Law and the New Religious Movements* (Chico, Calif.: Scholars Press, 1985), 20.
47. See *Unification Church v. I.N.S.*, 547 F.Supp. 623 (1982), and *In the Matter of the Holy Spirit Association for the Unification of World Christianity v. The Tax Commission of the City of New York*, 435 N.E. 2d 662 (1982).
48. Robert Wuthnow, "The Cultural Context of Contemporary

Religious Movements," in *Cults, Culture, and the Law: Perspectives on New Religious Movements*, Thomas Robbins, William C. Shepard, and James McBride, eds. (Chico, Calif.: Scholars Press, 1985), 43.

49. See *Founding Church of Scientology of Washington, D.C. v. United States*, 409 F.2d 1146 (1969). The Church of Scientology has had many challenges to its tax-exempt status for federal income tax purposes, but those challenges are not to its "religious" character, but usually to its failure to satisfy the I.R.C. Section 501(c)(3) requirement that income not inure to the benefit of private individuals. See, for example, *Founding Church of Scientology v. United States*, 412 F.2d 1197 (1969), and *Church of Scientology of California v. Commission of Internal Revenue*, 823 F.2d 1310 (9th Cir. 1987).

50. See *International Society for Krishna Consciousness, Inc. v. Barber*, 650 F.2d 430 (1981).

51. *Wisconsin v. Yoder*, 406 U.S. 205 (1972).

52. Ibid. at 215-16.

53. Terry Slye, "Rendering Unto Caesar: Defining 'Religion' for Purposes of Administering Religion-Based Tax Exemptions," *Harvard Journal of Law and Public Policy* 6 (1983): 234.

54. *Wisconsin v. Yoder* at 216.

55. Ibid. at 247-48 (Douglas, J., dissenting).

56. *Malnak v. Yogi*, 440 F.Supp. 1284 (D.N.J. 1977), affirmed at 592 F.2d 197 (3rd Cir. 1979).

57. Ibid., 440 F.Supp. at 1305-08.

58. Ibid., 592 F.2d at 208.

59. Ibid. at 213.

60. Ibid. at 214. The court rejected the defendant's argument that a narrower meaning of religion should be applied in Establishment Clause cases than in Free Exercise Clause cases. Such a dual definition is not, however, without considerable scholarly support. See, for example, Laurence Tribe, *American Constitutional Law* (Mineola, N.Y.: Foundation Press, 1978), 827-28, and Note, "Toward a Constitutional Definition of Religion," *Harvard Law Review* 91 (1978): 1084. In *Malnak*, the court preferred the unitary view because of its belief that the constitutional framers intended one meaning of religion to govern both clauses. Ibid. at 210-13.

61. *Malnak v. Yogi*, 592 F.2d at 208.

62. *Africa v. Pennsylvania*, 662 F.2d 1025 (1981).

63. Ibid. at 1026.

64. Ibid. at 1033-34.

65. Ibid. at 1034.

66. Ibid. at 1027.

67. *Callahan v. Woods*, 658 F.2d 679 (9th Cir. 1981).

68. Ibid. at 685.

69. Ibid. at 686.

70. Ibid. at 687.

71. Slye, "Rendering Unto Caesar," 240.

72. *Malnak v. Yogi*, 592 F.2d at 210; *Africa v. Pennsylvania*, 662 F.2d at 1032 n.13.

73. See *Church of the Chosen People, Etc. v. United States*, 548 F. Supp. 1247 (1982), and *Jacques v. Hilton*, 569 F. Supp. 730 (1983).

74. Slye, "Rendering Unto Caesar," 240.

75. *Lemon v. Kurtzman*, 403 U.S. 602 (1971).

76. *Africa v. Pennsylvania*, 662 F. 2d at 1033.
77. *Jacques v. Hilton*, 569 F. Supp. 730 (1983).
78. Ibid. at 732.
79. Ibid.
80. Ibid. at 735.
81. Quoted in *Context* 24 (1 March 1992): 3.
82. See, for example, James Hitchcock, "The Supreme Court and Religion: Historical Overview and Future Prognosis," *St. Louis University Law Journal* 24 (1980): 201, who asks, "But what will be excluded if religion is understood to be a person's ultimate philosophy of life, as *Seeger* and *Welsh* suggest it might be?"

6

Government Regulation of Religion through Labor and Employment Discrimination Laws

DAVID L. GREGORY

This essay assesses the policies, operations, and the ramifications of government regulation of religion through labor and employment discrimination laws. Special attention will be devoted to elucidating important decisions of the United States Supreme Court and federal appellate courts.

Given the nature of the conference at which these papers were originally presented, and given the Christian profession and identification of Baylor University, it is important to talk about the Constitution. It is even more important to structure the constitutional considerations within the spirit of the Declaration of Independence and its repeated invocations of God and of natural law. We must always remember that we have constitutions because of our antecedent fundamental natural law rights — rights with their source from God rather than in any secular constitution. And, most important and beyond all else, it is important to consider the centrality of Jesus in the world of work, as this chapter considers the degree to which government has, and should, regulate religion through contemporary labor and employment discrimination laws.

In capitalist political economy, the public is defined in large part by their work. Consider the question, "What do you do?" Most respond by identifying their position, career, or aspirations in their work— student, teacher, lawyer. Consider the quizzical look on the face of the questioner who initiated the exchange of pleasantries if one initially responds to the question "What do you do?" by first professing to follow Jesus. Capitalist political economy finds this sort of discourse foreign or offputting, to say the least. Yet Jesus is central to the world of work. He originally followed the example of his earthly father Joseph, who worked as a carpenter. In the Catholic tradition, Joseph the carpenter is the patron saint of all workers. Jesus was first fully grounded in the world of work as a prototypical blue collar, skilled worker. In his public life and ministry, Jesus was a white collar worker as a rabbi, teacher, preacher, and healer. But consider Jesus' primary audience. He began his public life by proclaiming the fulfillment of the prophecies of Isaiah, stating that he had come to the poor, to the prisoners, and to the afflicted, marginalized, and dispossessed—today, the unemployed, the underemployed, and those trapped for generations in cycles of grinding poverty and welfare statism.

The Scriptures are replete with examples of the transformation of the meaningless toil of slavery in Egypt to dignified work of free and autonomous people in the Promised Land. Throughout his ministry, Jesus continually reached out to the poor and the marginalized; his closest followers were blue collar workers— fishermen— and a socially despised and ostracized white collar worker, a tax collector. Some of his most poignant conversations were with the wealthy. Consider the parable of the necessity of being born again with his friend Nicodemus, and his plea to the rich young man to give all he had to the poor and to come and follow him. Beware the state. In some ways, it has been downhill since Constantine. If one gives to God what is God's, there should not be much left to Caesar.

With this focus on the individual person, the dignity of work, and the example of Jesus, one must consider the role of government regulation of religion in the world of work. Ideally, this author would prefer to see a perfect world where government intrusion and oversight was unnecessary to a workplace that valued the dignity and worth of every worker. But, until heaven is achieved, the world and all complex institutions within it will be imperfect and individuals will be left to the dubious mercy of collective corporate institutional powers. In these curcumstances, some degree of governmental oversight and protection of the individual worker will be necessary. Unfortunately, the contemporary legal regime generally indicates the prerogatives of the institutional employer at the expense of the individual employee. This legal regime's preferences for corporate power and disregard for the individual employee operates whether the parties are religious or secular. Jesus reminds us of the dignity and value of the individual worker, yet this country's legal structure generally subordinates the interests of the worker to corporate, institutional power.

The individual religious employee, who is most often in need of effective protection against unlawful discrimination in secular employment on the basis of the employee's religion, has been left largely bereft of constitutional and statutory safeguards. Meanwhile, the statist,[1] pro-management[2] Burger/Rehnquist Supreme Court has repeatedly enhanced the managerial prerogatives of the religious institutional employer and has essentially liberated the religious institutional employer's labor and employment practices from most government oversight.

This Supreme Court has consistently demonstrated inordinate judicial deference to institutional employer interests. This has occurred at the expense of the employee's constitutional right to the free exercise of religion in the workplace, and of the statutory right not to be discriminated against in employment on the basis of religion. The Supreme Court began this dramatic subordination of employee rights to the prerogatives of institutional employers in a series of important decisions beginning in 1977.[3] As the Burger and now Rehnquist Courts matured, this activist, proinstitutional, statist jurisprudence became increasingly inimical to the severely debilitated First Amendment[4] and Title VII[5] rights of religious employees, provisions which theoretically were designed to protect free exercise of religion and to protect employees against unlawful employment discrimination on the basis of religion. The sharply polarized salient decisions of the Burger Court of the late 1970s are now unproblematically accepted, largely without dissent, by virtually all of the members of the current Rehnquist Court. Several decisions by the Supreme Court and the courts of appeals between 1977 and 1992 powerfully exemplify the most troubling jurisprudential diminutions of the free exercise and Title VII rights of individual religious employees, and, correspondingly, the generally enhanced managerial prerogatives enjoyed when religion itself functions as the institutional employer in the secular employment arena.[6]

The first section of this essay analyzes the formally expressed but functionally feeble protections for the religious employee in the secular workplace. The primary focus will be upon the unprotected employee and the salient case law that has dramatically debilitated Title VII of the federal Civil Rights Act of 1964,[7] a statute designed to protect against discrimination in employment on the basis of, *inter alia*, the employee's religion. Concomitantly, the Supreme Court has largely vitiated the other major source of legal protections for the religious employee, the Free Exercise Clause of the First Amendment of the Constitution. The Supreme Court consistently has failed to protect the secular employment of the religious employee. Most recently, the Supreme Court has endorsed even the denial of unemployment compensation insurance eligibility of the employee terminated from secular employment for exercising purportedly protected religious observance.[8] In summary: employee rights? What rights? Section One charts this important chapter in the continuing tragedy of labor.

The second section will examine the significant prerogatives enjoyed by religion when it functions as the institutional employer. The contrast is quite dramatic, given the essentially unprotected religious employee in this employment regime. When the institutional mainstream religion functions as the employer, its managerial prerogatives have been enhanced by government deregulation, achieved especially through case law construction.

Is there any realistic basis to apprehend a specter of government regulation by undue intrusion into, or excessive entanglement of government with, religion through labor and employment discrimination laws? On the contrary!

Deregulation— the public policy paradigm of the past decade —
has been the prevailing motif as we approach the millennium.
Only when employees of religious institutional employers are
irrevocably and systemically marginalized while performing
wholly secular functions at the very bottom of workplace
hierarchies will they have any realistic hope of receiving some
passing judicial interest, and thus they may occasionally obtain
at least the bare protections of minimum wage or workers
disability compensation laws. Likewise, only marginalized and
decidedly non-institutional religious employers who deliberately
bear witness in opposition to the pernicious policies of the
government— for example, those employers who consciously
provide employment to undocumented aliens, because of the
employers' principled deliberate disregard of immigration
control laws— are at risk of intrusive and coercive government
regulation.

   The essay concludes with a critical assessment of this current
legal regime, and of its possible consequences for religion, the
world of employment (and unemployment), and public policy.

THE FAILURE OF GOVERNMENT REGULATION
TO PROTECT THE RELIGIOUS EMPLOYEE FROM
DISCRIMINATION IN THE SECULAR WORKPLACE

Title VII: Reasonable Accommodation of the Employee,
or the Employer's Undue Hardship

   Trans World Airlines, Inc. v. Hardison[9] marked the beginning
of the contemporary Supreme Court's debilitation of Title VII
protections of employees against unlawful discrimination on the
basis of religion. Justice Byron White wrote for the seven-
member Court majority, with Justices William Brennan and
Thurgood Marshall in dissent.

   Trans World Airlines ("TWA") hired Larry G. Hardison to
work in TWA's Stores Department. The Stores Department was
crucial to TWA's operations and found it essential, therefore, to
operate twenty-four hours per day, three hundred and sixty-five

days per year. Hardison was subject to a seniority system designed through a collective bargaining agreement that TWA had negotiated with the International Association of Machinists and Aerospace Workers, the union which represented Hardison's bargaining unit. Under the labor agreement, the most senior employees had first choice for job and shift assignments. In the spring of 1968, Hardison joined the Worldwide Church of God, which forbade its sabbatarian[10] members to work on the Sabbath and proscribed work on specified religious holidays. Hardison informed his supervisor of his work schedule shift conflict with his Sabbath. The problem was temporarily resolved by transferring Hardison to a different area. He later transferred voluntarily back to an area where he did not have enough seniority to avoid working on his Sabbath. Hardison was asked to work, and he refused to report. After a hearing, Hardison was discharged for insubordination for refusing to work his designated shift. Hardison claimed that his discharge constituted unlawful religious discrimination in violation of Title VII of the federal Civil Rights Act of 1964.

The Supreme Court held that TWA's discharge of Hardison did not violate Title VII. The Court explained that an employer must make reasonable accommodation of religious needs of employees. Based on the facts, however, the Court opined that TWA made reasonable efforts to accommodate Hardison's religious practices and Sabbath observance as required by Title VII. In addition, TWA had done all it reasonably could to accommodate the employee's religious practices within the bounds of the seniority system in the collective bargaining agreement. Therefore, stated the Court, the employer's duty to accommodate Hardison's religious observance and his refusal to work on his Saturday Sabbath did not require TWA to take steps inconsistent with the seniority system of the valid collective bargaining agreement.

The Court placed great weight on the seniority system of the labor contract. While the Court recognized that religious observances are a reality, religiously observant low seniority employees cannot always get first choice of shifts in order to remain observant. If there are not enough employees to work

Saturdays, the seniority system in this particular collective bargaining agreement made seniority the determinative factor in shift/days off assignments. Title VII does not stand for the proposition that the employer need deprive higher seniority employees of labor contract seniority and shift rights in order to accommodate junior employees' religious preferences. Neither the employer nor the labor union was required by Title VII to make special exception to the labor contract's seniority system to accommodate the employee's religious obligations. The Court found that "to require TWA to bear more than de minimis cost in order to give Hardison Saturdays off is an undue hardship not required by Title VII."[11] The costs of giving junior employees days off to accommodate their religion, while abandoning or violating the labor contract's seniority system, would result in unequal treatment of employees on the basis of religion.

The dissent, written by Justice Marshall in which Brennan joined, regarded the majority opinion as a fatal judicial blow to the Title VII statutory requirement to accommodate religious practices in the workplace. The dissent argued that accommodation should not be rejected simply because it involved unequal treatment. Title VII required employers to grant privileges as part of the accommodation process, and a huge carrier like TWA could have borne the burden of the extra costs without undue hardship, according to the dissent.

With the *TWA v. Hardison* decision, the employer's Title VII duty to reasonably accommodate the religious practices of the observant employee was utterly and literally minimized by the Court. According to the Court's calculus, any accommodation measure of the employee by the employer that resulted in more than a "de minimis" cost to the employer was an unreasonable "undue hardship," and thus was not required of the employer by Title VII. This effective judicial relief for the employer from its statutory duty to reasonably accommodate the employee's religious observance was, if possible, made even more complete by the Supreme Court in 1986. Chief Justice William Rehnquist wrote for the seven-member majority in *Ansonia Board of*

Education v. Philbrook,[12] with Justices Marshall and John Paul
Stevens filing opinions concurring in part and dissenting in part.

Ronald Philbrook was employed by the Ansonia School
Board since 1962 to teach business classes. In 1968, Philbrook
was baptized into the Worldwide Church of God. The church
required its members to refrain from working on designated
holy days, which caused Philbrook to miss six school days per
year. Pursuant to the collective bargaining agreement between
the school board and the teacher's union, teachers were granted
three days of annual leave for observance of religious holidays.
They could not, however, use any accumulated sick leave for
religious observances. Philbrook used the three days
contractually granted for religious holidays each year. Since
Philbrook needed three more work days annually free from
work in order to observe his religion, he asked the school board
either to adopt the policy of allowing use of three days of
personal business for purposes of religious observance, or, in the
alternative, to allow him to pay the cost of a substitute and
receive full pay for additional days off for religious observances.
The school board rejected Philbrook's alternative requests.

Philbrook sued, alleging that the prohibition on the use of
"necessary personal business" leave for religious observance
violated Title VII. He sought both damages and injunctive relief.
Although it remanded the case for further factual findings and
thus did not issue a dispositive decision, the Court reiterated
that the employer met its statutory obligations. Significantly, the
employer is not required to acquiesce to the employee's most
desired, most beneficial accommodation. As Chief Justice
Rehnquist summarized: "Thus, where the employer has already
reasonably accommodated the employee's religious needs, the
statutory inquiry is at an end. The employer need not further
show that each of the employee's alternative accommodations
would result in undue hardship. As *Hardison* illustrates, the
extent of undue hardship on the employer's business is at issue
only where the employer claims that it is unable to offer any
reasonable accommodation without such hardship."[13]

Through these two important decisions, the Supreme Court
essentially relieved the secular employer of its statutory duty to

reasonably accommodate the religious employee; anything beyond de minimis cost caused by the employer's accommodation of the employee will be an "undue hardship" to the employer, which is beyond the employer's statutory Title VII duty of reasonable accommodation of the observations, practices, and beliefs of the religious employee.

The Further (Un)Free Exercise of Religion: Loss of Employment and Loss of Eligibility for Unemployment Compensation Benefits

Employment Division, Department of Human Resources of Oregon v. Smith,[14] decided by the Supreme Court in 1990, quickly became one of the most controversial (un)free exercise[15] of religion decisions in First Amendment religion clauses jurisprudence. *Smith* may have effectively ended the isolated line of free exercise decisions that had previously sustained eligibility for state unemployment compensation insurance benefits by those whose exercise of religion precluded continuation of employment.[16]

Alfred Smith and Galen Black were members of the Native American Church. They ingested peyote sacramentally during the religious ceremonies of their church. Consequently, they were terminated from their employment as drug and alcohol counselors at the Douglas County Council on Alcohol and Drug Abuse, a private, non-profit rehabilitation center in Oregon. The state agency then denied them unemployment compensation benefits, based on the terminations for work-related misconduct.

Writing for the Court, Justice Antonin Scalia posited that the Court's precedents never held that an individual's religious practices relieved one from the duty to comply with a law prohibiting criminal conduct— in this case, drug use— that the state was free to regulate.[17] He went on to reject the prior test of compelling interest that had to be satisfied in order to sustain the constraint on the free exercise of religion.[18]

After *Smith*, the free exercise rights of the religious employee to retain employment or to obtain unemployment compensation benefits have been reduced to dependence upon the sufferance of the political majority. The Court has removed independent judicial protection of the free exercise rights of the religious employee in the secular workplace. The pernicious *Smith* decision especially encapsulates the major theme of the first section of this essay. In the current legal regime, and for the foreseeable future, the individual religious employee regrettably is left without viable legal protections from employment discrimination on the basis of religion or for the exercise of religious practices. The religious individual is at the dubious mercy of the secular employer and the pro-managerial legal regime.

GOVERNMENT REGULATIONS AND THE MANAGERIAL PREROGATIVES OF THE RELIGIOUS EMPLOYER

When a well-recognized, mainstream religious institution acts as the employer, the Supreme Court has been very deferential to the employer, often at the expense of the rights of employees. Those who advocate strict separation of church and state may see the Court's deference to the managerial prerogatives of the religious institutional employer as a violation of the Establishment Clause of the First Amendment.[19]   That, obviously, is not a perspective recently shared by the current accommodationist Court. The irony, of course, is that while this Court has increasingly "accommodated" government preferences for religion that would have been Establishment Clause violations during the Warren Court era, this Court has concomitantly vitiated the employer's Title VII duty to reasonably accommodate the religious employees's practices.

The internal labor relations of the religious employer generally will be free from the National Labor Relations Act and the jurisdiction of the National Labor Relations Board. The Court has made it virtually impossible for employees of religious employers to bargain collectively in a unionized context. The Court also has broadly interpreted the Title VII exemption for religious employers, thus enabling these employers to discriminate on the basis of otherwise protected classifications, in deference to the religious employer's doctrines.[20]

Fortunately, the religious employer has not had a complete carte blanche from the judiciary. When the religious employer is engaging in purely secular, commercial functions, the religious employer may be subject to secular labor and employment discrimination law regulations on those occasions. This has recently occurred, for example, in the contexts of federal courts of appeals mandating religious employers' compliance with the reporting requirements of the Immigration Reform and Control Act[21] and with the minimum wage provisions of the federal Fair Labor Standards Act.[22]

Labor Relations

In *National Labor Relations Board v. Catholic Bishop of Chicago*,[23] Chief Justice Warren Burger, writing for a bare five-member majority of the Court, opined that the National Labor Relations Board did not have jurisdiction to investigate unfair labor practice charges brought against the Catholic Bishop of Chicago. The Bishop was the employer of the complaining faculty members working in schools operated under the auspices of the Catholic Church.

The managerial prerogatives of this powerful institutional employer to avoid faculty unionization could have been somewhat constrained, if it had been subject to the National Labor Relations Act.[24] Although the Court majority expressed extreme sensitivity to the Free Exercise and Establishment Clauses of the First Amendment, it refrained from any substantive inquiry into the possible intersection of those clauses with labor law principles. Chief Justice Burger summarized: "Accordingly, in the absence of a clear expression of Congress' intent to bring teachers in church-operated schools within the jurisdiction of the Board, we decline to construe the Act in a manner that could in turn call upon the Court to resolve difficult and sensitive questions arising out of the guarantees of the First Amendment Religion Clauses."[25]

The National Labor Relations Board originally found that the Catholic Bishop, as the institutional employer of the lay faculty members at the schools operated under auspices of the Catholic Church, had violated the National Labor Relations Act and had committed unfair labor practices by refusing to recognize or to bargain with the faculty union. In 1974 and 1975, separate representation petitions were filed with the National Labor Relations Board by the faculty union. The Catholic Bishop challenged the assertion of jurisdiction by the National Labor Relations Board. The court of appeals agreed with the Catholic Bishop. The Free Exercise and Establishment Clauses precluded the National Labor Relations Board from exercising jurisdiction over the schools of the Catholic Church and over the Catholic Bishop as the institutional employer.

In a highly technical decision, which deliberately did not reach or address the underlying merits of the Bishop's unfair labor practices of refusing to recognize or to bargain with the faculty unions, the Supreme Court affirmed the decision of the Seventh Circuit Court of Appeals. In his opinion for the majority of the Court, Chief Justice Burger pointed to the legislative history of the National Labor Relations Act, which revealed nothing to indicate that church-operated schools would be within the jurisdiction of the National Labor Relations Board. The chief justice referred specifically to the debate behind an amendment to the National Labor Relations Act, which reflected certain First Amendment guarantees, and argued that "the absence of an 'affirmative intention of the Congress clearly expressed' fortifies our conclusion that Congress did not contemplate that the Board would require church-operated schools to [recognize] unions as bargaining agents for their teachers."[26] The Supreme Court, therefore, affirmed the decision of the Seventh Circuit. While the Court recognized that the Board's jurisdiction was broad, it again pointed to the legislative history of the National Labor Relations Act. Finding nothing in the legislative history that would endorse the Board jurisdiction sought by the faculty union in this case, the Court decided the Board must decline jurisdiction over labor law matters in church-operated schools. The alternative, noted the Court, would lead to "mandatory bargaining, which in turn would cause too many conflicts with church administrators."[27]

In a powerful, sharp dissent by Justice Brennan, and joined by Justices White, Marshall, and Blackmun, the majority opinion was characterized as a failed lesson in statutory construction. The dissent argued that the majority opinion failed to consider the National Labor Relations Act's language and history. The dissent further asserted that the majority failed to consider its own precedents, which held that the jurisdiction of the National Labor Relations Board is extremely broad. The dissent plainly would have included church-operated schools within the jurisdiction of the Board.[28]

Religious Employer Exemption from Title VII

In 1987, the Supreme Court sustained without dissent the religiously-affiliated institutional employer's prerogative to summarily terminate competent, long-service employees in *Corporation of the Presiding Bishop of the Church of Jesus Christ of Latter-day Saints v. Amos.*[29] The Deseret Gymnasium was a nonprofit facility open to the public and operated by the Corporation of the Presiding Bishop of the Church of Jesus Christ of Latter-day Saints and the Corporation of the President of the Church of Jesus Christ of Latter-day Saints. Both of these are religious entities associated with an unincorporated religious association sometimes called the Mormon Church. Arthur Frank Mayson worked at the Deseret Gymnasium for approximately sixteen years. He was discharged in 1981 because he failed to qualify for a "temple recommend," a certificate that he was a member of the Church and eligible to attend its temples. Mayson alleged that his discharge was unlawful discrimination on the basis of religion. The Church maintained that Section 702[30] of Title VII shielded it from liability. Mayson argued that if this federal civil rights statute permitted religious employers to discriminate on religious grounds in their employment of persons for obviously non-religious, secular jobs, Section 702 of

Title VII then would unconstitutionally violate the Establishment Clause of the First Amendment.

Without dissent, the Supreme Court reversed the decision of the lower federal court, which had found in favor of the former employee plaintiff. The Court examined whether Section 702 of Title VII was unconstitutional in light of the Establishment Clause. Specifically, did the Section 702 statutory exemption for the Church from Title VII have the primary effect of unconstitutionally advancing religion, in violation of the Establishment Clause? The Court resolved the question in the negative.

The Court measured the facts and the statute against the Establishment Clause, according to the classic multipart test set forth in *Lemon v. Kurtzman*. The Court concluded that, under the first prong of the *Lemon* test, it was permissible for the Congress to attempt to minimize governmental "interference with the decision-making process in religions."[31] Under the second prong, the Court stated that a law is not necessarily unconstitutional simply because it allows churches to advance religion. In order to violate this prong, the Court reasoned that it would be necessary to show that the government itself had advanced religion through its own activities and influence. Finally, under the third prong of the *Lemon* test, the Court concluded that there was no unconstitutional entanglement raised by Section 702 of Title VII.

Recent subsequent decisions by courts of appeals continue to follow the rationale of the Court in *Amos*.[32] Religious employers consequently remain free from government regulation that would otherwise risk running afoul of the Establishment Clause jurisprudence's excessive entanglement prohibition.

As the result of these salient Supreme Court decisions in *Catholic Bishop* and *Amos* and other court of appeals decisions in their wake, neither the legal regimes nor religion has been enhanced. Rather, on both conceptual and practical levels, labor law doctrine, the First Amendment religion clauses, and Title VII protections against discrimination in employment because of religion, have all been debilitated by the Court's jurisprudence.

The only consistent "winner" in these cases has been the institutional religious employer. Much more significantly and ominously, the Supreme Court has moved inexorably to a pro-institutional, "statist" bias, effectuating an insidious calculus of interests that routinely subordinates individual employees who generally lack corporate institutional power and influence. It is painfully ironic that institutional religious employers emulate Caesar, and take full advantage of this statist jurisprudence in order to insure the continued subordination of their employees and the debilitation of their employees' labor and employment discrimination law rights. This has not invariably occurred when neutral regulations in federal immigration and federal minimum wage law have been at issue. In these cases, when the religious employer is engaged in overtly secular employment functions quite distinct from the religious mission, the employer has been generally held subject to the neutral regulations of the secular legal regime.

Wage, Hour, and Worker's Disability Compensation Law

In 1985, in *Tony & Susan Alamo Foundation v. Secretary of Labor*,[33] the Supreme Court placed a partial judicial brake on what has otherwise been remarkable judicial deference to the managerial prerogatives of the religious employer. The Court unanimously affirmed that federal wage and hour laws protected employees engaged in the commercial, secular activities of the religious employer. The Alamo Foundation was a nonprofit religious organization incorporated under California law. Its professed primary mission was Christian evangelism and active corporal works of mercy to disadvantaged persons. The Foundation's income was generated from operating commercial businesses, ranging from service stations, hotels, farms, and construction companies to a candy producer and distributor. These businesses were staffed by three hundred of the Foundation's "associates." They received minimal food, clothing, and shelter, but not cash wages or salaries. Most characterized themselves as religious volunteers and disclaimed rights to any wages. Nevertheless, the Court affirmed the lower court's finding that they were covered "employees" within the meaning of the federal Fair Labor Standards Act (FLSA). The Foundation unsuccessfully argued that it should be exempt from the federal minimum wage and hour law because its commercial enterprises were "infused with a religious purpose."[34]   The Court, rejecting this position, summarized: "the Foundation's businesses serve the general public in competition with ordinary commercial enterprises . . . and the payment of substandard wages would undoubtedly give petitioners and similar organizations an advantage over their competitors. It is exactly this kind of 'unfair method of competition' that the [FLSA] was intended to prevent . . . and the admixture of religious motivation does not alter a business's effect on commerce.[35]

The core rationale of the *Alamo Foundation* decision has been reiterated in subsequent decisions of courts of appeals involving wage, hour, and worker's disability compensation law applied to religious employers. As this author concluded in an earlier law review article on the *Alamo Foundation* decision, "Religious organizations do not have carte blanche to exploit persons employed in their commercial ventures."[36]

The *Alamo* precedent has been closely followed in recent decisions in the courts of appeals. In *Brock v. Wendell's Woodworks, Inc.,*[37] the Secretary of Labor brought a Fair Labor Standards Act (FLSA) suit against two commercial enterprises, seeking to enforce the Act's minimum wage requirements and its prohibition of child labor.

Members of a separatist religious sect, the Shiloh True Light Church, rejected institutionalized formal education. They instead opted to teach their children at home "in relative freedom from worldly influences and in accordance with their parents' understanding of Scriptural teaching."[38] This parental instruction occupied half the usual institutional school day, thereby allowing the members' children's education to be supplemented by a vocational training program. Through an arrangement with the church, certain employers "having the same religious motivations as the parents" provided apprenticeship-type training. This was designed to "insulate the children from idleness, to teach them marketable skills, to provide them with savings . . . and to inculcate in them a scripturally mandated work ethic."[39]

Defendant Wendell's Woodworks used powersaws and forklifts in its woodwork manufacturing process. As part of their vocational training, members' children, some as young as nine and ten, operated power equipment. Wendell's controlling officers were church members. Defendant McGee Brothers, a masonry contractor, similarly employed church members' children as part of the vocational training program. The children were engaged in laying brick and cinderblock; they transported material and mixed mortar; worked on scaffolds and, when chimneys were being constructed, on rooftops. Four of the five owners of McGee Brothers were church members.

The Secretary of Labor sought to enforce the minimum wage requirements and the child labor proscriptions of the FLSA. The district court upheld the application of the FLSA. On appeal, defendants conceded application of the minimum wage requirements, but they contended that enforcement of the minimum age requirements would violate their First Amendment free exercise rights. Defendants therefore claimed an exemption from the child labor laws.

In upholding the district court's application of the FLSA to defendants' commercial enterprises, the fourth circuit emphasized the perilous nature of some of the positions which had been filled by church members' children. The court indicated that FLSA regulations classified some of these jobs as "hazardous" and not to be performed by anyone under eighteen years of age. The court further noted that the FLSA prohibits employment of anyone under fourteen.

Based on the analysis in *Alamo Foundation*, the court of appeals found that the federal government has a "substantial interest in regulating child labor, even to the point of prohibition."[40]   The government's interest was sufficiently compelling to override the church members' sincere convictions that they were rearing their children in the manner dictated by their religious beliefs. Although the court recognized the "spiritual worth" of the vocational training program, it concluded that those religious beliefs, served by employing children in "commercial enterprises that compete with other enterprises fully subject to labor laws," could not "immunize" the defendant employers from the proscriptions and requirements of the FLSA.[41]

In *Dole v. Shenandoah Baptist Church*,[42] the Fourth Circuit in 1990 again sustained the constitutionality of the child labor laws and minimum wage requirements of the FLSA to a church-operated school. The Shenandoah Baptist Church operated the Roanoke Valley Christian Schools to impart what the church regarded as a vital part of its mission of Christian education. The school's full-time curriculum include Bible study, and biblical materials were further integrated with traditional academic studies. The schools compensated the teachers with a six thousand dollar per year base salary. Because this low salary made it difficult to attract teachers, Shenandoah instituted a "head-of-household" salary supplement. The church's pastor explained that "the Bible clearly teaches that the husband is the head of the house. . . . We moved in that direction, thinking that our opportunity and responsibility of basing our practice on clear biblical teaching would not be a matter of question."[43] All married male teachers received the supplement, but married women were not eligible. However, three divorced females who had dependents did receive the supplement. Ninety-one persons who worked at Roanoke Valley as support personnel also were paid less than the hourly minimum wage. These workers included bus drivers, custodians, kitchen workers, bookkeepers, and secretaries.

The Secretary of Labor and the EEOC sued, asserting that Shenandoah had violated two components of the FLSA. The government alleged that Shenandoah paid support personnel less than the minimum wage, in violation of the FLSA minimum wage requirement, and had paid female teachers less than male teachers performing the same job, in violation of the equal pay requirements. The district court found that Shenandoah had violated both aspects of the FLSA, and it ordered Shenandoah to pay back pay to its support personnel and its teachers. On appeal, Shenandoah argued that Roanoke Valley was not subject to the strictures of the FLSA, and that applying the statute to a church-run school would violate the Free Exercise and Establishment Clauses of the First Amendment and the Equal Protection Clause of the Constitution.

The fourth circuit stated that two conditions are necessary for the FLSA to apply: Roanoke had to be an "enterprise" within the definition of the Act, and the teachers and support staff had to be "employees." The court of appeals held that the legislative history of a 1966 amendment to the Act, which brought public and private schools within the meaning of "enterprise," demonstrated Congress' intent to treat church-operated schools as enterprises. The amendment explicitly covered private non-profit schools, and deemed the activities performed in the operation of the school to be "performed for a business purpose."

Shenandoah nevertheless contended that the FLSA should not apply to its church-run school, because of the inseparable nature of the school and church. Relying on the *Amos* decision, Shenandoah first argued that the court was required to exempt its school from the FLSA. The court, however, pointed out that *Amos* stood for the proposition that Congress could provide for an exemption of religious institutions without running afoul of the First Amendment, but that such an exemption was not constitutionally mandated.

Shenandoah also argued that its teachers were not "employees," but instead were ministers and therefore included within the "ministerial exemption" from the Act. Relying on *Rayburn v. General Conference of Seventh-day Adventists*,[44] Shenandoah explained that the teachers taught from a "pervasively religious perspective," lead students in prayer, and, as a condition of employment, were required to subscribe to the "Shenandoah statement of faith."[45]

The court, however, distinguished *Rayburn*, which explained that the ministerial exemption "depended on the function of the position, not simply on ordination. . . . The teachers in the present case perform no sacerdotal function; neither do they serve as church governors. They belong to no

clearly delineated religious order."[46]   Construing the exemption
narrowly, the court ruled that the teachers at Roanoke Valley
were "employed as lay teachers in a church-operated private
school."[47]   The court therefore concluded that Congress
intended church-operated schools such as Roanoke Valley to be
covered by the FLSA, and that their teachers and support staff
were employees under the Act.

Shenandoah asserted that application of the FLSA would
unconstitutionally burden the church's free exercise of its
religious beliefs, unlawfully impair the church's ability to
administer its relationship with employees, and thereby its
"power to decide free from state interference, matters of church
government as well as those of faith and doctrine."[48]
Shenandoah further maintained that its "head-of-household"
salary supplement was based on sincerely held religious beliefs
— namely the biblical precept that established the husband as
the absolute head of the house. Finally, the support personnel,
intervenors in this action, claimed that allowing the government
to set their wages, rather than the church "acting under divine
guidance, would deprive them of blessings they would
otherwise receive by allowing their Lord to supply their
needs."[49]

In reviewing Shenandoah's free exercise claim, the court of
appeals applied a three-part analysis: it examined the burden on
the exercise of sincerely held religious beliefs; it determined
whether the state has a compelling interest to justify this burden;
and, it balanced the burden on the free exercise against the
hindrance to the state's goal that would arise from an exemption.
Under the first prong of this inquiry, the court found that any
burden on Shenandoah's free exercise rights that might arise by
application of the FLSA would be limited. The Bible does not
mandate a pay differential based on sex. Neither did church
doctrine prevent equal pay or minimum wage. Therefore, the
court concluded that "the pay requirements at issue do not cut to
the heart of Shenandoah beliefs."[50]   The court noted that the
church was presently in compliance with the FLSA, that
Shenandoah had no objection to complying with state fire,
health, and safety requirements, and that it had withheld income

tax from employees' wages and paid social security tax. The court also held that the increased payroll expenses that accompany FLSA compliance is not the type of burden that is determinative in a free exercise claim. The court followed the dictates of *Alamo*— if the support staff continued to object to the government mandated minimum wage, they had "the option of volunteering their services or returning to Shenandoah all or part of their back-pay awards."[51]

The court found that the government had a compelling reason to apply the minimum wage and equal pay provisions of the FLSA to Roanoke Valley. The government's interests in "maintain[ing] a minimum standard of living" and providing a "remedy [to the] serious and endemic problem of employment discrimination," the court concluded, were "interests of the highest order."[52]   Finally, weighing the limited burden of the free exercise rights of Shenandoah against the government's compelling interest in applying the statute, the balance was obviously resolved in favor of the application of the FLSA to Roanoke Valley. The court found that the state's goals would be undermined if it were to exempt Roanoke Valley from compliance with the FLSA. "There is no principled way of exempting the school without exempting all other sectarian schools and thereby the thousands of lay teachers and staff members of their payrolls. . . . Congress has here created a comprehensive statute, and a less restrictive means of attaining its aims is not available."[53]

The court found that application of the FLSA to the church-run schools would not be a violation of the Establishment Clause. Shenandoah asserted that the application of the FLSA would violate the second prong of *Lemon* because the ministerial exemption of the FLSA impermissibly favors the Roman Catholic Church by granting the exemption to nuns and priests, and not to the teachers and staff at Roanoke Valley. The court disagreed, and observed that the exemption "is facially neutral, encompassing ministers, deacons, and members of religious orders in any faith, not exclusively Catholic nuns and priests."[54]

This "accommodation of free exercise values," the court held, is not an Establishment Clause violation.[55]

Shenandoah also argued that the government inspection, monitoring, and review required by the FLSA would constitute an impermissible government entanglement with internal religious matters. The application of the FLSA to Roanoke would thus fail the third prong of the *Lemon* test. Citing *Alamo*, the court instead found that while the administrative requirements of the FLSA might impose a burden "in terms of paperwork," such a burden was "not significantly more intrusive into religious affairs" than other state administrative regulations with which Shenandoah had willingly complied.[56] Shenandoah's final constitutional argument asserted that the ministerial exemption violates equal protection guarantees in that it "creates a suspect classification which invidiously discriminates against adherents of religions that do not have formal religious orders."[57] The court, however, determined that once a statute passed the rigors of *Lemon*, all that was needed to uphold the statute was a showing that Congress had chosen a rational classification to further a legitimate end. The court upheld the exemption which it held to be a "rational means of creating a buffer between church and state."[58]

In *DeArment v. Harvey*,[59] in 1991, the eighth circuit also held that application of the FLSA to a church-operated school does not run afoul of the First Amendment religion clauses. D.L. Harvey was the pastor at the Rose City Pentecostal Church of God, which operated the Rose City Academy "as an integral part of the church."[60] The school, which provided education for children in grades kindergarten through twelfth grade, used a "self-study program" that taught all subjects from a "biblical point of view."[61] Each class was moderated by a supervisor, assisted by a classroom monitor. Neither the supervisors nor the monitors were required to be church members. Pastor Harvey testified that each supervisor and monitor must be a "born again" Christian. All of the supervisors and monitors had either high school diplomas or had completed a GED program. None of them, however, was certified by any association or body as being qualified for a teaching position. Both the supervisor and the monitors worked with the children, but they did not conduct formal classroom instruction. Supervisors graded papers, answered student questions, conducted prayer, and counseled the students. The court characterized the monitors' duties as equivalent to teachers' aides in the public schools. All monitors and supervisors who testified stated that they considered their teaching to be a part of their pastoral ministry.

The Secretary of Labor instituted suit to enforce the record keeping and wage-hour requirements of the FLSA. The district court found the church was an employer within the meaning of the FLSA; its supervisors and monitors were employees within the Act, and therefore the FLSA was applicable and had been violated. The eighth circuit held that the *Shenandoah* court had correctly decided the applicability of the FLSA to a church-run school and would be followed.

When operating a secular function, that aspect of the religious employer's function is subject to state workers' compensation law. In *South Ridge Baptist Church v. Industrial Commission of Ohio,*[62] the sixth circuit in 1990 rejected the church's challenge to the constitutionality of the application of Ohio's mandatory workers' compensation program to the non-profit religious corporation. Ohio's workers' compensation program mandates that all employers of at least one person in the state contribute semiannually to a state-administered insurance fund established for the payment of benefits to injured employees. The statutory scheme provides for two relevant exceptions. First, "employee" is defined not to include ministers of churches. Second, an employer can avoid paying premiums into the state fund by electing to self-insure and thus pay benefits directly to its injured employees.

South Ridge Baptist Church, a non-profit religious corporation located in Ohio, characterized itself as "an independent, fundamental, Bible-believing, Bible-teaching and preaching Church" which "strives to be absolutely obedient to fundamental doctrines of the Bible and seeks to operate and live in accordance with historical Baptist doctrine."[63] The church declared that its religious beliefs were founded on the conviction that the Bible is the "supreme and final authority in religious

faith and practice."[64] Based on biblical teachings, the church
asserted that its participation in the state's workers'
compensation program would "violate God's command that
Jesus is the head of the Church and that its funds are God's, to be
spent for Biblical purposes."[65] The church did not pursue the
self-insurance option. The church alleged that application of the
Ohio workers' compensation statute violated the Free Exercise
and Establishment Clauses. The district court held that the state
interest of compensating injured workers and protecting the
solvency of its compensation program were sufficiently
compelling to override the burden the program placed on the
church's free exercise rights. Further, the court held that the
scheme was the least restrictive means available, since it granted
an exemption to self-insured employers. Finally, the court held
that the system's administrative requirements did not
impermissibly entangle government in religion in violation of
the Establishment Clause.

On appeal to the sixth circuit, the church conceded that the
workers' compensation program advanced compelling state
interests. The church claimed, however, that the district court
erred in granting to defendants a summary judgment because
they had failed to prove as a matter of law that mandatory
participation of all employers, including churches, was the least
restrictive means available.

In resolving the free exercise claim, the sixth circuit applied
the three-part analysis utilized by the Supreme Court in *United
States v. Lee*.[66] It weighed the magnitude of the burden on the
exercise of religion; the existence of a compelling state interest
justifying the burden; and the extent to which accommodation of
the church would impede the state's objectives. The sixth circuit
found that the state's interest in preserving the solvency of the
workers' compensation program alone was sufficiently
compelling to dispatch South Ridge's free exercise claim. The
court placed heavy reliance on *Lee*, which held that the Free
Exercise Clause was not violated by compelling an Amish
employer to pay taxes into the federal social security system. In
Lee, the Supreme Court found that the federal government's
interest in maintaining the fiscal vitality of its old age and

unemployment benefits system through mandatory participation was "very high." The sixth circuit indicated that Ohio's interest is "at least as great since it is based on the state's fundamental police power to safeguard the welfare of its citizens."[67]   Although it failed to explain the nature of South Ridge's activities which subjected it to the workers' compensation program, the court of appeals implicitly characterized them as commercial: "Congress and the courts have been sensitive to the needs flowing from the Free Exercise Clause, but every person cannot be shielded from all burdens incident to exercising every aspect of the right to practice religious beliefs. When followers of a particular sect enter into commercial activity as a matter of choice, the limits they accept on their own conduct as a matter of conscience and faith are not to be superimposed on the statutory schemes which are binding on others in that activity."[68]

The sixth circuit also found that the Supreme Court in *Lee* had "implicitly incorporated the least restrictive means test . . . in stating that a restriction on religious liberty must be 'essential' to the compelling government interest."[69] South Ridge argued that Ohio's mandatory workers' compensation program was not the least restrictive means available, since it did not grant the church an exemption from coverage. The church invoked *Lee*, which found that an exemption from the social security tax for "self-employed persons in a religious community having its own welfare system"[70] would not unduly interfere with the fulfillment of the governmental interest. The sixth circuit, distinguishing the exemption in *Lee*, stated, "Confining the . . . exemption to the self-employed provided for a narrow category which was readily identifiable. Self-employed persons in a religious community having its own "welfare" system are distinguishable from the generality of wage earners employed by others."[71] Just as the ministerial exemption from Ohio's workers' compensation program, the self-employed exemption from the social security tax in *Lee* did not "operate to impose the employer's religious faith on the employee."[72] The court concluded that since the "limited and regulated self-insurance option [to Ohio's workers' compensation program] fully secures the state's interest in protecting its workers' it could be expected that a blanket exemption of churches would not."[73]   Finally, the court concluded that "decisions regarding the coverage of a tax program are properly for the legislative branch."[74]

The church alleged excessive entanglement of government with religion based upon inspection of church records, forced disbursement of church funds to a state program, record keeping and reporting, categorizing employees according to risk, and enforcement actions for non-payment of premiums. The court of appeals, following the guidance provided in *Presiding Bishop v. Amos*[75] and *Dole v. Shenandoah Baptist Church*,[76] held that the administrative burdens imposed on South Ridge under the Ohio worker's compensation program would not constitute an excessive governmental entanglement. "[R]outine regulatory interaction such as application of neutral tax laws which involves no inquiries into religious doctrine, . . . no delegation of state power to a religious body, . . . and no detailed monitoring and close administrative contact between secular and religious bodies, . . . does not of itself violate the nonentanglement command."[77]

Immigration Law

Religious employers who witness in opposition to the restrictive immigration policies of the government have predictably been subject to intrusive and coercive government regulation. "Divine obedience" will be regarded by Caesar as the most uncivil and unprotected disobedience, a further manifestation of the prevailing statist jurisprudence of the federal judiciary.

In *Intercommunity Center for Justice and Peace v. Immigration and Naturalization Service*,[78] in 1990, the second circuit decided that a religious organization is subject to the verification requirements and sanctions of the Immigration Reform and Control Act. The Intercommunity Center for Justice and Peace ("ICJP"), an organization of forty-one Roman Catholic communities, joined as plaintiffs to obtain a judgment that they were exempt from the employer verification and sanctions provisions of the Immigration Reform and Control Act ("IRC") of 1986 on the grounds that enforcement of the Act against them would violate the Free Exercise Clause.

The IRC requires employers to verify that each of their employees is authorized to work in the United States. Civil fines may be imposed if an employer violates these verification requirements or knowingly employs an unauthorized alien. Furthermore, a pattern or practice of knowingly employing unauthorized aliens may result in criminal punishment. The ICJP asserted that application of the IRC would violate their free exercise rights. They maintained that Roman Catholic Church teachings impose upon them a duty to provide "food, clothing, shelter and means to sustain their own lives" to all people without regard to residence, nationality or immigration status, and that they were compelled to "offer employment to people in need, without regard to immigration status, as part of their religious ministries."[79] Relying on *NLRB v. Catholic Bishop of Chicago*, the ICJP also argued that, absent an explicit statement in the Act that it should be applied to religious organizations, they are exempt. To apply the IRC to the ICJP would cause impermissible government entanglement with religion in violation of the Establishment Clause.

The court described the religion clauses of the First Amendment as "providing full protection for religious beliefs but only limited protection for overt acts prompted by those beliefs."[80] The First Amendment contains an absolute proscription of legislative regulation of religious beliefs. Religious practice, however, is not afforded absolute protection. The court did, however, recognize that Congress may not discriminate against religion by "banning acts only when they are engaged in for religious reasons or only because of the religious belief that they display."[81] The court of appeals analogized Congress's interest in controlling the flow of aliens to that of maintaining a uniform tax system, "which has been found to be a compelling governmental interest that overrides free exercise claims."[82] The court observed that although the ICJP sought an exemption only for its members, it was not alone — over one hundred amici of the Roman Catholic Church had

urged support for the ICJP. This obvious indication of the
potential for innumerable applications for religious exemption
would seem to implicate the third part of the *Lemon* test. In
dismissing ICJP's free exercise claim, the court relied on
*Employment Division, Department of Human Resources of Oregon v.
Smith*. "The [IRC] neither regulates religious beliefs nor
burdens acts because of their religious expression or motivation.
Rather, it is a valid, neutral law of general application that
happens to compel action contrary to certain religious beliefs.
No free exercise claim exists under such circumstances."[83]

The ICJP proposed that a limited exemption for "those whose
religion requires them not to discriminate on the basis of
immigration as an integral part of their religious mission" would
avoid the impermissible government entanglement that would
otherwise result from the application of the IRC to such a
religious organization.[84]   The second circuit, however, refused
to accept the notion that the application of the IRC here would
result in "governmental inquiries into religious beliefs."[85]   The
court opined that the existing exemptions for household
employees and employees hired prior to November 1986, unlike
the exemption proposed by the ICJP, has "no relation to religion.
No day-to-day inspection is required. . . . The proposed
exemption would require an inquiry into whether or not a
particular religious requirement is essential to an individual's
religious mission."[86]   Such an exemption, the court concluded,
would transform a neutral statute into one which would require
excessive governmental entanglement with religion. The court
accordingly rejected the Establishment Clause claim.

In *American Friends Service Comm. Corp. v. Thornburgh*,[87] the
ninth circuit in 1991 also upheld the constitutionality of the
verification and sanctions provisions of the Immigration Reform
and Control Act to a Quaker charity and relief organization. The
American Friends Service Committee (AFSC) was a Quaker
organization whose activities included charitable and relief
work. The AFSC failed to comply with the IRC because it
believed that to do so would violate the religious beliefs and
practices of its members. The AFSC contended that its beliefs
require that it not "refuse human beings work— thus depriving

them of the means to feed and clothe themselves and their children— simply because they may be strangers to our land." The ninth circuit applied *Employment Division, Department of Human Resources of Oregon v. Smith*, to find the IRC a "valid and neutral law of general applicability."[88]   Therefore, AFSC's free exercise claim failed because "prohibiting the exercise of religion is not the object of the [IRC] but merely the incidental effect of a generally applicable and otherwise valid provision."[89]

The court of appeals refused to accept AFSC's argument that its claims fell within the "hybrid claims" exception to *Smith*. Such claims, which contain another substantive constitutional challenge in addition to the free exercise claim, are "restricted to express constitutional protections such as freedom of speech, and firmly recognized substantive due process rights such as the privacy right in rearing children."[90]   The court declared that little would be left of the *Smith* decision if it were to accept the substantive due process "right to hire" claim— one of "slight constitutional weight— as an addition to a free exercise claim, sufficient to fall within the "hybrid claims" exception.[91]

CONCLUSION

The judiciary and the academic commentators have long recognized the potential tensions between the Establishment and the Free Exercise Clauses. The Title VII exemption which allows the religious employer to discriminate in employment, in order to carry on its activities, further exacerbates these tensions. Some courts have strongly suggested that the Title VII exemption may itself violate the Establishment Clause.[92]   Yet, the total absence of any exemption whatsoever would at least arguably unconstitutionally impinge upon the religious employer's free exercise rights. This author will refrain from proposing yet another sophisticated, multi-part test initially certain to harmonize the law, and thus even more certainly doomed to frustration.[93]   As concluded in an article written by this author in 1990, 'The tension in our religion clauses and Title VII jurisprudence can never be fully harmonized. However, with sensitivity and concern for everyone's rights, delicate balances can be achieved, if carefully and constantly recalibrated."[94]

It is highly unlikely that the current Supreme Court will sufficiently consider the interests of religious employees upon this theoretical balancing spectrum for the foreseeable future. Religious employers will probably continue to be privileged by the Court, not because of the Court's sensitivities to unconstitutional establishment or to the employers' free exercise claims per se, but rather due to the Court's near-automatic deference to the hierarchical institutional status of employers *qua* employers. When religious employers are judicially perceived as important statist instruments who are reinforcing the mainstream social, political, and legal order, they will continue to have virtual carte blanche in their labor relations and employment policies and operations. One of the deepest ironies in this highly skewed scenario is that the increasingly accommodationist Court only accommodates the religious employers, and remains hostile or oblivious to affording anything more than utterly de minimis "reasonable accommodation" to the religious employee of the secular employer.

The best instrumental means for at least partially rectifying this gross imbalance has been that proposed by Elizabeth Bradley in 1987 in the *Chicago Law Review*.[95] Bradley suggests that to resolve the "difficult and sensitive" issue of if and when the religion clauses compel or prohibit government regulation of the labor and employment sphere, the courts should concentrate on the job activities of the employee, rather than on the nature of the employer organization. This would, she argues, radically reconfigure the jurisprudential perspective from the employer to the employee: "The fact finder should determine, first, whether the employee was hired from the secular marketplace, and second, whether her employment activities can be distinguished from activities ordinarily performed in a secular setting only by reference to the theology of the religious organization. If the answer to both these questions is affirmative, or if an affirmative finding on one prong sufficiently outweighs a negative finding on the other, then Title VII, the NLRA, and other fair labor statutes are applicable. Otherwise, the particular activities in question should be exempt."[96] This test focusing on the employee's job activities will avoid the constitutional problem of excessive entanglement that the inquiry into the nature of the employer's organization invites. Whether this test will be recognized by this Court, whatever the test's jurisprudential virtues, is highly problematic because of the Court's congenital inability to appreciate— let alone adopt— the employee's perspective in any hierarchical employment relationship.

Apart from any possible recalibrations of the contour of statutory and constitutional law, religious employers have a greater, transcendent responsibility to treat their employees with the dignity and decency internally mandated by the tenets of the religion. Unfortunately, some religious institutional employers may be tempted to invoke the legalisms of the secular legal regime to avoid the higher internal obligations of the religion. If so, the institutional religious employers disingenuously will have assumed the role of Caesar in the workplace.

Last year marked the centennial of the Catholic papal encyclical *Rerum Novarum*. Pope Leo XIII forcefully articulated the dignity of all workers, the right to form labor unions, and of capital in service of human beings. That powerful document has inspired the Catholic Church's eloquent social teaching on labor throughout this century. Yet some Catholic institutions, as employers, have not implemented the Catholic Church's social teaching; instead, they insidiously have invoked secular labor law to deny the collective bargaining rights and aspirations of their workers, in contravention of the Church's pronouncements. These machinations of secular law by religious employers, often to avoid the teachings of their own religion, can be extraordinarily insidious and profoundly wrong. This can and must cease, not primarily through the counteruse or reform of secular law, but rather through the moral witness and suasion of the religious community and its workers upon its own internal institutional elites.[97]

Every religious employer first must answer the dictates of its religion: Is it treating its workers with the decency and dignity internally mandated by the religion? If the religious employer

instead is using the secular law to avoid its religious duties to its
workers, it will probably remain beyond the reach of the secular
law, given the pro-employer jurisprudence of this Supreme
Court. But, in this hellish scenario, the manipulative "religious"
employer who deliberately emulates Caesar ultimately will have
to answer to a court higher than this earthly High Court.

Government deregulation of religion through the judicial
vitiation of the labor and employment discrimination laws
ultimately will be much less significant in its ramifications than
whether religious employers and employees first comply with
their religion's own higher law by treating their workers with
dignity and decency, and thus making "society better, more just,
and more humane in the daily lives of all working people."[98]
This will occur through internal moral suasion brought to bear
upon the religious institutional employers among the
communities of believers, and not through secular law reform.
Once this is accomplished, a new judicial focus upon the role
and function of the employee, rather than the Court's skewed
deference to the institutional employer, may eventually become
possible and could result in more appropriate application of
secular labor and employment discrimination laws to protect
employees not essential to the core religious function and those
employees engaged in the secular, commercial functions of
religious employers. Until that occurs— and the prospects are
highly unlikely at the Supreme Court level for the foreseeable
future, absent congressional action to clarify intent and to
strengthen existing statutes— the legal regime will remain one
of deregulation of religion through the judicial vitiation of labor
and employment discrimination laws.

NOTES

1. For commentary on the statist ideology of the Burger/Rehnquist
   Court, see Cover, "The Supreme Court, 1982 Term: Foreword:
   Nomos and Narrative," *Harvard Law Review* 97 (1983): 4; Abner V.
   Mikva, "The Burger Court Evaluation: Some Good Marks from
   Unexpected Quarters," *Northwestern University Law Review* 82
   (1988):808; Charles Reich, "The Individual Sector," *Yale Law Journal*
   100 (1991): 1409; Rex E. Lee, "The Supreme Court's 1983 Term:

Individual Rights, Freedom and the Statute of Liberty," *Georgia Law Review* 19 (1984): 1.

2. This author has previously analyzed the pro-management jurisprudence of the Burger/Rehnquist Court and of the Reagan National Labor Relations Board. See generally, David Gregory, "Labor Contract Rejection in Bankruptcy: The Supreme Court's Attack on Labor in NLRB v. Bildisco," *B.C. Law Review* 25 (1984): 539; David Gregory and Raymond Mak, "Significant Decisions on the National Labor Relations Board, 1984: The Reagan Board 'Celebrates' the Fiftieth Anniversary of the National Labor Relations Act," *Connecticut Law Review* 18 (1985): 7.

3. *Trans World Airlines, Inc. v. Hardison*, 432 U.S. 63 (1977).

4. "Congress shall make no law respecting an establishment of religion, or prohibiting the free exercise thereof . . ." U.S. Constitution, Amendment 1.

5. "It shall be an unlawful employment practice for an employer to fail or refuse to hire or to discharge any individual, or otherwise to discriminate against any individual with respect to his compensation, terms, conditions, or privileges of employment, because of such individual's race, color, religion, sex, or national origin." 42 U.S.C. 2000e-2 (§ 703 (a)(1)).

6. Although it is beyond the scope of this essay, an interesting line of cases has begun to consider whether religious owners and senior managers within a secular employer may impose their religious norms upon subordinate employees. Thus far, Title VII has protected the subordinate employees: *EEOC v. Townley Engineering and Manufacturing Co.*, 859 F.2d 610 (9th Cir. 1988), cert. denied, 489 U.S. 1077, 109 S. Ct. 1527 (1989). *State v. Sport & Health Club, Inc.*, 370 N.W.2d 844 (Minn. 1985), dismissed for lack of juris, 478 U.S. 1015 (1986); *Young v. Southwestern Savings & Loan Association*, 509 F.2d 140 (5th Cir. 1975). See generally, David Gregory, "The Role of Religion in the Secular Workplace," *Notre Dame Journal of Law, Ethics, and Public Policy* (1990): 749; Laura S. Underkuffler, "'Discrimination' on the Basis of Religion: An Examination of Attempted Value Neutrality in Employment," *William and Mary Law Review* 30 (1989): 581.

7. 42 U.S.C. 2000e et. seq.

8. *Employment Division Department of Human Resources v. Smith*, 494 U.S. 872 (1990).

9. *Trans World Airlines, Inc. v. Hardison*, 432 U.S. 63 (1977).

10. See *Webster's Ninth New Collegiate Dictionary*, (1983), s.v. "sabbatarian." The term "Sabbatarian" refers to those who observe their Sabbath on Saturday. Anyone who observes a Sabbath, regardless of the day of the week on which it is observed, is a Sabbatarian. There are well over one million non-Sunday Sabbatarians in the United States, including Jews, Muslims, Seventh-Day Adventists, and members of the World Wide Church of God. James A. Kushner, "Toward the Central Meaning of Religious Liberty: Non-Sunday Sabbatarians and the Sunday Closing Cases Revisited," *Southwestern Law Journal* 35 (1981): 557.

11. "The term 'religion' includes all aspects of religious observance and practice, as well as belief, unless an employer demonstrates that he is unable to reasonably accommodate to an employee's or prospective employee's religious observance or practice without undue hardship on the conduct of the employer's business." 42 U.S.C. 2000e-j. (§ 701j).

12.   *Ansonia Board of Education v. Philbrook,* 479 U.S. 60 (1986).
13.   Ibid. at 68–69. Case law continues to follow these precedents. See, for example, *Ryan v. United States Department of Justice,* 950 F.2d 458, 57 FEP 854 (7th Cir. 1991) (FBI agent discharged for not investigating acts of civil disobedience against government policies).
14.   *Employment Division, Department of Human Resources of Oregon v. Smith,* 494 U.S. 872, 110 S.Ct. 1595 (1990). The decision immediately engendered a firestorm of very critical commentary. See Milner Ball, "The Unfree Exercise of Religion," *Capitol University Law Review* 20 (1991): 39; James D. Gordon, "Free Exercise on the Mountaintop," *California Law Review* 79 (1991):91; David Gregory and Charles Russo, "Let Us Pray ('But Not Them'!): The Troubled Jurisprudence of Religious Liberty," *St. John's Law Review* 65 (1991): 273; Michael McConnell, "A Response of Professor Marshall," *Chicago Law Review* (1991): 329; Michael McConnell, "Free Exercise Revisionism and the Smith Decision," *Chicago Law Review* 57 (1990): 1109; James E. Wood, Jr., "Abridging the Free Exercise Clause," *Journal of Church and State* 32 (Autumn 1990): 741; Richard K. Sherwin, "Rhetorical Pluralism and the Discourse Ideal: Countering *Division of Employment v. Smith,* A Parable of Pagans, Politics, and Majoritarian Rule," *Northwestern University Law Review* 85 (1991):388; Stephen D. Smith, "The Rise and Fall of Religious Freedom in Constitutional Discourse," *University of Pennsylvania Law Review* 140 (1991): 149; David E. Steinberg, "Religious Exemptions as Affirmative Action," *Emory Law Journal* 40 (1991): 77; Kenneth Marin, "Employment Division v. Smith: The Supreme Court Alters the State of Free Exercise Doctrine," *American University Law Review* 40 (1991): 1431; Thomas C. Rawlings, "Employment Division, Department of Human Resources v. Smith: The Supreme Court Deserts the Free Exercise Clause," *Georgia Law Review* 25 (1991): 567; Karin M. Rebescher, "The Illusory Enforcement of First Amendment Freedom: Employment Division, Department of Human Resources v. Smith and the Abandonment of the Compelling Governmental Interest Test," *North Carolina Law Review* 69 (1991): 1332; Danielle A. Hess, "The Undoing of Mandatory Free Exercise Accommodation," *Washington Law Review* 66 (1991): 587; but see William P. Marshall, "In Defense of *Smith* and Free Exercise Revisionism," *Chicago Law Review* 58 (1991): 308; William P. Marshall, "The Case Against the Constitutionally Compelled Free Exercise Exemption," *Case Western Reserve Law Review* 40 (1990): 357.
15.   For the interesting concept of (un)free exercise of religion, this author is indebted to Professor Milner Ball. See Ball, "The Unfree Exercise of Religion."
16.   See *Frazee v. Department of Employment Security,* 489 U.S. 829 (1989) (Christian refusing job requiring Sunday work could not be denied unemployment benefits under Free Exercise Clause); *Hobbie v. Unemployment Appeals Commission,* 480 U.S. 136 (1987) (Seventh-Day Adventist discharged for refusing to work on Sabbath could not be denied unemployment compensation benefits under Free Exercise Clause); *Sherbert v. Verner,* 374 U.S. 398 (1963) (Seventh-Day Adventist need not agree to work on Sabbath to be eligible for unemployment compensation benefits); *Thomas v. Review Board,* 450 U.S. 707 (1981) (Jehovah's Witness

quitting employment because religious beliefs prevented him from producing weapons entitled to unemployment compensation benefits under the Free Exercise Clause); but see, *Thornton v. Caldor, Inc.*, 472 U.S. 703 (1985) (Connecticut statute, which granted religious employees absolute right not to work on their Sabbath, violated Establishment Clause).

17. *Employment Division, Department of Human Services of Oregon v. Smith*, 110 S. Ct. at 1600.
18. Ibid. at 1595, 1603.
19. For extensive compilations of references to separationist and accommodationist theoreticians of Establishment Clause jurisprudence, see David Gregory, "The First Amendment Religion Clauses and Labor and Employment Law in the Supreme Court 1984 Term," *New York Law School Law Review* 31 (1986): 1, 7-10, n. 14-15; Gregory and Russo, "Let Us Pray," at 290-91, n. 60-63.
20. The Title VII exemption reads: "Notwithstanding any other provision of this subchapter, (1)it shall not be an unlawful employment practice for an employer to hire and employ individuals, for an employment agency to classify, or refer for employment any individual, for a labor organization to classify its membership or to classify or refer for employment any individual, or for an employer, labor organization, or joint labor-management committee controlling apprenticeship or other training or retraining programs to admit or employ any individual in any such program, on the basis of his religion, sex, or national origin in those certain instances where religion, sex, or national origin is a bona fide occupational qualification reasonably necessary to the normal operation of that particular business or enterprise, and (2)it shall not be an unlawful employment practice for a school, college, university, or other educational institution or institution of learning to hire and employ employees of a particular religion if such school, college, university, or other educational institution or institution of learning to hire and employ employees of a particular religion if such school, college, university, or other educational institution or institution of learning is, in whole or in substantial part, owned, supported, controlled, or managed by a particular religion or by a particular religious corporation, association, or society, or if the curriculum of such school, college, university, or other educational institution or institution of learning is directed toward the propagation of a particular religion." 42 U.S.C. 2000e-2(e)(1) (§ 702(e).)
21. 8 U.S.Code § 1324(a) (1988).
22. 29 U.S.Code § 201-219 (1982).
23. *National Labor Relations Board v. Catholic Bishop of Chicago*, 440 U.S. 490 (1979). For critical commentary upon the decision, see David Gregory, "Catholic Labor Theory and the Transformation of Work," *Washington and Lee Law Review* 45 (1988): 119; David Gregory and Charles Russo, "Overcoming *NLRB v. Yeshiva University* by the Implementation of Catholic Labor Theory," *Labor Law Journal* 41 (1990): 55; David Gregory, "The Right to Unionize as a Fundamental Human and Civil Right," *Mississippi College Law Review* 9 (1988): 138.
24. 29 U.S. Code § 151 et. seq.
25. *National Labor Relations Board v. Catholic Bishop of Chicago*, 440 U.S. at 507.

26. Ibid. at 505.
27. Ibid. at 503-504.
28. For an important limitation on the holding in *NLRB v. Catholic Bishop of Chicago*, see *NLRB v. Hannah Boy's Center*, 940 F.2d 1295 (9th Cir. 1991), where the court determined that the NLRB could assert jurisdiction over a church-operated school's employment practices when it involved action affecting only the school's secular, non-faculty employees. For other decisions recognizing the close relationship of the teaching function to the religion's mission, see *Dolter v. Walhert High School*, 483 F. Supp. 266 (N.D. Iowa, 1980) (Catholic school can discharge pregnant unmarried teacher for violation of church teachings); *Maguire v. Marquette University*, 627 F. Supp. 1499 (E.D. Wisc. 1986) (First Amendment precludes inquiry by court of whether plaintiff is qualified to teach in the theology department); *Pime v. Loyola University*, 803 F.2d 351 (7th Cir. 1986)(Jesuit Catholic University could reserve faculty tenure track opportunity for Jesuits, in order to preserve Jesuit Catholic character of institution); but see *Ohio Civil Rights Commission v. Dayton Christian Schools, Inc.*, 477 U.S. 619, 628 (1986) (pregnant teacher's contract not renewed, due to church's view that mothers should stay home with pre-school age children. Court found state civil rights agency had jurisdiction to investigate her complaint). *EEOC v. Mississippi College*, 626 F.2d 477 (5th Cir. 1980), cert. denied, 453 U.S. 912 (1981) (EEOC could investigate female professor's challenge under Title VII of college's practice of only male faculty teaching Bible courses). On 15 August 1990, Pope John Paul II promulgated an apostolic constitution on Catholic universities, entitled *Ex Corde Ecclesiae* (From the Heart of the Church). It requires the majority of faculty to be practicing Catholics, and requires all other faculty to be respectful of Catholic doctrine. See Charles H. Wilson, "Ex Corde Ecclesiae: The New Apostolic Constitution for Catholic Universities," *Catholic Lawyer* 34 (1991): 17.
    For articles examining the intersection of Title VII and the employment status of clergy, see Danielle Abuhoff, "Title VII and the Appointment of Women Clergy: A Statutory and Constitutional Quagmire," *Columbia Journal of Law and Social Problems* 13 (1977): 256; Bruce N. Bagni, "Discrimination in the Name of the Lord: A Critical Evaluation of Discrimination by Religious Organizations," *Columbia Law Review* 79 (1979): 1514. In 1991, the Executive Committee of the Association of American Law Schools adopted amendments to its Regulation 6.17, and now prohibits member law schools from discriminating in employment on the basis of sexual orientation. It remains to be seen whether any law schools with religious affiliations which continue to discriminate will be removed from AALS membership. Discussion Forum on Issues Involving the Amendment of Executive Committee Regulation 6.17 Law Schools·with a Religious Affiliation or Purpose, Association of American Law Schools Annual Meeting Proceedings, 5 January 1992.
29. *Corporation of the Presiding Bishop of the Church of Jesus Christ of Latter-day Saints v. Amos*, 483 U.S. 327 (1987). For commentary on the decision, see Frederick Mark Gedicks, "Toward a Constitutional Jurisprudence of Religious Group Rights," *Wisconsin Law Review* (1989): 99; Scott D. McClure, "Religious Preferences on Employment Decisions: How Far May Religious Organizations

Go?," *Duke Law Journal* (1990): 587; "*Corporation of Presiding Bishop v. Amos*: The Supreme Court and Religious Discrimination by Religious Educational Institutions," *Notre Dame Journal of Law, Ethics, and Public Policy* 3 (1988): 629; Scott Klundt, "Permitting Religious Employers to Discriminate on the Basis of Religion: Application to For-Profit Activities," *Brigham Young University Law Review* (1988): 221; Karen M. Crupi, "The Relationship Between Title VII and the First Amendment Religion Clauses: The Unconstitutional Schism of *Corporation of the Presiding Bishop v. Amos,*" *Albany Law Review* 53 (1989): 421.

30. See n. 20.
31. *Lemon v. Kurtzman*, 483 U.S. at 336.
32. See *Sharon v. St. Luke's Presbyterian Hospital*, 929 F.2d 360 (8th Cir. 1991) (chaplain's age and sex discrimination claims against hospitals could not be adjudicated without violating the First Amendment); and *Little v. Wuerl, Bishop of Pittsburgh*, 929 F.2d 944 (3rd Cir. 1991)(review of Catholic school's decision not to renew contract of non-Catholic lay teacher because her divorce and remarriage did not conform to Catholic mores not permitted because it would violate the school's free exercise rights. For earlier cases unwilling to examine the institutional religious employer's treatment of clergy as ecclesiastical matters, see *EEOC v. Southwestern Baptist Theological Seminary*, 651 F.2d 277 (5th Cir. 1981); *McClure v. Salvation Army*, 460 F.2d 553 (5th Cir.), cert. denied, 409 U.S. 896 (1972) (Court upheld dismissal of claim of sex discrimination brought by Salvation Army minister); *Rayburn v. General Conference of Seventh-day Adventists*, 772 F.2d 1164 (4th Cir. 1985), cert. denied, 478 U.S. 1020 (1986); Also, *Serbian E. Orthodox Diocese for the United States v. Milivoyevich*, 426 U.S. 696 (1976). See David A. Fielder, "Serving God or Caesar: Constitutional Limits on the Regulation of Religious Employers," *Missouri Law Review* 51 (1986): 779. Of course, it remains to be seen whether the courts will manifest the same degree of reluctance to examine whether the religious employer has reasonably accommodated disabled clergy within the meaning of the Americans with Disabilities Act of 1990. The accommodations required of employers by the ADA appear, at least in the statutory black letter, much more substantive that the de minimis standard of Title VII. Stephen A. Holmes, "When the Disabled Face Rejection from Churches that Nurture Them," *New York Times*, 30 September 1991, A10 (Presbyterian associate minister with multiple sclerosis quit her position, after church refused to redesign church sanctuary to accommodate her wheelchair; she felt humiliated at having to be carried to the pulpit.)
33. *Tony & Susan Alamo Foundation v. Secretary of Labor*, 471 U.S. 290 (1985).
34. Ibid. at 298.
35. Ibid. at 299.
36. See Gregory, "The First Amendment Religion Clauses and Labor and Employment Law in the Supreme Court 1984 Term," at 24.
37. *Brock v. Wendell's Woodworks, Inc.*, 867 F.2d 196 (4th Cir. 1989).
38. Ibid. at 197.
39. Ibid.
40. Ibid. at 199.
41. Ibid. at 198-99.

42. *Dole v. Shenandoah Baptist Church*, 899 F.2d 1389 (4th Cir.) cert. denied, 111 S. Ct. 131 (1990).
43. Ibid. at 1392.
44. *Rayburn v. General Conference of Seventh-day Adventists*, 772 F.2d 1164 (4th Cir. 1985), cert. denied, 478 U.S. 1020 (1986).
45. *Dole v. Shenandoah Baptist Church*, 899 F.2d at 1395.
46. Ibid. at 1396.
47. Ibid. at 1397.
48. Ibid. at 1397.
49. Ibid.
50. Ibid.
51. Ibid. at 1398.
52. Ibid.
53. Ibid.
54. Ibid. at 1399.
55. Ibid.
56. Ibid.
57. Ibid. at 1400.
58. Ibid.
59. *DeArment v. Harvey*, 932 F.2d 721 (8th Cir. 1991).
60. Ibid.
61. Ibid.
62. *South Ridge Baptist Church v. Industrial Commission of Ohio*, 911 F.2d 1203 (6th Cir. 1990), cert. denied, 111 S. Ct. 754 (1991).
63. Ibid. at 1204.
64. Ibid.
65. Ibid.
66. *United States v. Lee*, 455 U.S. 252 (1982). The Court held that the imposition of social security taxes on an Amish employer, who objected to the tax on free exercise grounds, was not unconstitutional.
67. *South Ridge Baptist Church v. Industrial Commission of Ohio*, 911 F.2d at 1208.
68. Ibid. at 1207.
69. Ibid. at 1208.
70. Ibid. at 1207.
71. Ibid.
72. Ibid.
73. Ibid. at 1209.
74. Ibid.
75. *Presiding Bishop v. Amos*, 483 U.S. 327 (1987).
76. *Dole v. Shenandoah Baptist Church*, 899 F.2d 1389 (4th Cir.), cert. denied, 111 S. Ct. 131 (1990).
77. *South Ridge Baptist Church v. Industrial Commission of Ohio*, 911 F.2d at 1210.
78. *Intercommunity Center for Justice and Peace v. Immigration and Naturalization Service*, 910 F.2d 42 (2d Cir. 1990).
79. Ibid. at 43.
80. Ibid. at 44.
81. Ibid.
82. Ibid. at 46.
83. Ibid. at 44.
84. Ibid. at 45.
85. Ibid.
86. Ibid.
87. *American Friends Service Comm. Corp. v. Thornburgh*, 941 F.2d 808 (9th Cir. 1991).

88. Ibid. at 810.
89. Ibid.
90. Ibid.
91. Ibid.
92. *Fedlstrin v. Christian Science Monitor*, 555 F. Supp. 974, 975-76 (D. Mass. 1983) (reporter not hired for paper because he was not a Christian Scientist); *King's Garden, Inc. v. FCC*, 498 F.2d 51, 55 (D.C. Cir.), cert. denied, 419 U.S. 996 (1974) (in strong dictum, the court suggested the Title VII Section 702 exemption unconstitutionally advanced and established religion, because the exemption "invites religious groups and them alone, to impress a test of faith on job categories, and indeed whole enterprises, having nothing to do with the exercise of religion."); but see, *Larsen v. Kirkham*, 499 F. Supp. 960 (D. Utah 1980), aff'd. without opinion (10th Cir. 1982), cert. denied, 464 U.S. 849 (1983).
93. To sample a variety of proposals purporting to resolve Title VII matters while avoiding constitutional problems, see, for example, Carl J. Esbeck, "Establishment Clause Limits on Governmental Interference with Religious Organizations," *Washington and Lee Law Review* 41 (1984): 347, 409, 420 ("pervasively religious" organizations "should be entirely exempt from equal employment legislation. . . . Governmental involvement should be prohibited when there is a measurable risk that worship, the religious teaching and propagation of the beliefs of the religious association, or the moral discipline of its members would be inhibited."); Gedicks, "Toward a Constitutional Jurisprudence of Religious Group Rights," (proposes absolute autonomy of religious groups in setting membership terms); Douglas Laycock, "Towards a General Theory of the Religion Clauses: The Case of Church Labor Relations and the Right to Church Autonomy," *Columbia Law Review* 81 (1981): 1373 (unless government can assert compelling interest, "churches have a constitutionally protected interest in managing their own institutions free of government interference"); Ira C. Lupu, "Free Exercise Exemption and Religious Institutions: The Case of Employment Discrimination," *Baylor Law Review* 67 (1987): 391, 395, 439 ("the right of a religious institution to discriminate in what would otherwise be unlawful ways should be viewed as driven by and coterminous with the associational rights of its members? that is, it can utilize its membership criteria as employment criteria. . . . Such associations may exclude from employment opportunities members of groups marked for protection by civil rights laws *if and only if members of those groups are also barred from membership in the church.* (emphasis in original.); Shelley K. Wessels, "The Collision of Religious Exercise and Governmental Nondiscrimination Policies," *Stanford Law Review* 41 (1989): 1201, 1204 ("I conclude that a religious interest should be absolutely protected against discrimination claims when the religious group advocates the religious interest in the context of its activity as a religious community 'turned inward,' a religious group should be required to adhere to antidiscrimination provisions, however, when it functions as community 'turned outward,' toward the world).
94. Gregory, "The Role of Religion in the Secular Workplace," 763.
95. Elizabeth Bradley, "A New Approach to NLRB Jurisdiction over the Employment Practices of Religious Institutions," *Chicago Law Review* 54 (1987): 243.

96. Ibid. at 244.
97. David Gregory and Charles Russo, "Overcoming *NLRB v. Yeshiva University* by the Implementation of Catholic Labor Theory," *Labor Law Journal* 41 (1990): 55, 63. "Decisions such as *NLRB v. Catholic Bishop of Chicago* should likewise become quickly irrelevant in Catholic employment environments. In light of the Church's unequivocal and powerful labor theory, it is simply morally preposterous that any Catholic employer continue to raise First Amendment or constitutional preemption claims in order to avoid collective bargaining with its workers, if and when the majority of the workers wish to unionize."
98. See Gregory, "The Right to Unionize as a Fundamental Human and Civil Right," 157.

7

Government Response
to the Sanctuary Movement

ROBIN JOHANSEN and KATHLEEN PURCELL

The history of government regulation of the sanctuary
movement is a story of politics and personalities. It is a tale of
powerful faith and prosecutorial power, and it is a lesson in law
and ethics.

Like the underground railroad before it, the sanctuary
movement posed a difficult and delicate problem for the
government. In a rare show of defiance, middle-class
churchgoers publicly challenged government policy by
harboring and transporting refugees from the political violence
that ravaged Central America during the 1980s. The movement
arose in the same Protestant and Catholic churches that the
Republican administration had long viewed as its strongholds.
The issue for the government was whether to prosecute these
churchgoers and, if so, how. That the government chose to
prosecute and even to infiltrate the sanctuary churches was
probably due not so much to the success of the movement in
smuggling refugees as it was to the fact that the movement had
embarrassed the government publicly by capturing the high
moral ground in an increasingly acrimonious public debate.

In the end, the government acted predictably, singling out a
pair of churches and their sanctuary workers for infiltration and
prosecution in the hope that a test case would intimidate others
and settle the law. The strategy worked at least in part. For
now, the law is settled, although wrongly, in the view of these

authors. Many were intimidated, but the extent of the fear will never be known, because the root conditions that caused the flood of refugees in the first place have changed. An uneasy peace exists, at least for now, in El Salvador. As the result of a government agreement, negotiated after the sanctuary prosecutions, Salvadoran and Guatemalan refugees were granted protected status, no longer subject to deportation. Although horrendous human rights abuses in Haiti continue to produce refugees in the thousands, the same public and media concern has not been sustained. World attention has shifted to other parts of the world and other issues. Chastened by losses in court and the need to adapt to changing conditions, the sanctuary movement has either gone underground or shifted its emphasis to meet new needs in the best way it can. But the legacy of that era remains for the churches and their members, a sense that their relationship with their government will never be the same again and, for the government, what may turn out to be some very costly victories over crimes of conscience.

THE BACKGROUND OF THE SANCTUARY MOVEMENT

The sanctuary movement in the United States officially began in March 1982 with a press conference in Tucson, Arizona. The Southside Presbyterian Church of Tucson, led by Rev. John Fife, and joined by six churches from the San Francisco area, publicly announced its practice and intention to aid refugees fleeing violence and political repression in El Salvador and Guatemala.

This press conference was, however, in some respects merely the organized formal announcement of activity that had been occurring for some time. The trigger for that activity was the arrival in the United States of increasing numbers of Salvadorans and Guatemalans reporting tales of atrocities, tortures, disappearances, and government-sponsored murders.

Statistics from governmental and non-governmental sources quantified the terror. In a speech to the American Chamber of Commerce on 29 October 1982, Deane Hinton, then United States Ambassador to El Salvador, stated that since 1979, among a total Salvadoran population of only 4.8 million, "perhaps as many as 30,000 Salvadorans have been killed illegally, that is, not in battle."[1] Legal aid offices of the Roman Catholic Church in El Salvador estimated that in the six months between January and June 1983, more than eighteen hundred noncombatant civilians died or "disappeared."[2] In 1984, the Organization of American States put the total number of noncombatant deaths at fifty thousand.[3] By the early 1980s, political violence had replaced infectious disease as the leading cause of death in El Salvador.[4]

Professional persons such as lawyers, judges, and doctors were particularly at risk, perhaps because they were viewed as potential witnesses of atrocity or because they had skills that were seen as serving the opposition. The International League for Human Rights concluded after a 1983 visit that medical practitioners were subject to grave human rights abuses in El Salvador, including disappearances, tortures, and murders.[5] The judge responsible for investigating the assassination of Archbishop Oscar Romero fled El Salvador after several death threats and an unsuccessful attempt on his life inside his home.[6]

Religious workers were in even greater danger.[7] The assassination of Archbishop Romero and the rape and murder of four American religious women proved beyond any doubt that the conventional respect shown the clergy in time of war did not exist in El Salvador.

If anything, the human rights situation in Guatemala was even worse. Since the mid-1950s, the people of Guatemala, under a series of governments, have suffered an unrelenting campaign of terror. As one source described it: "Arbitrary arrest, torture, disappearance, and political killings were everyday realities, affecting thousands of Guatemala's seven-and-a-half million people. . . . Evidence that [the] "death squads" were government created and supported and drawn from the ranks of the army and the police force was disregarded."[8] Rural massacres, sometimes involving entire villages, characterized the government of General Efrain Rios Montt from 1982 to 1983.[9]

Again, religious and human rights workers tended to be particular targets.[10]

Confronted with these facts and with real people fleeing the terror, United States church leaders and their followers drew on religious doctrine and tradition to formulate a response. What ultimately became known as the "sanctuary movement" was grounded in and emanated from the Judeo-Christian mandate to care for the stranger. Perhaps the most famous exhortation to care for the stranger comes from the evangelist Matthew's story of the last judgment,[11] but both the Old and the New Testaments are rich in this theme, ranging from the Old Testament temple sanctuary and cities of refuge to the New Testament story of the Good Samaritan and the commandment to "love your neighbor as yourself."[12]

Following the biblical command, many church communities started by working within the government system to ease the plight of Salvadoran and Guatemalan refugees. In Arizona, for example, church legal advocacy projects recruited lawyers to represent refugees in political asylum cases. Through bail programs, church members mortgaged their homes and raised over $1 million in Tucson and Phoenix to obtain refugees' release from what amounted to desert concentration camps.

The results were disappointing. During 1981-1982, fifty-five hundred Salvadorans filed for political asylum. Only two were successful. Between 1982 and 1985, the Immigration and Naturalization Service (INS) acted on 18,796 asylum applications.[13] Only 498 were granted, a 2.6 percent approval rate. Of 862 Guatemalans who applied for political asylum, only four succeeded.[14] The problem was compounded by the fact that it was the policy of the INS and the United States State Department to notify the individual's country of origin that an application for political asylum had been filed, thus placing the individual at even greater risk.[15] Rev. Fife concluded: "After that much involvement [with the legal system] and with defense efforts, I realized they were neither effective nor moral. . . . You recognize very quickly that nobody is going to get asylum except a tiny minority."[16]

As refugees continued to flow into the United States and the immigration system continued to reject pleas for asylum, the sanctuary movement grew. By virtue of their role as "founders" of the movement and because Arizona remained a key entry point for many refugees, the churches in Arizona continued to play a leadership role. However, by 1987, the sanctuary movement had spread throughout the United States to 370 religious congregations with more than seventy thousand workers. There were nineteen sanctuary cities and twenty sanctuary universities. Affirmations for sanctuary had been issued by numerous national governing bodies of religious entities, including the American Baptist Churches, the American Lutheran Church, the Disciples of Christ, the Presbyterian Church (USA), the Rabbinical Assembly, the United Church of Christ, the United Methodist Church, and the American Friends Service Committee.[17]

THE GOVERNMENT RESPONSE

For many months, the government response to the sanctuary movement was to ignore it. In part, this may have been due to a government perception— in large part true— that the sanctuary movement was not transporting a significant number of refugees, particularly when compared with employment-motivated coyote smuggling operations.[18] In part, however, the government's inactivity was a conscious effort to avoid confrontation with the churches.[19]

After a 12 December 1982 "60 Minutes" story on Jim Corbett, one of the sanctuary leaders, and the plight of Central Americans, the government approach shifted. Immediately after the "60 Minutes" program, the Western Region office of the INS directed the district office in Phoenix to conduct an investigation into the activities of Jim Corbett. This investigation, known as "Operation Sojourner" eventually expanded to encompass all of the sanctuary movement in Arizona.

The first several prosecutions of sanctuary workers were not so much products of the government investigation as they were decisions to arrest and prosecute in situations that the government in the past had intentionally passed over.[20]   Thus on 17 March 1983, border patrol agents stopped and arrested Phil Conger and Kathy Flaherty of the Tucson Ecumenical Council's Task Force on Central America as they were driving four Salvadorans on Highway 82 outside Nogales, Arizona. The Salvadorans faced deportation proceedings. Flaherty was never charged. Charges against Conger were dismissed after a federal judge found that the border patrol lacked a reasonable suspicion to stop the car. However, documents regarding the national sanctuary movement seized during the arrest helped to fuel the continuing investigation.

Stacey Merkt, an English teacher at Casa Oscar Romero, a religious "safe house" for refugees in southern Texas, was similarly stopped and arrested on 17 February 1984, while driving refugees to San Antonio where their asylum applications might receive a more favorable reception. Merkt was convicted on three felony counts of unlawful transportation and sentenced to two years' probation and a ninety-day suspended sentence. The conviction was later overturned on the ground that the jury had not been properly instructed about the intent required to violate the statute.[21]   The Salvadorans faced deportation.

On 13 April 1984, Jack Elder, the director of Casa Romero was arrested for transporting three Salvadorans to a nearby bus station. After two hours of deliberation, a jury found Elder not guilty. Jurors later explained that in their view the short ride to the bus station did not constitute a violation of law.

In December 1984, while Elder was still awaiting trial on his first case and Merkt was on probation, they both were indicted by a federal grand jury, Merkt on charges of transporting and conspiracy and Elder on charges of transporting, smuggling of undocumented persons, and conspiracy. The jury found Merkt not guilty of unlawful transportation, but guilty on the conspiracy count. Elder was convicted on all six counts against him. The judge revoked Merkt's earlier probation and sentenced her to serve the earlier 90-day sentence concurrently with 179 days of an eighteen-month sentence for the conspiracy conviction. She was allowed to remain free pending appeals so long as she disassociated herself from Casa Romero and did not speak publicly about the sanctuary movement. Elder refused those same conditions for probation and was sentenced to one year in prison, later reduced to 150 days in a halfway house.

While these piecemeal prosecutions were moving forward, so was "Operation Sojourner." Authorized from Washington, but directed by INS agent Jim Rayburn and Assistant U.S. Attorney Don Reno in Phoenix, Operation Sojourner was an undercover operation with sanctuary churches and sanctuary workers as its targets. The government used two informants, one of whom was a convicted felon, to infiltrate the movement and the churches that sponsored it. Acting the role of devout Christians and adherents to the movement, yet wearing concealed tape recorders, the two attended Bible study sessions and worship services at Tucson churches. They took down license plates of cars in the church parking lot. They taped prayers and sermons. When later questioned on this conduct, they insisted that what they infiltrated were political, not religious, meetings.

On the morning of 14 January 1985, the government struck. It issued and served a lengthy indictment, naming sixteen individuals and charging them with multiple felonies of smuggling, transporting, and harboring undocumented refugees. Those indicted included a Protestant minister, John Fife, two Roman Catholic priests, Father Ramon Quinones and Father Anthony Clark, and three nuns, Sisters Darlene Nicgorski, Ana Priester, and Mary Waddell. Others indicted included movement leaders Jim Corbett, Kathy Flaherty, Phil Conger, and people who had long been involved in offering sanctuary such as Mary Espinosa and Maria Socorro Aguilar — as well as a number of individuals who had only been briefly or marginally involved— Wendy LeWin, Ana Priester, Mary Waddell, and Nena MacDonald.[22] Prosecutor Don Reno explained the inclusion of these women as a signal to the religious community: "A conspiracy doesn't function without the gofers. . . . This prosecution was really for deterrence; it was not for punishment."[23]

While indictments against sanctuary workers were limited to Arizona, dozens of Central American refugees were arrested

around the country in the days that followed as a result of the
federal investigation. In Arizona, the INS had compiled
addresses of refugees from reports of government informants
who had driven them home from church.

THE JUDICIARY'S RESPONSE

As a team of attorneys worked to plan a defense strategy,
they also looked to whether the nature of the investigation and
its assault on church autonomy provided grounds to dismiss the
indictment. A motion to dismiss was rejected out of hand by
Federal district Judge Earl Carroll and his order was affirmed on
appeal.[24]

Other evidentiary rulings made in the criminal trial were
even more discouraging. Judge Carroll barred all testimony
regarding the religious motivation behind the defendants' acts.
He also barred all testimony about conditions in the countries
from which the refugees had fled and refused to permit the
refugees to tell their personal stories.[25]

Those rulings were upheld on appeal in a decision that also
rejected the defendants' claim that the religion clauses of the
First Amendment protected them from prosecution. In *United
States v. Aguilar*,[26] the Ninth Circuit Court of Appeals held that
the government's interest in controlling its borders outweighed
the religious interests of the defendants.

The court's approach to the First Amendment problem is a
classic demonstration of how the outcome of a constitutional
issue can be made to depend entirely upon how the question is
framed. It is predictable that when constitutional rights are
raised and government practice challenged, the government will
describe its "compelling state interest" in the broadest possible
terms and the challenger will do just the opposite. That is
precisely what happened with the sanctuary movement cases.
The government described its interest as that of controlling the
borders, a grandly stated interest that courts have frequently
recognized as compelling.

Aware of the problem, the sanctuary lawyers tried to focus the inquiry several levels lower in abstraction. The government does indeed have a *right* to control the borders, they argued, but its actions belie the importance of the right in this particular context. And indeed, the lawyers' argument was quite sound, given that there exists a glaring exception to the so-called compelling need to keep undocumented refugees from entering the country: the statute allowed employers to bring in undocumented workers at will.[27] It is difficult to understand how the government could argue that it had a compelling interest in excluding political refugees when it was willing to admit those who would pick strawberries for the minimum wage. It is equally difficult to understand how the government could argue that the sanctuary movement interfered with the state's interest in controlling the borders when a key government official had testified to the contrary.[28]

None of that mattered, the courts held. The government's right to control the borders is plenary; it cannot be diminished by the fact that Congress creates exemptions or the threat posed by criminal activity is small. The *Aguilar* court's opinion on the First Amendment issue ignores any dissonance between what the government says and what it does and refuses to question the "fit" between the government's asserted interest and the need to preclude the sanctuary movement's activity.[29] Demonstrating that courts, too, can use different levels of abstraction to set the terms of discourse, the *Aguilar* court rejected the suggestion that a limited exemption should be made for those whose religious convictions compel them to give sanctuary: "Courts cannot possibly grant an exemption to certain members of a [religious] group while denying it to others of that same group. The only basis for distinction would be the sincerity of the member's belief, a standard which is ill-suited for adjudication."[30]

The *Aguilar* court's statement ignores the many areas of the law in which motive and sincerity, not to mention intent, are routinely the dispositive issue in a case. The U.S. Supreme Court has held that the test for a religious exemption from the draft is whether the defendant acted on the basis of a belief system that "occupies a place in the life of its possessor parallel to that filled by the orthodox belief in God of one who clearly qualifies for the exemption."[31] Juries are frequently called upon to determine whether an employer harbored a discriminatory intent, whether a claim of self-defense was based on a reasonable and sincerely held belief of imminent harm, or whether the sale of a house with a leaky roof was an honest oversight or calculated fraud. Nevertheless, the *Aguilar* court found the problem a convenient excuse for avoiding more difficult constitutional questions.

Simultaneously with the criminal trial in *Aguilar*, the Presbyterian Church (U.S.A.), the American Lutheran Church, and their affected local churches in Arizona filed a civil suit challenging the government's surveillance and infiltration as violations of the churches' First and Fourth Amendment rights. The outcome was a mixed bag, to say the least. The Ninth Circuit rejected most of the churches' free exercise claims, finding a narrow right to sue for prospective injunctive relief against future government misconduct. Noting that the case would be moot if the government conduct were discontinued and there were no reasonable expectations that it would recur, the Ninth Circuit remanded to the district court to allow it to take more evidence on mootness and standing and then, if appropriate, to adjudicate the First Amendment claim.[32]

Ultimately, the district court held that the government demonstrated "a significant and intimate relationship between the conduct in which it engaged and the government interest sought to be achieved."[33] The court thus refused to condemn the government surveillance. Instead, it identified two narrow limitations on government investigations when groups are engaged in protected First Amendment activities: First, the investigation must be in "good faith; i.e., not for the purpose of abridging first amendment freedoms."[34] Second, undercover informers must "adhere scrupulously to the scope of the defendant's [church's] invitation to participation in the organization."[35]

In short, the government response to the sanctuary movement was an investigative and prosecutorial arm that saw no religious or moral dimensions[36] to the "crime" and a judiciary that refused to permit any evidence of such considerations. This approach accurately divined the direction in which the increasingly conservative Supreme Court was headed. Only a year after the Ninth Circuit decisions, the United States Supreme Court held that generally applicable, religion-neutral criminal laws that burden a particular religious practice need not even be justified by a compelling state interest.[37] The precise holding in *Employment Division v. Smith* was that the state may include religiously inspired use of peyote within the reach of the state's general criminal prohibition on the use of that drug, stating: "It may fairly be said that leaving accommodation to the political process will place at a relative disadvantage those religious practices that are not widely engaged in; but that unavoidable consequence of democratic government must be preferred to a system in which each conscience is a law unto itself or in which judges weigh the social importance of all laws against the centrality of all religious beliefs."[38]

Thus, for now at least, a claim of individual conscience will rarely weigh heavy enough to overcome a "legitimate state interest," and those who dare to act upon their conscience must expect to pay the price.

LAW, ETHICS, AND MORALITY

From a legal point of view, it is hard to deny that the sanctuary movement lost far more battles than it won. Unlike the underground railroad, which resulted in few criminal trial and even fewer convictions, the sanctuary movement suffered losses in both the civil and criminal courts. Even in the face of testimony from the INS regional director that the sanctuary movement did not pose any serious threat to the administration's efforts to control the borders, the Ninth Circuit held the prosecutions to be justified by the government's "compelling" interest in policing the borders;[39] the court found that this proposition "hardly needs testimonial documentation."[40] In light of this conclusion, the sincerity of the sanctuary defendants' religious beliefs and the doctrinal basis for their actions became factually, if not legally, irrelevant.[41]

Would the sanctuary movement have been better off if it had followed the example of the underground railroad and avoided a direct challenge if it could? Legally, that may be the case. Certainly there are judicial opinions now on the books that were not there a decade ago and that definitively reject a First Amendment exemption for sanctuary activity. Nevertheless, the movement had a profoundly radicalizing effect on millions of Americans. Not since the 1960s have so many of this country's middle class overtly challenged the legitimacy of government policy on moral grounds. Not since the 1960s has the government squared off against the churches in such a public way. And we know of no time— in the 1960s or at any other time in the history of this country— in which the government boldly infiltrated the religious community and spied on its followers.

That the government went to such lengths to stop the movement is testament to the movement's success in dramatizing the refugees' plight to the rest of the country. The legal outcome aside, the sanctuary movement adds to a vibrant tradition that has been pivotal in the development of American law and democracy— the tradition of civil disobedience.

Not everyone in the movement is pleased with the comparison. The sanctuary movement long harbored an internal debate over whether to characterize sanctuary activity as protected by the First Amendment and international law and hence as the best expression of the legal order (i.e. legal activity) or as conscious lawbreaking designed to challenge and change law and policy (i.e. civil disobedience). The characterization as legal activity was, of course, encouraged as lawyers developed defenses against criminal prosecution on First Amendment and international law grounds. That self-identification was also grounded in the process of religious discernment whereby, as Jim Corbett put it, "Churches and synagogues must decide whether they will adhere to the prophetic faith they proclaim."[42] There were certainly private sanctuary givers, persons who without any public or political statement offered safe haven for refugees.[43] Additionally, some may have been concerned that material aid for the movement, money, food, clothing, would be less available if its adherents described themselves as lawbreakers.

On the other hand, there is no question that sanctuary workers from both schools of thought selflessly exposed themselves to the possibility of criminal prosecution and prison. That some saw their activity as intrinsically legal while others saw it as not, made little difference in the face of a government response that treated all as felons.

Moreover, while the disagreement within the movement was real, the difference in articulation and specificity of purpose should not disguise its shared goal— to change how the United States government and the people of the United States dealt with Salvadoran and Guatemalan refugees. All of the participants in public sanctuary were committed to seeing the story of Central American refugees told. The refugees themselves sought opportunities to speak out at grave personal risk. This shared vision served to harmonize and bind diverse schools of thought. As the *National Catholic Reporter* put it: "For most of the people involved [in the sanctuary movement], there is no overriding political ideology, but there may well be an underlying dynamic of faith. At bottom, it is not so much a political confrontation between church and state as it is a religious challenge to what has become the American Way."[44]

For now, the judicial decisions denying any religious exemption to sanctuary workers have effectively mooted the debate over whether the sanctuary movement is legal or in violation of law. But like the underground railroad before it, the true impact of the sanctuary movement will not be felt so much in American jurisprudence as in American collective history. Its importance lies in the example it provides of otherwise law-abiding citizens compelled by conscience to break a law that they felt was both morally and legally wrong. As with other major protests in our nation's history— from abolition to the civil rights movement— many churches were at the center of the controversy, adding both numbers and moral authority to the cause.

The ultimate outcome of all this is not easy to assess. There can be no doubt that government infiltration had a profoundly chilling effect on the ministry of the targeted churches.[45] Members were lost, distrust was sown, and fear replaced the comfort that many had previously found there. But the churches survived, and those who remained were strengthened by the experience.

At the national level, too, the experience seems to have stiffened the denominational resolve. The Presbyterian Church (U.S.A.) and the American Lutheran Church joined the targeted churches in suing the government and offered them steady support. And Rev. John Fife, one of those convicted in the *Aguilar* case, now heads the Presbyterian Church (U.S.A.) as its moderator.[46]

Thus, although the government prevailed in the courts, it has by no means won the war. There remains in this country a strong tradition of conscientious objection to government policies that conflict with deeply held religious convictions. Because it is selfless and often grounded in the "mainline" churches, that strain of stubborn resistance can often be deeply embarrassing to an administration that seeks to repress it. Thus, from the government's point of view, the less said about government infiltration and conspiracy convictions for ministers and nuns, the better.

For the churches and the individuals who worked (and still work) in the sanctuary movement, an important point has been made and some important lessons learned. There will always be a tension in any such movement between the need to publicize in order to gain popular support and the need to remain underground so as not to sacrifice effectiveness. Like the Civil Rights Movement, the sanctuary movement ultimately became a very public one, challenging the government at every turn and almost daring it to prosecute. That the government did prosecute was expected; that it used trickery and lies to do so caught nearly everyone by surprise. For many members of the religious community, the experience extinguished their sense of trust in their government, their belief that "it couldn't happen here." However much they disagreed with the government, many people felt that it would play fair and that it would honor the sanctity and integrity of their churches. That it did not, that instead it treated the churches as any other gang of criminal conspirators, may ultimately be the most indelible lesson learned from the sanctuary movement and not one that those involved will soon forget. It is a lesson that will shape the government's relations with the religious community for many years to come.

NOTES

1. Amnesty International, *Extrajudicial Executions in El Salvador* (1983), 6.
2. Ibid. For a review of the continuing human rights abuses, see Americans Watch, *Report on Human Rights in El Salvador* (New York: Random House, 1982) and the annual Supplements thereto.
3. Douglas F. Colbert, "The Motion in Limine: Trial Without Jury," *Hofstra Law Review* 15 (1986): 5, 29, n.125.
4. The Committee for Health Rights in El Salvador, "Health Care Under Siege: El Salvador," *Science for the People* (May/June 1982); *El Salvador: War and Health*, COPROSAL (Committee for Professional Health Workers), 1981.
5. Ibid., 17.
6. Americas Watch, *Report on Human Rights in El Salvador*, 55.
7. Ann Crittenden, *Sanctuary: A Story of American Conscience and Law in Collision* (New York: Weidenfeld and Nicholson, 1988), 16-17.
8. Amnesty International, *Guatemala: The Human Rights Record*, (London: Amnesty International Publications, 1987), 5.
9. Ibid., 3-4; Americas Watch and British Parliamentary Human Rights Group, *Human Rights in Guatemala*, (The Americas Watch Committee USA, 1987), 1.
10. *Guatemala: The Human Rights Record*, 18, 23-33.
11. "When the Son of Man comes in his glory, escorted by all the angels of heaven, he will sit upon his royal throne, and all the nations will be assembled before him. Then he will separate them into two groups, as a shepherd separates sheep from goats. The sheep he will place on his right hand, the goats on his left. The king will say to those on his right: 'Come. You have my Father's blessing! Inherit the kingdom prepared for you from the creation of the world. For I was hungry and you gave me food, I was thirsty and you gave me drink. I was a stranger and you welcomed me, naked and you clothed me. I was ill and you comforted me, in prison and you came to visit me.' Then the just will ask him: 'Lord, when did we see you hungry and feed you or see you thirsty and give you drink? When did we welcome you away from home or clothe you in your nakedness? When did we visit you when you were ill or in prison?' The king will answer them: 'I assure you, as often as you did it for one of my least brothers, you did it for me.'" Matthew 25:31-40, Standard Version
12. See, for example, 1 Kings 1:50-53 and 2:28-29, 1 Maccabees 10:43-44, Numbers 35:9-15, Deuteronomy 19:10, Exodus 21:12-14, Joshua

20:1-9, Exodus 22:21 and 23:9, Isaiah 16:3-4, Luke 10:25-37, Matthew 22:34-40, Hebrews 13:2. The image of Jesus as the stranger to be welcomed and cared for is apparent throughout the Christian tradition. At Jesus' birth, the place of refuge was a stable offered by a considerate innkeeper. Later, the Holy Family, fleeing persecution in Judah, sought refuge in Egypt. After Jesus' death, the two apostles who extended their hospitality to a wandering stranger on the road to Emmaus recognized him as Jesus only *after* they invited him to supper.

13. Colbert, "The Motion in Limine," 34.

14. By comparison, during 1983, 72 percent of the Iranians who applied for political asylum were accepted, 62 percent of the Afghanis, and over 30 percent of the Poles. Colbert, "The Motion in Limine," 35. Ninety percent of the refugees admitted to the United States after World War II under political asylum laws were from Communist countries; see Crittenden, *Sanctuary*, 18.

15. "A Symposium on the Sanctuary Movement," *Hofstra Law Review* 15 (Fall 1986) : 37.

16. Ibid., 38.

17. As the movement grew, so did tensions within it. One of the key debates revolved around the question of whether this was primarily a political or religious movement, or whether the two elements were inseparable. Thus in 1985, the Chicago Religious Task Force wrote: "For us, to love is to create a movement capable of stopping U.S. intervention in Central America, a movement not simply of protest or witness but of resistance. This effort is profoundly religious and inevitably political." Quoted in Ignatius Bau, *This Ground is Holy* (Mahwah, N.J.: Paulist Press, (1985), 31. Sanctuary leaders in Arizona, on the other hand, often viewed the movement as a religious response to the immediate needs of the refugees, without any particular political or foreign policy objectives. Ibid. Significantly, both of these perspectives can and did spring from religious faith.

18. See Bau, *This Ground is Holy*, 87-88; Crittenden, *Sanctuary*, 104, 140.

19. See Bau, *This Ground in Holy*, 88-89; Crittenden, *Sanctuary*, 101.

20. The summaries of these cases set forth below are based upon the information collected in Bau, *This Ground is Holy*, 76-83.

21. *United States v. Merkt*, 764 F.2d 266 (5th Cir. 1985).

22. For good measure, the government also indicted two women from Phoenix, Bertha Martel-Benavidez and Cecilia Del Carmen Juarez de Emery, who were not part of the movement but had unwittingly used government agents to help bring family members into the United States.

23. Quoted in Crittenden, *Sanctuary*, 193.

24. *United States v. Aguilar*, 883 F.2d 662 (9th Cir. 1989) at 696-705.

25. The defense argued that this evidence went to the defense of necessity which requires a criminal defendant to demonstrate four elements: (1) that he was faced with a choice of evils and chose the lesser evil; (2) that he acted to prevent imminent harm; (3) that he reasonably anticipated a causal relation between his conduct and the harm to be avoided; and (4) that there were no other legal alternatives to violating the law. The Ninth Circuit relied on the fourth element to affirm the exclusion of evidence, stating that the defendants "failed to appeal to the judiciary to correct any alleged

improprieties by the INS and the immigration courts." In earlier prosecutions, specifically the first prosecution of Stacey Merkt, much more evidentiary latitude was permitted. In Merkt's prosecution, for example, the individual refugees' stories were told in detail, evidence regarding conditions in El Salvador as well as the INS record on Salvadoran refugees in the area was admitted, and extensive testimony on the religious basis for sanctuary, including testimony from the local Roman Catholic bishop, was presented; Bau, *This Ground is Holy*, 78-79. The judiciary's increasing unwillingness to have the justifications for sanctuary presented became apparent not only in the *Aguilar* case but also in the conditions for release pending appeal imposed on Stacey Merkt after her second conviction; namely, that she not speak publicly regarding the sanctuary movement. Ibid. at 83.

26. *United States v. Aguilar*, 883 F.2d 662 (9th Cir. 1989).
27. Ibid., 883 F.2d at 696, n.34.
28. *United States v. Aguilar*, U.S.D.C. Nos. 86-1208 to 86-1215, Pretrial Transcript at 347 (testimony of Ruth Ann Myers, INS District Div. for Phoenix District).
29. *Aguilar*, 883 F.2d at 695-97.
30. Ibid. at 696.
31. *United States v. Seeger*, 380 U.S. 163 (1965) at 166.
32. *The Presbyterian Church (U.S.A.) v. U.S.*, 870 F.2d 518 (9th Cir. 1989) at 528-29.
33. *The Presbyterian Church (U.S.A.) v. U.S.*, 752 F.Supp. 1505 (D. Ariz. 1990) at 1515. The court reached the First Amendment issues rather than finding the case moot "[b]ecause the government has taken a position that it can continue to pursue criminal investigations in this manner. . . ." Ibid. at 1510.
34. Ibid. at 1515, quoting *Aguilar*, the criminal case against the individual sanctuary workers.
35. Ibid.
36. Indeed, it may be that the investigation and indictments would never have proceeded were it not that Jim Rayburn was convinced that the sanctuary movement was some sort of communist plot. See Crittenden, *Sanctuary*, 140-41.
37. The case, *Employment Division v. Smith* 108 L.Ed.2d 876 (1990) at 884-89, represented a radical departure from existing precedent that had allowed religious exemptions to a variety of otherwise neutral laws. To avoid overruling these exemptions, the court simply grandfathered them in. Thus, post-*Smith*, a free exercise claim of exemption to a facially neutral law can prevail, it at all, only if it falls into one of the exceptions used by the Court to distinguish prior precedent: (1) if the law somehow violates the right to religious belief and profession as opposed to the right to perform or commit a physical act (see *United States v. Ballard*, 322 U.S. 78 [1944] at 86-88, in which the government prosecuted for mail fraud an evangelist who promised divine intervention to his contributors); (2) if the law violates the right to religious speech, presumably not because it is religious but because it is speech; see *Cantwell v. Connecticut*, 310 U.S. 296, 303, 84 L.Ed. 1213, 60 S.Ct. 900 [1940]; *Murdock v. Pennsylvania*, 319 U.S. 105, 87 L.Ed. 1292, 63 S.Ct. 870 [1943], which invalidated a licensing system and a flat tax, respectively, on religious solicitation; (3) if the law interferes with parental control of education for their children; see *Wisconsin v.*

Yoder, 406 U.S. 205, 32 L.Ed.2d 15, 92 S.Ct. 1526 [1972]; (4) if the law calls for "individualized governmental assessment of the reasons for the relevant conduct," such as in *Sherbert v. Verner*, 374 U.S. 398, 10 L.Ed.2d 965, 83 S.Ct. 1790 [1963], an unemployment compensation case holding that the government cannot deny benefits to individuals whose religious beliefs prohibit them from working on Saturday; and (5) if the law is not truly neutral. The Court never defines neutrality, but leaves open the possibility that motivation to harm religion renders a law suspect though harmful impact does not. The motivation concept is a familiar one in the establishment context. See *Wallace v. Jaffree*, 472 U.S. 38 (1985), a moment-of-silence case in which the legislative history of the Alabama law left no doubt that the purpose was religious. If this is the standard for religious motivation, then the exception will not amount to much.

38.   *Smith*, 108 L.Ed.2d at 893.

39.   *United States v. Aguilar*, 883 F.2d at 694-96.

40.   Ibid. at 695.

41.   Before the recent Supreme Court decision in *Employment Division v. Smith*, a showing that government action interferes with the religiously based activity shifted the burden to the government to show that the limitation on religious liberty is "essential to accomplish an overriding governmental interest." *United States v. Lee*, 455 U.S. 252 (1982) at 257-58. Although this test sounds extremely deferential to religious liberty, in practice the government regulation often prevailed. As noted above, the *Smith* decision has changed the test and eliminated even the formal requirement for a showing of governmental interest so long as regulation infringing religious liberty is not targeted at churches or religious activities.

42.   Jim Corbett, "A View from the Border," (unpublished manuscript), 8 September 1984, p. 1; and TEC Task Force Letter, "Basta!", Tucson edition, January 1985, p. 20, quoted in Bau, *This Ground is Holy*, 34.

43.   For whatever reason, these individuals sought to fulfill the mandate of conscience without confronting the government. Their analogue is, of course, the secret sanctuary that some European individuals and communities offered to Jews during the Holocaust.

44.   Editorial, "Sanctuary: Rooted in Values that Confront the American Way," *National Catholic Reporter* 21 (22 February 1985), 12; quoted in Bau, *This Ground is Holy*, 194, n.51. One need only change "religious challenge" to "values challenge" and all viewpoints are represented.

45.   The impact of the infiltration is described in *The Presbyterian Church (U.S.A.) v. United States*, 870 F.2d at 521-23 and *Presbyterian Church (U.S.A.) v. United States*, 752 F.Supp. at 1510.

46.   *Los Angeles Times*, "Presbyterians Elect Activist Pastor as National Leader," 6 June 1992, Part B, p.5, col.5.

8

Regulating Religious Broadcasting: Some Old Patterns and New Trends

JEFFREY K. HADDEN

The movement of a few television preachers into politics during the early 1980s led to the widely held perception that the televangelists have trespassed the serpentine wall that has traditionally separated religion and politics.[1] If Jerry Falwell's creation of the Moral Majority at the beginning of the decade evoked memories of Father Charles E. Coughlin, it was the financial scams and sex scandals of Jim Bakker and Jimmy Swaggart near the end of the decade that served to recall *Elmer Gantry*, the slick-talking, hypocritical, barn-storming tent preacher of Sinclair Lewis's 1927 novel of the same name. As the tormented details of money and sex unfolded— not in the supermarket tabloids but on the evening television news and ABCs *Nightline*— millions of Americans concluded that the televangelists were living beyond the edge of accountability.

This essay pursues two broad objectives. The first is to examine the history of regulation of religious broadcasting from the very beginning of radio through the current crisis of confidence that has rocked the industry since 1987. The second objective is to assess the probable direction of regulation of religious broadcasting in light of (1) the scandals, (2) technological and economic developments that are impacting broadcasting, and (3) the structural and cultural trends that are likely to be manifest in an evolving legal interpretation of religious liberty.

A SOCIAL HISTORY OF RELIGIOUS BROADCASTING

Radio and television broadcasting in the United States has experienced three discrete stages of development. The televangelism scandals which commenced with the PTL sex and financial scandals in 1987 marks the beginning of a fourth stage. The defining features of this fourth stage are still emerging. Each stage corresponds roughly to the regulatory environment,[2] but the formal regulatory structures are themselves determined by technological and social organizational developments.

The emphasis and main conclusion of this inquiry into the history of religious broadcasting is that the social organization and informal structures of broadcasting have been more important than the role of government in regulating religious broadcasting.[3] While the regulatory, legislative, and judicial structures of government did not move precipitously to control religious broadcasting in the wake of the scandals, there is substantial evidence to suggest that greatly enhanced regulation is in the offing.

Phase One: Unregulated Broadcast Experimentation (1906-1927). Reginal Fessenden's offshore airwaves transmission on Christmas Eve of 1906 inaugurated broadcasting and the ensuing phase of experimentation. The technology was quickly grasped and widely explored around the globe. The first regularly scheduled radio broadcasting in the United States commenced in November 1920 in Pittsburgh. Owned by Westinghouse Electric, radio station KDKA was created to stimulate the sale of radios. Many others stations quickly commenced regular broadcasting. In less than two years there were 382 stations in operation, in just over four years there were over 600 stations on the air, and by 1927 the number had escalated to 732.[4] Religious organizations were into broadcasting from the beginning. Of the 600 stations identified by *Popular Radio* magazine in January

1925, sixty-three were owned by churches and parachurch organizations.[5]

The Radio Act of 1912, which actually preceded regular broadcasting, did not adequately anticipate the problems of this new communications medium. Indeed, these early days of broadcasting were characterized by few regulations. A talented engineer could build a station for a few hundred dollars, and anyone could obtain a license for the asking. These have been characterized as the "wild and wooly days of radio"[6] and a "frenzied frequency free-for-all. . . ."[7] Ben Armstrong, former executive director for the National Religious Broadcasters, described what happened: "Stations competed for the airwaves all across the frequency band, drowning one another in bedlam of squeaks, whistles, and disjointed words."[8]

One of the most celebrated renegades of this early era was Aimee Semple McPherson, an early superstar of radio evangelism. McPherson's shifting of power and frequency was sufficiently annoying that Secretary of Commerce Herbert Hoover ordered her station in Los Angeles closed. Enraged by this action, McPherson fired an angry telegram to Hoover which read: "Please order your minions of Satan to leave my station alone. You cannot expect the Almighty to abide by your wave length nonsense. When I offer my prayers to Him I must fit into his wave reception. Open this station at once."[9] In the end, Hoover did not have the authority to shut down McPherson's station. It took the Radio Act of 1927, which created a federal agency with the power to license and regulate, to bring radio broadcasting under some semblance of control.[10]

This episode is worth remembering because it serves as an exemplar of several important issues that remain with us today concerning the relationship between religious broadcasters and public policy.

First, from the very beginning of broadcasting there was little doubt but that regulation would be necessary. In addition to safeguarding stations from technical interference by other stations, other issues were early identified as providing cause for regulation. It was obvious, for example, that the spectrum for transmission of radio, and later television, signals was quite limited.

If anyone could rush in and, by fiat, stake a claim on a broadcast frequency, this scarce commodity would quickly be exhausted. Thus was recognized both the need to conserve a scarce resource and to assure that this scarce resource was utilized in a manner that could be judged to be in the public interest. Yet another reason for regulating the airwaves was to prevent misuse by those who might influence society in ways judged to be harmful.[11]   These factors in combination virtually assured from the early days of broadcasting that government would play a critical role in regulating radio and television broadcasting.[12]

If the Hoover-McPherson confrontation presaged the inevitability of government regulation of the airwaves, there is a second lesson that is too frequently overlooked— Aimee Semple McPherson was not the only broadcaster to violate what would seem to be norms of civility with respect to avoiding interference with other broadcasters. Clearly the government could not stand by while renegade broadcasters sent their signals in whatever direction caught their fancy, or owners of more high powered equipment drowned out lower powered stations. If the government had not stepped in to solve the problem, crime syndicates would likely have done so.

As to Aimee Semple McPherson's being singled out for punitive attention, the historical record as to whether her practice was more egregious than others is not clear. In all probability, it was not. It is likely that McPherson was singled out because of the content and style of her broadcasts. Whether or not these speculations are correct, one should examine the behavior of religious broadcasters in the light of broadcasting industry standards rather than from the perspective of externally imposed standards. To demand that regulatory agencies hold religious broadcasters to higher standards than other broadcasters is to introduce prejudice, which if acted upon would likely result in violation of the Free Exercise Clause of the First Amendment.

In recent years religious broadcasters have deservedly been the subject of intense public scrutiny. But fair minded assessment of their behavior will recognize that every misdeed of religious broadcasters can be matched by parallel misdeeds by secular broadcasters. Indeed, most of the abuse and questionable behavior on the airwaves is not committed by religious broadcasters.

A final important lesson that is highlighted by the confrontation between Hoover and McPherson is that many religious broadcasters do believe that they are entitled to special treatment that precludes regulatory interference. For many broadcasters, this view is grounded in the belief that the air waves are quite literally an instrument given by God to facilitate the mission of preaching the Gospel to all the nations. They take seriously Christ's commandment to go into all the world and preach the gospel to every creature (Mark 16:15). The ability to transmit the voice and the visual image of the preacher has, for the first time in history, made it possible to reach all humankind with the Gospel message.[13]

When this perspective is taken seriously, it is understandable why some evangelicals might view God's law and purpose as loftier than man-made laws. To understand the social history of broadcast regulation, it is also very important to note that this perspective focuses on the biblical commandment to preach the Gospel rather than the constitutional right to do so.

From the public's perspective, the real issue is not a lofty principle or higher law so much as an arrogance of power. This arrogance stems from the belief that religious broadcasters are accountable to the Almighty and, hence, any other accountability would be superfluous. At a press conference following Jerry Falwell's assuming leadership of PTL in April 1987, he confessed this to be the case— albeit in an underwhelming way: "We have had *a little sense* of arrogance out there in the [electronic] church that it is none of your business or anybody else's what we do or how we do it" (emphasis added).[14] Falwell promised that "the arrogance is over," but five years after the televangelism scandals came to public light, a large proportion of America's religious broadcasters have stubbornly refused to open their

books to outsiders or to subject themselves to the discipline of a
self-regulatory agency.

In summary, the 1925 confrontation between Hoover and
McPherson provided three important lessons. First, it pointed to
the need for government regulation of access to the airwaves.
Second, while the incident of a flamboyant and highly visible
female preacher helped lend credence to the perception that
preachers are the principal abusers of the airwaves, in reality
abuse of the airwaves is by no means restricted to religious
broadcasters. Third, notwithstanding the inevitability of
government regulation, religious broadcasters have tended to
see their mission as special, and therefore, believe that they
should not be subject to oversight by any worldly authority.

*Phase Two: Sustaining Time and the Politics of Exclusion
(1927-1956).* By the mid-1920s station owners discovered that
they could sell time to business organizations to promote
products and the rush to develop privately owned commercial
radio was underway. Religious stations did not fare well under
the stiff competition of a market that quickly turned commercial.
Many of these radio pulpit preachers turned out to be short both
on capital to keep up with the rapidly rising costs of the
technology of broadcasting and the social capital to protect them
from the assaults of those who coveted their license for
commercial purposes. Some were blasted off the air by stations
with greater frequency, others faced license challenges by
commercial stations, a few were squeezed out by heavy-handed
deals, some sold their licenses, and still others simply ceased to
broadcast. They would face even stiffer challenges during the
second phase of broadcasting.

During the first phase of experimental radio, commercial
broadcasters had ample opportunity to observe that religious
broadcasters tended to be noisy, often intolerant, and otherwise
controversial. Moreover, they came in large numbers seeking
access to the airwaves. Dealing with them posed no small
problem.

Most station owners would have preferred to have the liberal
Protestants on the air rather than the fundamentalists and
pentecostals who were clamoring for the opportunity. But from

the beginning, the liberal Protestant traditions were very much underrepresented. Part of the problem was that they were ambivalent about broadcasting. Liberal Protestants saw the possibility of some positive benefits, but they could also see potential negative consequences.[15]

If liberal church leaders were generally unenthusiastic about broadcasting, some were vociferous in their condemnation of the evangelical broadcasters. This condemnation of evangelical broadcasters provided the legitimacy for the policies of both the networks and the Federal Radio Commission [forerunner of the Federal Communications Commission]. These policies had the net effect of significantly restricting evangelicals' access to the mainstream of broadcasting for nearly three decades.

The formal and informal mechanisms that restricted evangelical access to the airwaves first became evident in the late 1920s with the creation of the Federal Radio Commission (FRC) and the formation of radio networks.[16] In its early years of operation, the Radio Commission used its broad authority in a rather heavy-handed way. During the late 1920s the FRC reassigned some religious stations to low-powered frequencies, determined not to grant any new licenses to religious stations, and used their broad regulatory powers to examine complaints that the religious stations were not operating in the "public interest."[17]

NBC, the first radio network, was founded in 1926. It determined at the onset not to accept paid religious broadcasting. Time allocated for religious broadcasting would be free (or "sustaining time" as it is called in the industry) and it would be available "only [to] the central national agencies of great religious faiths."[18] The Federal Council of Churches, the leading cooperative for liberal Protestant groups, was solicited for counsel and manpower for religious broadcasts. NBC's policy explicitly excluded "individual churches or small group movements where the national membership is comparatively small." Small denominations and independent evangelical broadcasters were thus caught in a double bind, excluded by network radio and squeezed out by the FRC. But for the free enterprise character of broadcasting, evangelicals might have been excluded from the airwaves altogether.

When the CBS radio network was formed in 1927, it needed cash and thus determined to sell air time for religious broadcasting, but in 1931 CBS shifted to a policy of sustaining time religious broadcasts only.[19]   For the next four years, the only access to the airwaves for evangelicals was on local stations, but even this was often difficult. Many local stations adopted the networks' policy of sustaining time only and, further, many accommodated only "mainline" religious groups.[20]

A major breakthrough for evangelicals came in 1935 with the formation of the Mutual Broadcasting Network. Mutual accepted paid religious broadcasts and Charles E. Fuller's "The Old-Fashioned Revival Hour" quickly became Mutual's largest account. By 1940 paid religious broadcasting accounted for more than one-quarter of the network's revenues. In 1943, however, Mutual seemed ready to join NBC and CBS in a policy of sustaining time only for religious programming, but then reversed its decision and announced, instead, restrictive policies. Most important among the restrictions was the banning of on air solicitation of money from listening audiences. The prohibition against asking audiences to help pay for the programs made it impossible for some broadcasters to continue.

It is widely believed that Mutual's decision to restrict access was the result of pressure from liberal church groups.[21] Whether or not there was a conspiracy to exclude them from the air, evangelicals clearly understood that they were having a difficult time gaining access to the air. In 1942 they created the National Association of Evangelicals (NAE) and one of the first official acts of that organization was to create a radio committee to explore the problem of discrimination in access to the airwaves.

In April 1944, just a month after Mutual announced its policy changes, 150 evangelical broadcasters met in Columbus, Ohio, and formed the National Religious Broadcasters.[22] Their first official act was to retain a Washington-based communications attorney.[23]   The NRB claimed some early successes including gaining access to some sustaining time on Mutual and NBC's newly created Blue Network (forerunner to ABC), but then lost some of its initial zeal and vitality.[24]

The rapid expansion of television in the 1950s, like the initial expansion of network radio, caught evangelicals off-guard. NBC turned again to the Federal Council of Churches and representatives of Catholicism and Judaism, and moved swiftly to put in place a policy that would exclude evangelicals. CBS, leery of earlier conflict with evangelicals, added the Southern Baptists to its consortium of liberal Protestants, Catholics, and Jews. The Southern Baptists, of course, were evangelical and, under the able leadership of Paul Stevens, produced some of the most creative and effective religious broadcasting in the history of the medium. But Southern Baptists were not members of NRB. Thus, the large body of small evangelical denominations and independent broadcasters were effectively denied access to national television even as they were still struggling to keep a foothold in national radio.

To summarize, the period from the late 1920s, when the networks were formed, through the mid-1950s, when television was rapidly expanding, found the evangelical broadcasters on the margin.[25] With the benefit of hindsight and an awareness of the emerging role of litigation in the settlement of disputes, one can easily pose questions of prejudice and First Amendment rights of access. But these questions are essentially moot today. If the evangelical preachers perceived their problem in constitutional terms of free access, they did not take their fight to the courts. The most important datum is the fact that the evangelical religious broadcasters were not organized to challenge those who did not want them on the airwaves. Once they organized, the problem of access changed dramatically.

Phase Three: Free Market Access (1956-1987). From the Radio Act of 1927, it has always been understood that an important criterion for retaining a broadcasting license is "public service" broadcasting. Just how much public service time is necessary has never been explicitly defined, but it has always been clear that religious programming constitutes public service. In 1960 the Federal Communications Commission (FCC) ruled that there was no intrinsic relationship between sustaining time and public service.

The implication of this ruling was monumental. It meant that local stations could sell air time for religious programs and still get "public interest credit" in the eyes of the FCC. By this time, the big action had shifted from radio to television. Two important developments followed the ruling. First, it buoyed the commitment of evangelical broadcasters to buy commercial time, and fierce competition ensued. Second, this competition enhanced the value of the time slots, with the result that many local stations, which previously had adhered to network policy not to sell air time for religious broadcasting, decided to cash in on the new demand.[26]

In the course of two decades, the landscape of religious broadcasting was transformed from the rule of sustaining time to the dominance of free market access. By 1977, 92 percent of all religious broadcasting in the U.S. was paid-time program.[27] The overwhelming proportion of that time was being purchased by evangelicals.[28]

The 1960 ruling of the FCC was a watershed — not the beginning or the culmination — in the long struggle of evangelicals to gain access to the airways. The year 1956, however, rather than 1960, was the beginning of this free market phase of religious broadcasting because 1956 was the year that James DeForest Murch became the executive director of the National Religious Broadcasters. Murch took several important initiatives that quickly made NRB a big player in the communications business. The most important step was to take the annual meetings of the NRB to Washington, D.C. In his autobiography, Murch explained his reasoning: "I felt that our position would be immensely strengthened if we could take our national convention to the Nation's Capital. This was the seat of the Federal Communications Commission and the lawmakers who could assure our constitutional rights to freedom of religion and freedom of speech on the airwaves. It was also the seat of the industry's National Association of Broadcasters and the leading trade journal of the industry, *Broadcasting* magazine."[29]

One of Murch's early and most important moves was to call on Sol Taishoff, editor and publisher of *Broadcasting*. Murch persuaded Taishoff that evangelicals had a legitimate complaint and became a champion of NRB's campaign to purchase air time. Murch and other NRB leaders also found their way to the offices of the FCC and pleaded their case for fair treatment.

The evangelicals moved beyond gaining parity with the mainline church traditions to absolute dominance in access to the airwaves. And having gained dominance, they have successfully protected their turf. The annual meetings of NRB are still held in Washington. Two features of the program are indicators of the NRB's influence. First, it has an annual luncheon for the commissioners of the FCC and attendance by commissioners is very good. A former FCC commissioner recently commented that the religious broadcasters "have a lobbying capability that makes the National Rifle Association seem like a bunch of rank amateurs."[30] The second program feature which is an indicator that the broadcasters know their way around Washington is the annual appearance of the president of the United States at the annual meeting.

The liberal Protestant and Catholic traditions have tried to check the influence of the evangelical broadcasters.[31] Two principal strategies have been advanced. First, they argue that a license to broadcast is a public trust. Those who hold this trust, they argue, are obliged to offer sustaining time for religious programming and ought to make the mainline churches the recipients of that gratis air time. The second strategy is a two-pronged attack aimed at evangelical religious broadcasters on the one hand, and television itself on the other. The heart of the message of this second strategy is that televangelists are scoundrels using a medium that is inherently corrupting.[32] Thus we have the ambivalence liberals have felt toward the medium of broadcasting for most of this century. It is difficult to argue entitlement to a medium that you really do not trust.

The growth of syndicated religious broadcasting occurred as individual televangelists purchased air time station-by-station.

During the 1980s the marketplace of syndicated religious broadcasters became saturated. This led to increased competition that drove the cost of air time beyond the means of the broadcasters to pay, i.e., beyond their capability to raise money from the small proportion of the viewers who were willing to send in a donation. One theory advanced regarding the underlying conditions precipitating the scandals was that the market had become oversaturated and some broadcasters were covertly seeking to reduce competition.[33]

Conclusions. Before turning to an analysis of developments that have occured in the five years since the scandals of televangelism began to unfold, some reflections regarding the regulation of religious broadcasting up to this point are offered.

Historical analysis of religious broadcasting reveals that regulation has taken place on two levels. First, religious broadcasters have been subjected to essentially the same regulatory principles that govern all broadcasting in America.[34] If the radio and television preachers sometimes appear to be operating in a relatively unfettered fashion, it is because broadcasting in the United States operates with greater latitude and freedom from government interference than broadcasting in any other nation. The religious broadcasters are a mirror image of the broadcast industry itself.

The second level of regulation of religious broadcasters is a complex web of informal social controls. These informal mechanisms operate at three levels: (1) the broadcast networks, (2) local radio and television station managers and owners, and (3) the viewing and listening audiences which financially support the religious broadcasters and thus provide them the resources required to access the airwaves.

These informal regulatory mechanisms have not always produced felicitous outcomes. The second stage saw conservative traditions substantially excluded from broadcasting, while the third stage saw liberal traditions lose ground to the point that they had very limited access. There was one important difference. Conservatives were excluded as a result of policies that sought to exclude them, whereas liberals were excluded because they elected to or have not been able to play by the rules of the free market.

The televangelism scandals of 1987-88 have not diminished the dominance of evangelical broadcasters over mainline or liberal Protestants in access to the airwaves.[35] It is abundantly clear that the scandals had a profound impact on the access of many individual broadcasters.[36] In the post-scandal era, the former constituencies of religious broadcasters have played an important role in the regulation of religious broadcasting— they put away their checkbooks and switched the dials on their television sets. In this respect, it may be said that the free market principle continues to do the job of policing religious broadcasting.

But this is only part of the story. In the wake of the scandals, several other trends, most of which have been emerging for a long time, are now coming into central focus. These trends and an assessment of their likely impact for the future of religious broadcasting are discussed next.

ASSESSING THE PRESENT AND LOOKING AHEAD

The scandals have had a dramatic impact on the course of religious broadcasting, but even without the scandals, the industry has been on a course of dramatic change. The most immediate developments precipitating this change are economics and technology. Less immediately evident, but no less significant, are the evolving cultural perceptions of the role of the state in the lives of its citizens. Nowithstanding popular public rhetoric about the desirability of less government, the general drift of the modern welfare state is toward greater involvement of government in virtually every aspect of public and private life. This development has important long range implications for all religious institutions.

Impact of the Scandals. Few developments in American religion during the twentieth century rival the attention the mass media devoted to the televangelism scandals. Sinclair Lewis's 1927 novel about a conniving and lecherous evangelist had been resurrected many times in made-for-television movies and dramatic series in which Elmer Gantry became a television preacher. With the scandals, real life was imitating art. Sex, money, power, and politics all wrapped together in an intrigue that appeared to involve an ever-expanding circle of televangelists.

If ever the time appeared right for the government to step in and regulate religious broadcasting, this was it. In October 1987, Congressman J.J. Pickle (D-Tex), chairman of the Oversight Subcommittee of the House Ways and Means Committee, held hearings on religious broadcasting.

Several of the nation's leading religious broadcasters were called to testify before the subcommittee. Most spoke softly, but one by one they told Congressman Pickle and his colleagues that they were quite capable of regulating themselves. The one heavy who went on the attack during the hearings was Ben Armstrong, the executive director of NRB, the broadcaster's trade association. Armstrong labeled the Pickle hearings an "insidious" attack and "the beginning of a new inquisition" against religious broadcasters.[37]

But the "inquisition" has not been forthcoming. No one appears to be anxious to rush to judgment or regulation. To date, neither the Pickle subcommittee nor any other legislative committee has introduced regulatory legislation. Subsequent to the Pickle hearings, the IRS investigated at least thirty religious broadcasting organizations. In each instance, the IRS chose to work quietly with the ministries in question to resolve some apparent problems. For example, the IRS found that Liberty Federation, a Jerry Falwell-founded, non-profit educational organization, operated too closely with the Moral Majority, a political lobbying organization, and proposed a revocation of its tax-exempt status. Falwell elected to formally disband the Moral Majority and the IRS proposed no adverse actions.[38]

In this and other instances, authorities from the IRS, the FBI, the U.S. Postal Service, and the Federal Election Committee have gone about their business without whipping up a witch hunt atmosphere. The present mood in Washington appears to be one of minimal interference with religious broadcasters so long as broadcasters take steps to regulate themselves. But the process of moving toward genuine peer accountability has been slow and, at times, painful. Religious broadcasters were prominent in the leadership that founded the Evangelical Council for Financial Acccountability (ECFA) in 1980, but only a few broadcasters actually became members.

The failure of NRB members to join ECFA led that organization's leaders to propose their own self-regulatory organization. Several months before the scandals broke, the NRB drafted and approved in principle a plan to create an Ethics and Financial Integrity Commission (EFICOM). Following the scandals, ECFA was contracted to independently manage EFICOM. Initially NRB talked tough. All NRB members would have to meet the membership requirements of EFICOM or be dropped from NRB.

Five years after the scandals and three years after EFICOM was formally inaugurated, NRB faces a quiet crisis as it struggles to bring members into compliance.[39] Many members are resisting pressure to comply with accountability standards. One critic recently stated that EFICOM is going to keep lowering their standards for membership until every organization qualifies. This is not quite true. NRB has dropped members and will soon face another significant trimming of membership for lack of compliance.[40] Another problem with self-regulation is that several highly visible radio and television ministries have never been NRB members. All of this leads to the troubling question of whether NRB is capable of pursuing an agressive leadership role in regulating the industry. Further, the apparent absence of outside influence on the boards of directors of many broadcast ministries raises serious questions about their ability to responsibily govern themselves.

Investigative reporting continues to lend credence to the popular perception that religious broadcasting has not rehabilitated itself. A recent edition of ABC's "Prime Time Live" presented an indicting probe of three Texas television ministries.

In each instance there were strong implications of deception, fraud, and financial mismanagement.[41]

The scandals and developments during the past five years have not altered this author's view that the majority of religious broadcasters are honest and their listeners and viewers receive a spiritual benefit. And a small proportion who receive spiritual benefits reciprocate with financial contributions— just as millions of Americans support public broadcasting.

By far the most important consequence of the scandals is that they have underminded the confidence of a significant number of viewers and contributors. Virtually all religious broadcasters faced a drop in support and have had to rebuild confidence. Honest broadcasters are paying a price for the misdeeds of ministries of questionable integrity. But religious broadcasting remains substantially a marketplace regulated by consumer behavior.

Rapidly Changing Economics and Technology. The economics and technology of broadcasting are changing very rapidly, and with these changes will come sweeping changes in the availability of religious programming. On the economic side of the equation, the cost of syndication on conventional VHF commercial stations is rapidly becoming prohibitive. During the 1980s a dozen televangelists appeared at least weekly, on 150 or more stations. A few appeared on more than three hundred stations. In 1990 there were only two broadcasters on more than 150 stations.

The scandals hastened the process of economic crisis for religious broadcasters, but they did not fundamentally alter the pattern of soaring costs which led to an industry-wide retrenchment. During the 1980s televangelists aggressively engaged in bidding wars against each other for choice stations and time slots. In the course of the decade, the cost of air time for choice slots typically tripled. During this same time frame, most religious broadcasters experienced only modest growth in audience size while others were losing viewers. The precipitious loss of audience and revenues in the wake of the scandals forced many televangelists to retrench. The thinning out of competition, however, did not bring a drop in the cost of air time or make space for new televangelists.

What happened? Beginning in the early 1980s, the success of the televangelists enticed others to explore the economic viability of the Sunday morning time frame. By the time the scandals hit, video magazines, news analyses, and other types of programming produced both locally and by networks, were alreadying squeezing religious broadcasting into a tighter time frame. One of the fastest growing competitors in many markets was the "infomercial"— program-length commercials thinly disguised as talk shows or entertainment programming.

Syndicated religious broadcasting will probably not disappear, but the continued inflation of air time costs will make it increasingly difficult for established broadcasters to hold onto markets and even more difficult for new syndicators to break into good markets.

The future of religious broadcasting is in satellite delivery via cable television. If religious broadcasting is almost certain to survive on the UHF channels of cable television, it is equally clear that individual broadcasters are destined to have much smaller audiences than many obtained when they bought time on local network affiliates in a large number of markets. Still, without cable outlets, religious television might virtually disappear.

The process of building cable outlets for religious television began in 1977 when the Christian Broadcasting Network (CBN) transmitted its first satellite broadcast. In rapid succession Trinity Broadcasting Network (TBN) was formed in southern California followed by the PTL Network (PTL) in North Carolina. CBN, PTL, and TBN all had state-of-the-art technology poised to deliver religious programming to this expanding audience potential.[42] In fact, they were ahead of themselves as the task of wiring the nation for cable took place during the decade of the 1980s.

In the early 1980s there was not enough audience to support three full-time religious networks. Pat Robertson recognized this and elected to shift the focus of CBN from full-time religious broadcasting to family oriented programming. Aside from the daily airing of "The 700 Club," Robertson's Family Channel currently restricts religious broadcasting to weekends. This format has been very profitable, but it has resulted in a reduction in the availabilty of air time for religious telecasting.

Before the end of the decade, Jim Bakker's greed and mismanagement put his PTL network out of the picture, thus further reducing outlets for religious broadcasting. This left only TBN, founded by Paul Crouch, as a full-time religious network with significant cable outlets. There are other cable networks including VISN, Eternal Word, the Southern Baptists' ACTS, and the New Inspirational Network, but none has the capability of delivering significant audiences. TBN has also acquired ownership or affiliation with a significant number of low and medium powers television stations. Indeed, Crouch has developed a legacy for what might be called "religious PAC MAN." Having assisted several smaller stations in getting started, he has gobbled them up when they became financially vulnerable.[43] With little opportunity for the development of new networks with large cable outlets, Crouch appears to be positioned to be a major player in the future of religious broadcasting.

The Future of Access, Accountability, and Religious Liberty. The history of religious broadcasting has not always been a felicitous one, nor has the protection of First Amendment rights always been the paramount concern of the actors in the struggle for access to the airwaves. Neither of these conclusions should be particularly surprising. Given the high stakes, and the longstanding antagonism between evangelicals and mainline Protestants, what is really surprising is the fact that there have been very few judicial cases involving religious broadcasting. There are several reasons for the the absence of litigation.

First, evangelicals saw the battle in religious rather than constitutional-legal terms. To be sure, they saw themselves as victims of discrimination by secular broadcasters and errant brethren in liberal churches, but the resolution of the problem was faithfulness to God and hard work to overcome the obstacles. There is no evidence that it ever occurred to the evangelicals to take their struggle to the courts.[44] Part of the explanation for this would appear to be the simple fact that the culture was much less litigious in those days.

Another important reason evangelicals did not fare well in the early decades of broadcasting was that they were not organized. Once organized, their access to the airwaves changed dramatically. Their present airwave dominance stems directly from the FCC ruling that uncoupled the link between free air time and public service. Theoretically, the adversaries of evangelicals might find a way to challenge this ruling, but this will be difficult because the 1960 ruling is so totally consistent with the free market character of American broadcasting.

The case for the proposition that church liberals are victims of discrimination is very weak. If they want to get on the air, all they have to do is lay down the cash and step up to the microphone.[45] That mainline churches have been unsuccessful or unwilling to raise the funds to buy air time speaks to a host of issues that say a lot about their priorities.

For the immediate future the advantage in access to broadcasting seems likely to remain with the evangelicals. As long as the White House is controlled by conservatives, whether Republican or Democrat, a radical restructuring of free market policies of broadcasting in America is unlikely. So long as the NRB maintains effective communication with the executive branch of government, FCC appointees committed to upsetting the status quo seem improbable.

Dominant power relationships seldom remain unchecked for long periods of time. There is evidence that a new power dominance is emerging. This is not a shift away from evangelical influence in broadcasting, but a consolidation of power within that sector. Transformation in the technological delivery of broadcasting is at the heart of this shift. Litigation may become the principal instrument by which this new dominance is forged.

But there may be a more imminent danger to the religion clauses of the First Amendment than wars of corporate litigation among big religious broadcasters: the encroachment of the modern welfare state. The benevolent welfare state of today is

increasingly responsible for those who have been victimized —
victimizations of almost every kind imaginable. The modus
operandi of those who seek to protect the vulnerable is litigation
and legislation.

In the domain of religion, cults, sects, and religious
broadcasters are unpopular. There is public sentiment for the
proposition that they victimize those who get "caught up in their
webs" and, for the protection of these victims, that they should
be held accountable. Court decisions deriving from litigation
against unpopular religious groups seem much less likely to be
scrutinized for First Amendment implications. The
"brainwashing" argument, for example, contends that a person
who has come under the influence of an unpopular religious
group is not of his or her own mind and, thus, has no First
Amendment rights. The goal of "deprogramming," "exit
counseling," or "post-traumatic stress counseling" is to restore
their mental facilities. Only when this is achieved can one speak
of "rights."[46]

Generally, this author is skeptical of so-called "slippery slope"
or "camel's nose under the tent" theories. In the case of legal
actions against unpopular religious groups, however, it is
important to consider carefully the implications of actions
against them for the broader culture. If no one objects when
Rev. Syung Moon goes to jail, or the Scientologists are harassed,
or Jimmy Swaggart is taxed, or Native American Indians are
prohibited from using peyote in their ancient ritual ceremonies,
then perhaps there will be no objections as the courts rewrite the
long established meanings of the Establishment and Free
Exercise Clauses in the United States Constitution.

The argument of this essay has been that religious
broadcasting has had its own built-in checks and balances. If
there has been little discussion of the First Amendment, it is
because constitutionally guaranteed religious liberties have not
heretofore been threatened by the activities on litigation brought
against religious broadcasters. For all of the rancorous carrying
on by and against religious broadcasters, this enterprise has not
posed a serious threat to the First Amendment. This status quo
may now be threatened, not so much because the world of

religious broadcasting is changing— although it clearly is— b u t rather because the cultural attitude toward litigation has changed.

Aimee Semple McPherson, like Tammy Faye Bakker, was a source of amusement for some and the focus of immense hostility for others. But in a world in which litigation was not second nature to the culture, McPherson's excesses did not even remotely pose the possibility of a threat to the religious liberties of a whole culture. That is no longer true today. Because television preachers are unpopular, their perceived misdeeds are potentially the source of imaginative and novel legal challenges. One may not like many of the televangelists, or what they do, but the decisions made against them could have very serious impact on the religious liberties of the nation.

NOTES

1. This was not the first time that religious broadcasters had stepped over the line from preaching to politicking. The most celebrated case was that of Father Charles E. Coughlin, a Roman Catholic parish priest from a Detroit suburb, who began radio broadcasting in 1926. Gradually his sermons became highly politicized. In 1932 he actively supported the presidential candidacy of Franklin D. Roosevelt and then later became Roosevelt's bitter enemy. So daunting were Coughlin's attacks that Roosevelt had Coughlin's mailing privileges revoked under the Espionage Act of 1917 and considered having him indicted for sedition before choosing to persuade the priest's archbishop to silence him.
2. Kimberly A. Neuendorf, "The Public Trust versus the Almightly Dollar," in Robert Abelman and Steward M. Hoover, eds., *Religious Television: Controversies and Conclusions* (Norwood, N.J.: Ablex Publishing, 1990), 72.
3. The dates attached to each stage are only rough approximations. Beginning dates correspond to specific developments, but the real impact of that development may not be felt for several years. And, similarly, the denotation of a new phase does not usually represent a sharp departure from the previous phase.
4. Dennis N. Volkuil, "The Power of the Air: Evangelicals and the Rise of Religious Broadcasting," in Quentin J. Schultze, ed., *American Evangelicals and the Mass Media* (Grand Rapids, Mich.: Zondervan, 1990), 71.
5. Jeffrey K. Hadden and Charles E. Swann, *Prime Time Preachers* (Reading, Ma.: Addison-Wesley Publishing, 1981), 73-4.
6. Voskuil, "The Power of the Air," 72.
7. Neuendorf, "The Public Trust versus the Almighty Dollar," 73.
8. Ben Armstrong, *The Electric Church* (Nashville, Tenn.: Thomas Nelson Publishers, 1979), 24.

9. Cited in Hadden and Swann, *Prime Time Preachers*, 188-89. Whether Aimee Semple McPherson believed the Department of Commerce agents literally to be "minions of Satan" or merely intrusive bureaucrats, it is clear that she believed they had no legitimate basis for interfering with her broadcasting. There remain today a significant number of religious broadcasters who share that view.

10. This was one of the classic confrontations in the politics of American broadcasting. McPherson was a self-made evangelist without professional credentials, yet she was one of the most gifted radio evangelists of the twentieth century. In her indomitable resistance she succeeded in facing down a powerful Washington politician who just three years later would become the president of the United States.

11. For a more detailed discussion of the rationale for broadcast regulation, see Sydney W. Head, "Broadcasting Laws," *World Broadcasting Systems* (Belmont, Cal.: Wadsworth Publishing Co, 1985), 129-61.

12. Clearly, preventing technical interference and protecting a scare resource are more readily defined and executed than determining "the public interest" and "misuse" of the airwaves. The first two objectives have been managed relatively easy by the regulatory agency, while the latter two have periodically engaged the executive, judicial, and legislative branches of government.

13. The history of electronic communication is intertwined with religious significance and symbolism which serves to affirm these evangelical Christians' belief that this medium has providential purpose. In 1844 when Samuel F. B. Morse completed the installation of the first telegraphic line he seemed to have experienced a sense of awe, even sacredness, in what he was doing as is evidenced by the choice of his first transmission: "What hath God wrought"; Head, *World Broadcasting Systems*, 108. Radio dates from 1896 with Guglielmo Marconi's discovery of wireless communication, but the first successful voice transmission occurred a decade later when a Canadian engineer, Reginal Fessenden, beamed a signal from the coast of Massachusetts to ships at sea on Christmas Eve 24 December 1906. The content of the first transmission was a religious service. Hadden and Swann, *Prime Time Preachers*, 8-9; Marconi provided technical assistance in the construction of Vatican Radio and introduced the pope to the world in the inauguration of the first global network; Donald R. Browne, *International Radio Broadcasting: The Limits of the Limitless Medium* (New York: Praeger Publishers, 1982), 306. These and other early developments in radio and television provide the rationale that evangelicals express frequently for the providential character of broadcasting.

14. "Excerpts from the Rev. Jerry Falwell's News Conference," *The Charlotte Observer*, 29 April 1987, 11A.

15. For a treatise that personifies the ambivalence of liberal church leaders toward radio and television broadcasting from the onset, see John W. Buckman, *The Church in the World of Radio-Television* (New York: Association Press, 1960). Their response was not totally negative. As Buckman says, "As early as 1923 the Federal Council of Churches [the forerunner of the National Council of Churches] . . . officially encouraged local church federations to develop cooperative radio ministries." Voskuil, "The Power of the Air," 76. This counsel was followed in some measure but liberal

church leaders just never got as excited about the possibilities of broadcasting as did the evangelical traditions.

16. The FRC was created by the Radio Act of 1927 which empowered an independent agency to assign frequencies, license stations, review the performance of those licensed, and otherwise exercise broad authority in the regulation of broadcast communications.

17. In 1931 the license of a powerful and controversial Los Angeles religious broadcaster, "Fighting Bob" Shuler, was withdrawn.

18. From the policy statement of the NBC Advisory Committee on Religious Activities; quoted in Hadden and Swann, *Prime Time Preachers*, 77.

19. Ostensibly, this policy shift was to bring CBS into conformity with the other network. In reality, it was a means of getting rid of Father Charles Coughlin whose sermons were considered too controversial. CBS, like NBC, called upon the Federal Council for assistance in programming.

20. Voskuil, "The Power of the Air," 76. When evangelicals did get on local stations, they were twice as likely to be charged for the air time as were Roman Catholics and mainline Protestants.

21. Martin, "Giving the Winds a Mighty Voice," 63. Federal Council officials denied this and investigators of the controversy have failed to find a smoking gun. It is also likely that both networks and local stations were pressured by prospective advertisers for these choice time slots; Lowell Saunders, "The National Religious Broadcasters and the Availability of Commercial Radio Time," (Ph.D. diss., 1968). In perhaps the most comprehensive investigation of the controversy, Saunders concluded that the charges against the Federal Council could only be considered hearsay. He further concluded that there existed a high correlation between the economic health of the broadcasting industry and their willingness to sell time to evangelicals. When local stations or networks needed money, they sold time to evangelicals. While there may have been no overt conspiratorial activities to exclude evangelicals, there can be no question that the Federal Council preferred to have its own members represented on the network airwaves rather than nonmember churches. Furthermore, it is clear that many liberal church leaders were openly hostile toward the evangelical broadcasters as is evidenced in the editorial policy of *The Christian Century*, long the most prominent independent publication of liberal Protestantism. When Mutual announced its decision to restrict access, *The Christian Century* published an article bitterly complaining that they had not gone far enough: "The network religious radio program racket, capitalized by independent superfundamentalist revivalists, will not be eliminated nationally until Mutual goes the whole way and bans paid religious programs altogether, as the other networks have done." Charles W. Crowe, "Religion on the Air," *The Christian Century* 61 (23 August 1944): 973-74.

22. Ralph M. Jennings, "Policies and Practices in Selected National Religious Bodies as Related to Broadcasting in the Public Interest, 1920-1950" (Ph.D. diss. New York University, 1968), 317.

23. James DeForest Murch, *Adventures for Christ in Changing Times* (Louisville, Ky.: Restoration Press, 1973), 173.

24. Jeffrey K. Hadden and Anson Shupe, *Televangelism: Power and Politics on God's Frontier* (New York: Henry Holt and Company, 1988), 48.

25. A few radio broadcasters, such as Charles E. Fuller and Walter E. Maier, gained network access and, thus, large national audiences. But on the whole, evangelicals found themselves struggling for access in local markets. The combination of a competitive free market and an unsympathetic Federal Radio Commission made it difficult for them to own radio stations. The policies of NBC and CBS offered access only through sustaining time, and the cozy relationships the networks formed with the Federal Council of Churches alliance substantially blocked access to outlets for reaching a national audience.
26. Hadden and Shupe, *Televangelism*, 51.
27. Report by the Communications Committee of the U.S. Catholic Conference; quoted in Peter G. Horsfield, *Religious Television: The American Experience* (New York: Longman, 1984), 89.
28. The networks produced their sustaining time religious programs for more than a decade, but with the lure of big bucks from the syndicated televangelists, local affiliates elected not to run the network productions.
29. Murch, *Adventures for Christ*, 179.
30. Personal interview with this author, 17 May 1991.
31. The office of the assistant general secretary for communications of the National Council of Churches has been the focal point of the counterattack.
32. William F. Fore, until recently the assistant general secretary for communications of the National Council of Churches, is the most important spokesperson for this argument. For an introduction to this perspective, see William F. Fore, *Television and Religion* (Minneapolis, Minn.: Augsburg Publishing, 1987).
33. This thesis can be pursued in many possible directions. For example, when Marvin Gorman, an Assemblies of God minister began to develop a significant television ministry in Louisiana, Jimmy Swaggart brought changes of sexual misconduct before the Assemblies of God. Gorman was defrocked and subsequently lost his New Orleans church and television ministry. Swaggart subsequently threatened to bring Jim Bakker's sexual improprieties before the Assembly of God. When this became public knowledge, Swaggart denied that he had his eye on the PTL Network. Jerry Falwell similarly denied that his motivation for taking over PTL had anything to do with acquiring a network for his own broadcasting ambitions. The truth of the "economic motivation" thesis will probably never be proven. For some of the best investigative research on this thesis see: Charles E. Shephard, *Forgiven* (New York: Atlantic Monthly Press, 1989); and Larry Martz, *Ministry of Greed* (New York: Weidenfeld and Nicolson, 1988).
34. The primary regulatory agency is the Federal Communications Commission. An examination of the regulatory functions of the FCC is beyond the scope of this inquiry.
35. The scandals clearly had a role in facilitating the creation of Vision Interfaith Satellite Network (VISN) an interdenominational cable consortium. VISN is owned and operated by The National Interfaith Cable Coalition, Inc., a not-for-profit 501(c)(3) corporation. Currently twenty-eight "mainline" faith groups from Protestant, Roman Catholic, Eastern Orthodox, and Jewish traditions are affiliated. VISN offers an impressive twenty-four-hour program schedule, but it has yet to develop sufficient cable outlets to be a major player in religious broadcasting.

36. In the five years since the scandals broke, virtually every indicator of broadcast viability is off sharply. Arbitron and Nielsen ratings report sharp declines in individual and overall religious broadcast viewing. Many ministries have reported significant revenue declines. Significant ministries have disappeared from television and others seem almost certain to follow.
37. Michael Isikoff, "The Preachers' Complaint," *The Washington Post*, October 1987, C-4.
38. "Three Year IRS Audit of Liberty University Concluded," Liberty University News Release, 18 December 1991.
39. In January 1992, EFICOM had 104 broadcasters that were "fully certified members" and another 91 who met all standards for membership by virture of being ECFA members. Three hundred and sixteen were exempt from membership for various reasons: for-profit organizations (170), broadcasters with incomes of less that $150,000 (94), and non-U.S. organizations (52). David Clark, NRB president announced at the annual meetings that an additional 162 non-complying organizations would be dropped pending another phone call and registered letter seeking compliance with EFICOM membership standards. These numbers account for a total of 673 organizations, which is 136 fewer organizations than had been accounted for a year earlier. The number of "fully certified" and ECFA members remained essentially unchanged from figures released in January 1991. See "NRB Moves Slowly to Enforce Ethics Code," *Christianity Today* 9 March 1992, 59.
40. Ibid. The actual loss of membership is not clear. In 1989 Ben Armstrong, then executive director of NRB, claimed a membership of 1,450 members. Art Borden, then president of ECFA, placed NRB membership at 825 An NRB press release at the 1992 annual meetings claimed a membership of 940 organizations. This figure is in sharp variance with the 673 total reported by David Clark, a figure which includes 162 non-complying organizations. Clark estimates the membership roster could drop to as low as 565. Given that NRB had virtrually no success in bringing organizations into compliance between January 1991 and January 1992, a more realistic membership figure may be around five hundred.
41. One of the trio, Larry Lea, was incorrectly portrayed as an NRB member in good standing and keynote speaker at the most recent convention. In fact, Lea had not complied with the EFICOM certification requirements and while he had earlier addressed the NRB convention, he was not the keynote speaker. "Prime Time Live" did not correct these and other factual errors.
42. The presence of these networks spawned a great interest in the production of religious programming. Many television ministries began on one of these networks and then expanded to syndicated programming in the VHF commercial market. By 1983 there were almost a hundred syndicated religious programs.
43. Mark I. Pinsky, "Evangelist Plays Hardball in Christian TV," *Los Angeles Times*, Orange County Section, 9 April 1989. Pinsky, an Orange County reporter for the *Times* has reported regularly on the financial dealings of the expanding TBN empire.
44. If some religious broadcasters might have considered legal action, the long shadow of the Scopes Trial in 1925 may have left them doubting the prospects of getting a fair day in court. Furthermore,

most of the broadcasters did not have the financial resources to
make their claims of prejudice before a court.

45. In 1988, in the wake of the televangelism scandals, a coalition of
the Protestant, Jewish, Roman Catholic, and Eastern Orthodox
faith groups created a cable television network called Vision
Interfaith Satellite Network (VISN). The network was made
possible through a combination of loans and grants from a
coalition of cable system owners. As of mid-1991, VISN was
broadcasting twenty-four hours per day, seven days a week and
was available on approximately two thousand cable affiliates.
VISN policies prohibit proselytizing and on-air solicitation of
funds. VISN has survived longer than many experts predicted.
Without on-air solicitation, or some other significant infusion of
operating funds, VISN will continue to be a precarious operation.

46. For two complimentary discussions of the dangers of the
"brainwashing" assault on religious liberty, see James T.
Richardson, "Cult/Brainwashing Cases and Freedom of Religion,"
Journal of Church and State 33 (Winter 1991): 55-74; and Dick
Anthony, "Religious Movements and Brainwashing Litigation:
Evaluating Key Testimony," in Thomas Robbins and Dick
Anthony, eds., *In Gods We Trust: New Patterns of Religious
Pluralism in America* (New Brunswick, N.J.: Transaction Publishers,
1990), 295-344.

The Role of Government in Regulating New and Nonconventional Religions

DAVID BROMLEY and THOMAS ROBBINS

This essay examines state regulation of new and/or nonconventional religious movements. The primary emphasis is on the cohort of new religious movements, popularly labeled "cults," that became the source of a major public controversy during the 1970s and 1980s. Beginning early in the 1970s and continuing through the present, there have been a number of initiatives designed to exert social control over these movements. This essay begins by observing that state regulation of religion has varied historically, considering the unique challenges new religions pose to the social order, and by identifying different types of regulation of religion. Building upon this discussion, the sources, substance, and implications of regulation of NRMs are considered, with primary emphasis on regulation of the means by which new religious groups recruit and socialize new members and finance their organizations.

THE CONTEXT OF REGULATION
OF NEW RELIGIOUS MOVEMENTS

The significance of the issue of regulation of new religious groups gains force from several important trends and events. First, beginning with the free exercise and establishment provisions of the U.S. Constitution, the United States has guaranteed religious liberty as a fundamental right. Although there have been ebbs and flows during particular historical periods, a long succession of U.S. Supreme Court decisions, many involving new or nonconventional religious groups, have reiterated the commitment to this right. Of course, as all of the major works on American religious history record, religious countermovements and religious repression have been commonplace. However, the state has not been empowered to use its monopoly on coercive power to suppress new religious groups.

Second, recent history may have witnessed a high-water mark in religious libertarianism. In their seminal article, "Religious Marginality and the Free Exercise Clause," political scientists Frank Way and Barbara Burt report on the pattern of judicial legitimation of marginal religious movements.[1] Surveying all reported state and federal judicial opinions pertaining to free exercise claims by religious groups in two periods, 1946-1956 and 1970-1980, Way and Burt found significant increases in the percentage of successfully litigated claims in the 1970s, although in both periods the majority of claims were rejected. More provocatively, they found that religionist success in free exercise litigation in the 1970s appeared to be positively related to those factors which identify the litigants as marginal movements. Indeed, marginal groups were more likely to have their claims vindicated in the 1970s than mainline churches. The finding that the legitimation of marginal movements by the American judiciary has for a certain period (1970-1980) been a function of their marginality arguably contravenes the thrust of social science and legal scholarship,[2] which relates legitimacy to the shedding of marginal characteristics through processes of institutionalization.

It is likely, as Way and Burt note, that the patterns they uncovered pertain to a special (and very possibly aberrant) "countercultural" period of American religious and legal history in which libertarian norms were widely deferred to and nonconformity respected. Indeed, it was the *Sherbert* (1963) and *Yoder* (1972) balancing test that reshaped free exercise litigation in a libertarian direction, thus commencing what seemed to be a tradition of "religious exemptions" that arguably tended to favor marginal groups. As applied in specific cases, if a court found that a governmental measure placed a "burden" on an individual's or group's religious "free exercise," the state then was required to show a "compelling state interest" to justify the regulatory burden. Because marginal groups have been viewed as more likely to be significantly "burdened" by given state regulations, the *Sherbert-Yoder* balancing test, which became "a focal point of judicial methodology,"[3] partly served to legitimate marginality.

Finally, the recent *Employment Division of Oregon v. Smith* (1990) case may be a harbinger of change. In that case, a Native American was denied unemployment compensation by the state after being fired for using peyote, which is used ceremonially in Native American Church rituals. Notwithstanding ambiguities, the general thrust of Justice Antonin Scalia's majority opinion in the *Smith* case has been widely viewed as undercutting the "compelling state interest" norm and giving the state substantial-ly greater regulatory leeway to constrain free exercise.[4] Justice Scalia seems to move constitutional interpretation back toward the restrictive doctrine of the Mormon polygamy cases, especially *Reynolds* (which his opinion cites) and away from the jurisprudence of the libertarian 1960s and 1970s.[5] As Scalia acknowledges, it is the small religious groups which will largely bear the cost of his constitutional interpretation, as they must now appeal to a political process in which they may have little leverage.[6]

In political terms, the constitutional Free Exercise and Establishment Clauses have had the effect of "privileging" religion. The longer and more fully institutionalized the tradition of religious liberty (as defined by these clauses) has become, the more powerful the coalition that would be required to alter these basic normative parameters. At the same time, it is clear that the nature and extent of state regulation of religion historically has fluctuated around these normative precepts. The recent past has witnessed a relatively libertarian period during which, the evidence suggests, marginal religious group appeals have actually been received more favorably by the courts than those from established churches. Current events suggest that the recent libertarian period may now be ending.[7] Whatever trends develop in the future, it is marginal and nonconventional groups that tend to constitute the leading edge of change. Therefore, tracking developments in the patterning of judicial decisions with respect to these groups constitutes one important means by which the church-state normative boundary can be assessed. From a social science perspective, the location of this boundary influences the degree and kind of social control levied on developing religious organizations.

CHURCH, STATE, AND "CULT"

New and nonconventional religious groups historically have been central to the elaboration of the free exercise and establishment provisions of the U.S. Constitution, and that pattern is likely to continue. Indeed, in an essay on "New Religions and the First Amendment," James E. Wood, Jr. refers to "the disproportionate number of church-state cases to reach the United States Supreme Court on behalf of religious groups outside of the mainline religious denominations."[8] And as two sociologists of religion have noted, "The dominant focus of American legal history has not been on church versus state so much as *sect versus state* . . . [and in this process] far from being neutral, the courts have exercised considerable influence over the forms and functions of sectarian religiosity."[9] Many older and now well-established groups— such as Baptists, Methodists and Mormons — "began as unfamiliar, high-demand, proselytizing religions, greeted with deep hostility by more sedate and longer established faiths."[10]

Why have conflicts involving new religious groups— both nineteenth century "sects" and contemporary "cults"— loomed so large in church-state litigation in the United States? It has been argued, on the one hand, that the fundamental answer is *discrimination*: marginal and exotic groups have been victimized by an institutional system which tends to accommodate to the more powerful and established competitors of marginal movements; that is, "the courts have aligned with the churches in their struggle against sects."[11] On the other hand, it has also been argued that, at least in the current milieu, "cults" represent a sinister menace that has confronted courts and other law enforcement agencies with unique control problems. Several sociologists who are not "anti-cult" crusaders have contended that the intensity of government controls which have been brought to bear on certain controversial groups has been partly a function of the success with which certain manipulative movements were initially able to utilize legal guarantees of religious freedom and the regulatory exemptions granted churches to protect and expand their operations. The result was that the explosive growth of exploitive and abusive patterns eventually elicited extreme hostility and devastating state intervention.[12]

Both of these arguments have merit. However religion is defined, it clearly involves "ultimate concerns," and religious belief systems formulate the ultimate assumptions upon which social life is based (i.e., those which require no higher level legitimation and from which other principles are derived). Sects may be understood as religious groups that both reject and are rejected by the society of which they are a part. Sectarian groups typically condemn the existing social order, predict its demise, construct a vision of an alternative order, separate members from conventional social relationships, establish parallel institutional forms to replace "corrupted" institutions, and maintain limited loyalty to existing normative arrangements.

The most radical sectarian groups are those that develop apocalyptic ideologies and communal organizations, which have the effect of maximizing internal group commitment and distance from conventional society.[13] To the extent that new religious groups approach this position, which is not uncommon during at least the early histories of many sectarian movements, conflicts between movement and society are likely to be intense. The challenge such groups pose to the fundamental assumptions on which the social order is founded and the limited investment such groups have in institutional arrangements produce the mutual rejection that is characteristic of sect-society relationships.

Viewed from a civil liberties perspective, it would always be sectarian groups that most fully exercise the entire range of religious liberties, pushing up against or crossing normative boundaries. The combination of full exercise of religious liberty and conflict with the larger society makes new religions an important set of groups to observe, for it is here that governmental regulation is likely to begin and it is here that normative boundaries are likely to be redrawn.

REGULATION

In understanding the social control of new religious groups, the concept of regulation should be broadly defined to incorporate endogenous and exogenous sources of control. In "settled times" with "settled religious groups" the social control system may approach endogenous regulation, in which the control system incorporates the basic assumptions and principles upon which major institutional units operate and operational procedures are reasonably consensual. Under such conditions dispute resolution becomes a matter of comparing specific claims against these overarching principles.[14] In "unsettled times," when prevailing principles and practices are under challenge, it is much more likely that exogenous regulation will occur. Exogenous regulation involves the introduction of principles and procedures that are not formally incorporated into the control system. Exogenous regulation is likely to involve, first, the expansion of grounds upon which claims can be brought against groups (increased legal accountability) or the contraction of the grounds upon which claims can be resisted by groups (decreased legal entitlement), and, second, the expansion of enforcement of rule violations by groups (increased legal prosecution) or the contraction of enforcement of rule violations committed against groups (decreased legal protection). It is precisely this situation that religious movements are likely to confront because they arise during historical periods and/or among segments of the population in which prevailing social arrangements are experienced as problematic, and they are likely to organize in a manner that maximizes tension with the larger society.

Given the constitutional proscription on close, invasive regulation of religious organizations, situations in which conflict between new religious groups and mainstream institutions erupt are likely to eventuate in exogenous forms of social control involving increased normative liability, decreased normative assets, increased prosecution, and decreased protection. For example, in the last decade a number of civil suits have been brought by ex-members against controversial "cults." The state controls the viability of such suits and that of the targeted movements through the decisions made by the courts with regard to the interpretations of rules governing the admissibility of evidence and "expert" testimony, as well as by the judicial response to the constitutional issues which are claimed by defendants to pose a barrier to the litigation. The courts will necessarily encourage or discourage such suits through their response to novel concepts such as "brainwashing," which are introduced as essential to support key causes of action. Judicial decisions in these realms will always be to some degree "arbitrary" as they do not emerge automatically and inevitably from the application of consensual principles to substantive data; rather they are influenced by exogenous factors such as the climate of public opinion, media treatment of "cults," and so on. The state cannot, therefore, be viewed entirely as a mere neutral referee or umpire without a regulatory agenda concerning religious minorities. The state necessarily regulates or deregulates as it interpretively defines the "rules of the game" governing private actions in this area. To take a second example, the state is indirectly regulating or deregulating controversial religious groups when it decides to protect such groups and their adult members from forcible abductions by "deprogrammers," or when, conversely, courts decline to intervene and implicitly define such coercive actions as private "family matters."

CATEGORIZING CASES

In his famous dissent in *U.S. v. Ballard*,[15] Justice Robert H. Jackson asserted that "The chief wrong that false prophets do their following is not financial. . . . The wrong of these things, as I see it, is not the money the victims part with half so much as the mental and spiritual poison they get" (emphasis added). Of course, it was Jackson's opinion that it was precisely this insidious "poison" which the Constitution puts beyond legal regulation. For purposes of the analysis developed here, what is noteworthy is that Justice Jackson's comment identifies metaphorically two broad, important categories into which many "cult" cases or regulatory conflicts tend to fall. First, there are conflicts dealing mainly with allegations about personal harm ("poison") inflicted upon members (or occasionally non-members) through group processes of conversion, indoctrination, and recruitment. Second, there are cases dealing largely with financial arrangements ("money"), such as regulatory conflicts involving the financial and commercial practices of movements, their relations with the Internal Revenue Service and state and local taxing authorities, their employment practices, the services they provide, and so on. Arguably the history of the 1970s and 1980s with respect to new religions has been one of initiatives that would expand state regulation of religious organization and practice, either from endogenous or exogenous sources.[16]

PERSONAL HARM ("POISON")

The most sensational and potentially innovative recent legal cases involving controversial religious movements or "cults" are those involving claims that overpowering psychological coercion has rendered individuals essentially involuntary participants, unable to evaluate rationally their continued participation.[17] These cases fall into four categories: allegations of brainwashing against specific individuals, deprogramming cases, ex-member civil suits, and proselytization cases.[18]

Brainwashing Cases

Given the centrality of brainwashing allegations to the new religions controversy, it might be regarded as surprising how few cases there have been in which individuals have been identified and accused of brainwashing specific victims. Groups rather than individuals generally have been charged with brainwashing while coercive persuasion has been attributed to social processes rather than individual actions. Further, prosecutions of individuals specifically for brainwashing (or kidnapping/imprisonment via brainwashing) have generally been unavailing in the absence of physical constraint.[19] For example, in 1976 a Hare Krishna devotee, twenty-three-year-old Merylee Kreshower, attempted to press kidnapping charges in a Queens, New York court against her mother and a deprogrammer following an unsuccessful deprogramming. Instead of a probe of Kreshower's abduction and deprogramming, the assistant district attorney converted the case into a grand jury investigation of Hare Krishna. The grand jury subsequently dismissed the charges against the two defendants and instead indicted two local Hare Krishna leaders for using mind control to imprison Kreshower and a fellow adherent unlawfully. The New York Superior Court ultimately dismissed the false imprisonment charges brought against the Krishna leaders. In his decision, Judge John Leahy observed, "The said two individuals entered the Hare Krishna movement voluntarily and submitted themselves voluntarily to the regimen, rules and regulations of said so-called Hare Krishna religion, and it is also conceded that the alleged victims were not in any way physically restrained from leaving the defendant organization."[20]

There have been a few instances in which brainwashing charges have been employed in prosecutions of group members for criminal acts as a way of generalizing responsibility beyond the immediate perpetrator(s) to the "cult" and its leadership and in criminal defenses designed to mitigate the legal responsibility of a defendant who participated in a nonconventional group. In the "Stonegate" case in West Virginia, for example, both occurred. A husband and wife, who were convicted in the beating death of their infant son, cooperated with the district attorney in the successful prosecution of the female leader of the Christian commune for unduly influencing them to engage in the corporal punishment that led to the infant's death. The commune leader was sentenced to a longer prison term than the couple, who apparently averted loss of custody over their other children in return for their testimony.

Deprogramming Cases

The most sensational use of "brainwashing" claims involves cases in which a putatively brainwashed adherent has been physically abducted, forcibly constrained, and subjected to counterindoctrination.[21] In these cases, rather than NRM's being charged with brainwashing (i.e., psychological programming), the effort has been to establish a presumption of, or standard for, demonstrating brainwashing so that "de-programming" is legitimated either through legal or extra-legal means. Although the term "deprogramming" has been broadened by advocates to include voluntary information-giving or "exit counseling," the deprogramming controversy emerged in the 1970s over two involuntary modes: simple abductions without prior legal authorization (but legally defended after the fact through a defense of necessity), and authorized actions transpiring under state law, usually in the form of a temporary guardianship or conservatorship orders granted by courts (often in ex parte hearings) to relatives of adherents.

After a relatively brief history, deprogramming under the aegis of guardianship or conservatorship orders rapidly disappeared. One of the most significant cases in creating this impetus was *Katz v. Superior Court*.[22] In that case, a California superior court judge initially awarded five sets of parents thirty-day custody over their adult offspring, who were affiliated with the Unification Church, for purposes of conducting deprogramming. The judge specifically declined to enjoin deprogramming during the conservatorship but did require that the parents be present at all times during the process. An appeal by the five Unificationists resulted in a ruling by an appellate court forbidding the parents from engaging in deprogramming activity prior to a review of the constitutionality of the conservatorship laws. A few weeks later, a court order was issued dismissing the temporary conservatorships and releasing the five individuals from custody. The court ruled that "in the absence of such actions as render the adult believer gravely disabled . . . the process of this state cannot be used to deprive the believer of his freedom of action and to subject him to involuntary treatment."[23] The court suggested that when it was asked to determine whether a change of religious attitude "was induced by faith or by coercive persuasion, [was] it not investigating and questioning the validity of that faith?"[24]

Although only a binding precedent in California, this case appears to have discouraged the use of conventional guardianship and conservatorship statutes to legalize the involuntary deprogramming of devotees who could not be deemed "gravely disabled." In the early 1980s, bills were introduced in numerous state legislatures aimed at circumventing the *Katz* precedent. The objective of these bills was the amendment of state probate codes to provide for temporary custody orders which could be obtained by parents who could show that their adult children had been subjected to systematic coercive persuasion and deception and that they also had suffered harm. The watershed for such legislation came in New York where a guardianship bill was passed in two successive terms by both houses of the New York legislature but vetoed each time by Governor Hugh Carey. Similar bills introduced elsewhere attracted little support following the defeats in New York.

Professor Richard Delgado has most systematically developed the basic rationale for a qualified legalization of deprogramming and, more generally, for an activist regulatory posture on the part of the state toward the high-pressure and "coercive" proselytization and indoctrination tactics of "cults."[25]

In Delgado's view, state intervention is justified if harm (including psychological harm) is inflicted on a devotee by participation in a cult and if the process of joining a harmful movement does not meet criteria of informed consent. Delgado argues that the posited components of informed consent, knowledge and capacity, are manipulated by cults in such a manner that a pre-convert cannot simultaneously experience both attributes. That is, recruits are initially deceived as to the identity and practices of the group; later when the veil of deception drops, they have allegedly lost the capacity to evaluate rationally their continued participation. Delgado further argues that the inconvenience which involuntary treatment (deprogramming) visits upon a possibly voluntary adult adherent is outweighed by the greater risk of withholding such treatment from a psychologically imprisoned devotee who is trapped indefinitely in an encapsulating extremist group.[26] In a later article on deprogramming, Delgado made explicit what was implicit in his earlier work, that only the truly "free" (as formulated in his argument) exercise of religion (and not coercive cultism) is constitutionally protected.[27]

The inability of deprogramming proponents to translate this position into statutory provisions resulted in the virtual elimination of such court-authorized deprogrammings following *Katz*. However, extra-legal abductions continue to occur, even if in much smaller numbers than during the 1970s.[28] When charges are brought against deprogrammers, an exculpatory outcome is more likely if a defense of necessity or justification is permitted by the trial judge. A variant of the defense of necessity is the balancing choice-of-evil rule whereby a jury may acquit defendants if it feels that the evil or harm avoided through the forcible "rescue" of a convert outweighs the evil of the abduction and the attendant violation of the subject's rights.[29]

The choice-of-evil/necessity defense is usually grounded in allegations of cultic brainwashing and tends to entail substantial testimony about the beliefs and practices of a group in question. In one recent case, jurors acquitted deprogrammers of second-degree kidnapping who had abducted a twenty-nine-year-old Swedish member of the Unification Church.[30] The Colorado

Supreme Court eventually ruled in 1990 that the defendants had been allowed too much latitude in presenting evidence concerning the indoctrinative and recruitment methods of the church. Such evidence was not deemed sufficiently pertinent to the nature and severity of the deprogrammee's allegedly consequent disability.[31] The court further stipulated that the jury had wrongly been invited to consider "the morality and desirability of church doctrine and practices rather than whether in fact the victim was threatened by the prospect of a grave, imminent injury."[32]

A defense of necessity sometimes has been supplemented, particularly in civil actions against deprogrammers, by a defense of consent, which alleges that the abductees did not consistently object to the forceful actions of parents or deprogrammers or that they would not have objected had not the abductee's judgment been impaired by cultic mind control. The most influential successful application of the defense of consent to deprogramming has been *Peterson v. Sorlien*.[33] In that case, the parents of a twenty-one-year-old member of The Way International arranged for her deprogramming; the daughter was held for a total of sixteen days. Her participation in the deprogramming clearly was involuntary for the first three days and less decisive for the remainder of the period. Following a telephone conversation with her boyfriend, who also was a member of The Way, she returned to the group and ultimately brought suit against the deprogrammer for false imprisonment.

A two-to-one Minnesota Supreme Court decision held that a civil action for false imprisonment of a convert cannot be sustained if parents or their agents are convinced that the judgment of an adult child is impaired and if at some point the child consents to actions intended to extricate the person from what the intervenors reasonably believe is a dangerous "cult."[34] Since the consent which invalidates a suit for false imprisonment need not be manifested at the outset of the abduction or the deprogramming process, presumably the plaintiff must be able to show consistent and continuous resistance to support a false imprisonment claim.

A different result emerged in *Eilers v. Coy*. In that case, William Eilers, a member of a small evangelical sect, the Disciples of the Lord Jesus Christ, was abducted and physically restrained during a five-day deprogramming that ended with his escape. Eilers brought suit against his parents and wife, who had engineered the deprogramming, as well as against the deprogrammers.[35] The federal district judge, who directed a verdict for the plaintiff on the issue of false imprisonment, declared that apparent temporary consent is not a sufficient defense against a claim of false imprisonment. According to the judge, "The defendants had to establish three points to justify the abduction of the plaintiff: (1) that there was imminent physical danger to Eilers or others; (2) that Eilers was confined only long enough to get him to the proper authorities; and (3) that the 'least restrictive means' available were employed to restrain Eilers."[36] The judge concluded that a defense of necessity is not allowable unless the defendants, having physically seized a putatively troubled individual, immediately turn him or her over to proper authorities.

Partly in response to defeats such as *Peterson* and earlier setbacks, a coalition of opponents of deprogramming mobilized in the late 1970s and early 1980s to formulate a legal remedy for coercive deprogramming that would avoid reliance upon state courts and false imprisonment tort claims through a broad interpretation of sections of the Ku Klux Klan Act [now 42 U.S.C section 1985(3)]. Proponents argued that this act should be construed as protecting the civil rights of members of religious and racial minorities from private conspiracies, as well as conspiracies transpiring under the color of state law. To sanction coercive deprogramming (or "faith-breaking" as some critics refer to it) is arguably to actively persecute and discriminate against minority faiths. From this perspective, the federal government has an affirmative duty to mandate compensation for harms arising from such invidious discrimination, whether or not state and local authorities have been directly involved.[37]

Civil suits over alleged conspiracies to deprive plaintiffs of their civil rights have produced mixed results at the appellate level. One case favorable to the plaintiff, *Ward v. Connor*, involved a 1981 suit by an unsuccessfully deprogrammed member of the Unification Church. In that case, Thomas Ward, a member of the Unification Church, was physically restrained and deprogrammed over a thirty-five-day period. The federal district court in Virginia dismissed the section 1985(3) portion of his suit, asserting that "members of the Unification Church did not qualify as a class, that the defendants' benevolent concern negated the requisite discriminatory animus, and that alleged deprivation of the right to travel was secondary to claimed interference with Ward's First Amendment rights of freedom of religion and association."[38] Charges against the deprogrammers were reduced to wrongful taking of private property. The United States Court of Appeals for the Fourth Circuit reversed the lower court decision, ruling that civil rights laws passed to protect racial minorities might also be applied to religious minorities. The court stated that "religious discrimination, being akin to the invidious racial bias, falls within the ambit of section 1985(3)" and that "the plaintiff and other members of the Unification Church constitute a class" protected by the civil rights law. However, the U.S. Supreme Court has avoided reviewing (sometimes contradictory) circuit court opinions in this area.[39] It is conceivable that an increasingly conservative high court, which tends toward restrictive interpretations of civil rights, will limit the applicability of the Klan Act to conspiracies against racial minorities and/or conspiracies involving state action.[40]

It is not clear whether there will be a definitive legal resolution of deprogramming. Court-sponsored deprogramming drastically declined in the wake of *Katz*, but coercive abductions have continued. During the mid-1970s there was a virtual epidemic of coercive deprogrammings,[41] and law enforcement agencies often were extremely permissive in their response to coercive deprogramming. The FBI declined to become involved in abductions from marginal spiritual groups even when deprogrammees were transported across state or international boundaries.[42] Local police officials sometimes assisted deprogrammers or declined to intervene on behalf of adult deprogrammees even when the individuals asserted that they were being forcibly detained. Within a few years, however, police officials came under increasing pressure to interrupt deprogramming activities even though the FBI continued to resist involvement.[43] Some local prosecutors also began filing criminal charges against deprogrammers, and some deprogrammees brought civil charges against their deprogrammers. Even though outcomes were quite mixed, the mere potential of civil and criminal actions and the costs of mounting a legal defense dramatically raised the stakes on coercive deprogramming.

Further, it was during the early to mid-1970s that many of the new religious movements at the heart of the cult controversy experienced their highest rates of membership growth. As a result, there was a large pool of candidates for deprogramming. Just a few years later these same movements were confronted with low recruitment rates and high defection rates, making deprogramming a less important option for resolving family conflicts.

Finally, the anti-cult movement (ACM) began to retreat from espousing coercive deprogramming. Professional therapists, who became an increasingly powerful component of the ACM, were unwilling to accept abducted individuals as clients, and deprogrammers discovered that voluntary forms of deprogramming were as effective as coercion in many cases. Still, coercive deprogramming persists, and it is not easy for deprogrammees to obtain remedy in civil or criminal courts. As juries tend to sympathize with troubled families who have "lost" a member to a "cult" and there is reluctance to interfere in "family matters," the prospects of prosecutions and civil actions against deprogrammers and relatives who have employed them remain indeterminate.

Ex-member Civil Suits

Ex-member suits are linked to the anti-cult movement in the sense that the plaintiffs are generally deprogrammed former adherents who have become involved in counseling services and support groups that are part of an anti-cult organizational network. They generally involve causes of action such as false imprisonment, fraud, intentional infliction of emotional distress, and, occasionally, interference with the custody of a minor. Ex-member civil suits are potentially devastating mechanisms of social control because plaintiffs generally seek punitive damages. Juries have granted awards exceeding $30 million. Awards as high as $3 million have survived appeals, and interest accrued during the appeals process can elevate the ultimate liability above $5 million.[44] The survival of religious groups against which these verdicts are registered is placed in jeopardy.

Whatever the formal causes of action, such suits generally depend upon allegations of intense psychological coercion (claims regarding physical coercion are rare) supported by testimony from reputed "experts" in brainwashing or coercive persuasion."[45] The basic rationale for ex-member suits that incorporate claims of psychological coercion is found in Delgado's model, which asserts that involvement is basically non-consensual because participation involves a manipulative sequencing of deception and incapacitating mind control such that either knowledge or capacity is absent at each stage of conversion.[46]

In practice, in these cases the plaintiff's counsel has attempted to demonstrate the implausibility or the emotionally deleteriousness of the defendant movement's beliefs.[47] As Douglas Laycock asserts, "The trials of these cases are generally characterized by attempts to incite the jury to fear and hatred of a strange faith."[48] The role of prejudice may be magnified by the intrinsic subjectivity of "coercion" claims which are not based on tangible physical action or threat but on the inferring of harms from verbal communications often expressive of religious belief.[49] As Laycock comments: "From beginning to end these cases consist of subjective and intangible elements . . . it is difficult to separate the actionable wrongdoing, where there is any, from protected free exercise. These cases provide maximum opportunity for juries to act on their prejudices and minimum opportunity for judges to control juries."[50] An example is found in a very recent case, *Murphy v. ISKCON* (1991).[51] In that case, Susan Murphy, then legally a minor, became involved with Hare

Krishna. She and her mother subsequently brought suit against
ISKCON for intentional infliction of emotional distress and
interference with the custody of a minor. During the trial the
judge allowed large amounts of testimony describing Hare
Krishna beliefs. The Massachusetts Supreme Court overturned
that part of the award charged to emotional distress while
allowing a smaller component of damages relating to
interference with the custody of a minor. The court held that the
claim of intentional infliction of emotional distress could not
stand in the case in the absence of copious testimony concerning
the group's religious beliefs. The defendants, the court opined,
had been placed in the position of having to defend their
unpopular beliefs in court. The court concluded that "the essence
of what occurred in the trial is that the plaintiffs were allowed to
suggest to the jury extensively that the exposure to the
defendant's religious beliefs was sufficient to cause tortious
emotional damage and to separate Susan from her mother."[52]
The judgments were vacated and the case was remanded for
retrial.

It is precisely this line of reasoning that makes the recent
Molko and Leal v. Holy Spirit Association case so potentially
significant.[53] This suit was brought by two former members of
the Unification Church in California, David Molko and Tracy
Leal. Molko was approached by Unificationist street recruiters in
January 1979 shortly after he had graduated from law school.
Molko agreed to attend several church workshops and asserted
that he did not learn of their connection to the Church for twelve
days, although he consented to remain after learning of the
relationship. About a month later he decided to join the Church.
His legal training was of interest to the Church, which paid for
his preparation to take the California Bar examination. Shortly
thereafter, Molko was forcibly abducted and deprogrammed
over a three-day period by deprogrammers retained by his
parents. Leal was approached by street recruiters as a nineteen-
year-old college student. Like Molko, Leal asserted that she did
not learn of the connection between the group of individuals
who recruited her and the Unification Church for twenty-two
days; by this time, she asserted, she was incapable of making an

informed decision about affiliation with the Church. Leal also was affiliated with the Church for a period of several months and was subsequently deprogrammed. Molko and Leal brought charges of fraud (based on allegations of deception as to the group's identity during the recruitment process), intentional infliction of emotional distress (through use of coercive persuasion techniques), and false imprisonment.

In *Molko*, after several levels of litigation[54] the California Supreme Court by a six-to-one decision in 1988 reinstated the suits for infliction of emotional distress and fraud while upholding lower courts' dismissals of the tort claim of false imprisonment. The vindicated causes of action partly depended upon claims of brainwashing. In an opinion clearly influenced by Richard Delgado and by the Minnesota Supreme Court's opinion in *Peterson v. Sorlien*, the majority discussed brainwashing theories and, while acknowledging an absence of consensus, seemed disposed to allow a jury to resolve the basic issues. Prior to *Molko*, the courts generally were reluctant to accept novel concepts such as brainwashing or to equate psychological and social pressure with tangible physical duress. So, for example, in *Meroni v. Holy Spirit Association* (1986), a New York appellate court affirmed the dismissal of the claim on behalf of a deceased (suicide) ex-member's estate that psychological injury had been caused by mind control.[55] The court ruled that in order to support a tort claim based on mind control theory, a plaintiff must present evidence either of false imprisonment or of having been subjected to violence.

The question thus becomes how much latitude the California Supreme Court is granting through its decision in *Molko*. According to one extensive analysis,[56] the California high court created a narrow exception to received extrapolations of the First Amendment which had implied that processes of religious conversion were not justiciable. It appears that absent the boundary condition of extreme deception in the form of initial concealment of the identity of the group, religious speech acts putatively constituting "coercive persuasion" would enjoy First Amendment protection, but the presence of blatant deception opens the door to causes of action which may be supported by arguments alleging mind control. The crucial issue may turn out to be whether the legally empowering condition of blatant deception, which renders triable tort claims depending upon psychological coercion, can be generalized beyond concealment of group identity (e.g., to the failure to warn participants of the possible pathological consequences of rituals such as repetitive chanting, meditation, etc.). This line of reasoning, which would greatly extend indirect state regulation of religious movements, was not accepted by a California appellate court in *George v. ISKCON*, in which the Court narrowly interpreted *Molko* and reduced the trial court award, although the court's opinion was decertified by the state supreme court.[57]

The battleground seems to have shifted in ex-member suits very recently from constitutional issues to procedural decisions regarding the admissibility of "expert" testimony on psychological coercion and brainwashing under the *Frye* standard and equivalent state rules.[58] Courts have considered the admissibility of expert testimony in several recent cases including both ex-member civil suits and criminal prosecutions in which the defendant's prior experience of disorienting processes in a nonconventional religious or therapeutic group has been advanced as a factor mitigating criminal responsibility. For example, in a criminal prosecution of an ex-Scientologist, proffered expert testimony was rejected by a district judge as not being "generally accepted" in the scientific community.[59] In a civil suit against Transcendental Meditation, a federal judge declined to apply the *Frye* standard of "general acceptability" but ruled expert testimony inadmissible under the more permissive standard of "sufficient acceptability."[60]

Regulating Proselytization Activity

Disclosure legislation has been advocated to disrupt sequences of deception/mind control in "high demand sects." Proponents have argued that such legislation "would represent a valid secular regulation of the 'manner of recruitment' to protect the public from fraud."[61] Such bills are presented as consumer protection legislation that would obligate the state to prosecute deceptive and psychologically destructive practices through which incompetent or unscrupulous gurus and healers allegedly beguile and harm their followers. In a free-market, consumption-based economy, the state enhances its legitimacy through consumer protection, which is depicted as neutral regulation of free but fair markets.[62]

One particular statute, apparently aimed at regulating the Church of Scientology, was narrowly defeated by the Nevada legislature in the mid-1980s. In its original version the bill was primarily directed at providing that members or former members of a "cult" could bring a civil action against the cult for offering or promising psychological benefits to individuals for a fee unless a licensed psychologist or psychiatrist was present. A later version dropped the term "cult" but retained the same objective. Amid intense lobbying, the bill passed the Senate but was defeated in the Assembly, primarily as a result of Mormon influence.[63]

FINANCIAL AND COMMERCIAL PRACTICES ("MONEY")

Litigation and regulatory issues concerning the economic and financial practices of sectarian religious movements constitute the second category of social control initiatives. As James Beckford notes in his book, *Cult Controversies*, religious groups that are regarded as defenders of the culture and whose practices and doctrines are compatible with utilitarian individualist ideology have customarily been granted privileges and regulatory exemptions. Therefore, sectarian religious movements' conflicts with public authority have tended "to widen out into more general conflicts centering on the definition of 'authentic' religion." One of the primary issues has been economic organization and practices— for example, how funds are raised, how money is used, and what constitutes a religious purpose with respect to monetary practices. In the course of these conflicts, "Courts of law, administrative tribunals and individual law enforcement agents . . . find themselves obligated to decide what is to count as 'religion' for legal purposes."[64]

There are various possible explanations for conflicts over finances. Alternative religions tend, at least initially, to have small congregations and may have difficulty financing their operations largely by donations from members. They are thus frequently led to seek funding from the general public, either through direct solicitation or through commercialization in terms of the sale of goods and services. However, a financial outreach to the general public is significantly more legally precarious than internal donative funding, and arguably entails diminished accountability relative to internal funding. Moreover, commercial financing enhances the probability of "goal displacement" whereby profitability becomes an end-in-itself.[65] The disproportionately charismatic leadership of new movements also has clear implications for both the greater volatility and lesser financial accountability of "cults" compared to older churches, as does the tendency toward youthful leadership and membership and the intense emotional fervor which characterizes many younger movements.[66]

Of all the governmental agencies, none has been more influential with respect to financial practices than the Internal Revenue Service. Indeed, the IRS plays a crucial role in the very survival prospects and adaptive evolution of new religious movements. "IRS regulations and rules concerning the 'proper' use of money, types of activities that might be conducted (particularly the exclusion of political action), and the types of property that can be tax exempt, have all engendered controver-sy."[67] Dramatic changes in some groups' organizational and even doctrinal patterns have transpired as a movement's attempt to maintain its tax status in the face of shifting tax policies and official interpretations. As one social scientist observed: "It is clear that the IRS is a major instrument of social control of new religions and that IRS regulations dictate not only substantive considerations, but also the 'rules of the game' whereby substantive rules are applied."[68] Sociologist Rodney Stark put it even more bluntly:

American tax laws induce religious movements to become formally organized at a very early date and this may make them visible sooner than is true of similar groups in Europe. As a result, the primary regulators of our religious economy are state and federal tax collectors. This situation is reflected in the fact that the founders and leaders [of NRMs] appear to be the single highest risk group in terms of tax violations. Unwittingly perhaps the IRS serves as a functional equivalent of the Holy Inquisition in the officially unregulated religious economy of the United States.[69]

The IRS is hardly alone in developing initiatives to regulate financial practices of new religious groups. A variety of state and federal agencies also have been involved in such regulation. Perhaps the two most significant types of regulation involve the granting/withholding of tax-exempt status and control of the various processes by which funds are raised and used.

Tax Exemption

One of the most critical areas of conflict involving new religious groups' finances is what is to be regarded as tax exempt on religious grounds. In this regard it is worth noting the difficulty communally organized religious groups face in gaining exemptions. The IRS appears to grant more or less automatic exemptions to organizations associated with familiar institutions (e.g., Catholic monastic orders) but to deny them to exotic or esoteric communitarian groups. As Meade Emory and Lawrence Zelenak note: "In denying exempt status to communitarian religious organizations, the service has made two basic arguments: that such organizations are not organized and operated exclusively for exempt purposes because furnishing the necessities of life to their members is a significant non-exempt purpose, and that the net earnings of such organizations inure to the private benefit of their members, through the members' receipt of food and shelter."[70] The resistance to granting tax-exempt status to communitarian groups is unusually significant for sectarian movements because, as noted earlier, they are particularly likely to organize communally in order to strengthen their internal solidarity and distance themselves from the influences of the larger society.[71]

One important case in a related area is the 1989 U.S. Supreme Court decision in *Hernandez v. Commissioner of Internal Revenue*.[72] The Court was asked to determine whether fees from the therapeutic process of "auditing" transpiring under the auspices of the Church of Scientology were tax deductible. In deciding that they were not, the Court ruled that the fees have "a quid pro quo character [and] are of a commercial nature."[73] As one analysis of the decision observed:

Based on its doctrine of exchange, "fixed contributions" are set forth in schedules and the prices charged vary according to the sessions' length and sophistication. The CoS [Church of Scientology] rewards advance payments with a 5% discount and refunds unused portions of prepaid services with the deduction of an administrative charge. CoS also distributes "account cards" on which those who prepaid can determine which services have not been claimed yet. The Court also noted that auditing and training sessions may never be offered free, because "processing is too expensive to deliver."[74]

The *Hernandez* decision indicates the legal risks of commercial and educational diversification as an alternative to lay donations as a means of organizational funding. Auditing was treated by the Court as a professional service provided to clients on a fee-for-service basis rather than a religious activity. Again, it is much more likely that new religious groups will develop innovative means of financing that are consistent with emerging forms of religious expression. To the extent that new religious movements are regarded as illegitimate, it is unlikely that such practices will be viewed as having a religious purpose.

Tax-exemption cases have not always involved federal agencies. For example, The Way International was assessed $156,000 for purchases it made between 1974 and 1976. An appeal to the Board of Tax Appeals led to a ruling that The Way is not a church and hence fails to qualify for religious exemption. This ruling was reversed on appeal to the Ohio Supreme Court which found that sales of books and tapes to adherents was a means to advance its religion and not a business enterprise.[75]

Regulating the Process by Which
Funds Are Raised and Used[76]

One of the most significant examples of regulation of the process of financing new religions is the 1982 *Larsen v. Valente* case. That case involved a suit brought by the Unification Church to challenge an amended Minnesota statute. The state amended its charitable solicitation law so as to impose an obligation on religious organizations which obtained less than half of their financing from membership donations or parent or affiliate organizations to file a comprehensive financial report. It seemed clear that the intent of the statute was to write legislation that would not impact established denominations. The Supreme Court, in a five-to-four decision written by Justice William J. Brennan, upheld the decision of the circuit court that differential treatment contravened the Establishment Clause of the First Amendment.[77]

The most conspicuous recent case involving the use of church funds is the successful prosecution of Sun Myung Moon for criminal income tax evasion in the early 1980s. For several years in the mid-1970s Reverend Moon deposited funds in a Chase Manhattan Bank account in his own name. The account earned one hundred and twelve thousand dollars interest over a three year period which Moon did not report on his income tax return. The defense contended that Moon was holding the money in trust for the church, and that it therefore was not taxable. The government denied the relevance of Moon's role as founder of a church in the case and referred to him as "an ordinary high-ranking businessman." From the prosecution's perspective, the matter was a simple case of white-collar crime. It objected when the defense attempted to introduce evidence that Moon was acting as a trustee of a religious body. Whatever the merits of the charges against Moon, the case clearly involved governmental specification of the financial structure of tax-exempt religious entities.[78]

Internal use of church funds (involving allegations of financial mismanagement and corruption) also was central in the attorney general of California's action placing the controversial

Worldwide Church of God in temporary receivership in 1979.[79]
The church was nearly five decades old at the time of the legal
action and at the time still led by its founding prophet, Herbert
Armstrong. The attorney general launched an investigation of
the church following complaints from dissident members of
financial improprieties, and appointed a receiver to prevent
destruction of church records during the investigation. The
receivership lasted for three months until church members were
able to post a $2 million bond. The attorney general's action was
predicated on the theory that churches are charitable
organizations and therefore subject to the law of charitable
trusts. According to this theory, there are no "private interests"
involved, and due process is therefore unnecessary. That is, the
state should view churches as embodying "public trusts," which
means that they should be accorded less legal protection against
regulatory intrusion than a secular private business. Had the
attorney general viewed churches from the perspective of
"corporate free exercise," whereby a church is the collective
embodiment of the consciences of its members, then churches
would enjoy a protection closer to that of an individual believer.

Considerable litigation has involved the right of exotic "cults"
or aggressive evangelical groups to solicit funds and proselytize
in public settings such as parks, state fairs, airports, malls,
stadiums, etc. One recent case reached the U.S. Supreme Court,
Heffron v. ISKCON (1981), but it is actually of rather limited
generality.[80] The Court upheld, as a legitimate restraint on the
time, place, and manner, a "booth restriction" at the Minnesota
State Fair whereby Hare Krishna devotees could only solicit
funds or distribute free literature from specified booths assigned
to activist groups on a first come-first served basis.

Numerous other cases have involved airports and other
transportation centers. Extremely broad laws have been struck
down,[81] but no decisive trend has emerged. Cases involving
privately owned shopping malls are particularly important to
new religious groups because urban ecological trends are
leading to the decay of central urban marketing and recreation
areas and their replacement by outlying (and often privately
owned and enclosed) malls, whose owners have viewed

solicitation and politico-religious proselytization with a jaundiced eye. The Supreme Court has granted the state a regulatory option here and state supreme courts have produced inconsistent outcomes in response to suits by political, religious, and environmentalist groups alleging unconstitutional restraints on freedom of speech. Arguably the interaction of urban ecological trends and judicial indulgence of private regulation is creating a climate in which it will be difficult for faith and issue-oriented minorities who lack access to major media to disseminate their "message."[82]

A recent case in this area, *ISKCON v. Lee*, is potentially significant. In the spring of 1991 a federal appeals court reversed a lower court's ruling and reinstated a ban on solicitation by religious groups in airports, although free literature may be distributed. The U.S. Supreme Court recently reviewed the case and in a six-to-three vote upheld the appellate court's ruling that airport officials may prohibit public solicitation of funds. However, in the same ruling the court rejected the airport's ban on literature distribution.[83]

CONCLUSION

The establishment and free exercise provisions of the Constitution set the basic parameters for the social control of religiosity, and historically there clearly has been an ebb and flow of legislative and judicial control initiatives around those parameters. The recent past may have been a period of exceptional religious libertarianism, and there are some indications that there will be a retreat from this position. Should a pronounced, extended trend of this type develop, as some recent court cases suggest, the results would be particularly consequential for new and nonconventional groups in a high state of tension with the larger society.

The cult controversy of the 1970s and 1980s witnessed a continuous series of initiatives to expand social control over new religious groups. Recruitment/socialization and financial practices have been two of the primary arenas of exogenous control initiatives. These have included initiatives to expand the grounds on which claims can be brought against groups (e.g., conservatorship laws and ex-member suits based on assertions of coercive persuasion), contraction of the grounds on which claims can be resisted (e.g., cases in which religious beliefs are put on trial rather than constituting a barrier to judicial inquiry or narrowing of the definition of religious purpose in tax-exemption decisions), expansion of enforcement of rule violations by groups (e.g., prosecution of the Moon tax case and the Worldwide Church of God receivership case), and contraction of enforcement of rule violations committed against groups (e.g., direct or indirect sanctioning of coercive deprogramming).

It is difficult to assess the overall impact of these various initiatives. Some groups have reacted to conflicts with the larger society by becoming more radical and separatist, others by becoming more accommodationist. Some groups have changed their organizational style to reflect the contemporary expectations for legitimacy, thus altering to some degree the form in which religiosity is expressed. Certainly the most significant trend cutting across all of the control initiatives discussed here is the reshaping of religion in individual-contractual rather than collective-covenantal forms.[84] Treating religion as a commodity subject to consumer protection provisions, subjecting conversion experiences to informed consent standards, economically disadvantaging communal organization in which collective good supercedes individual good, and extending bureaucratic and accounting-principle logic to religious communities would have a long-term impact on the form that religion assumes. Mainline churches already have largely assumed that form, and the impact of such measures on new religions may substantially influence the shape of religion in the future.

NOTES

1. Frank Way and Barbara J. Burt, "Religious Marginality and the Free Exercise Clause," *American Political Science Review* 77 (1983): 652-65.
2. Leo Pfeffer, "The Legitimation of Marginal Religions in the United States," in *Religious Movements in Contemporary America*, ed. Irving Zaretsky and Marc Leone (Princeton: Princeton University Press, 1974). More generally this finding contravenes the sociological church-sect literature.
3. See Way and Burt, "Religious Marginality and the Free Exercise Clause," 661.
4. Douglas Laycock, "The Remnants of Free Exercise," *Supreme Court Review 1990*. Reprinted for private circulation by the University of Chicago, 1991.
5. *Reynolds v. United States*, 98 U.S. 145 (1878).
6. Professor Angela Carmella argues that the severe mitigation of the compelling state interest standard by Justice Scalia and the majority in *Smith* was facilitated by the tendency in recent decades for free exercise litigation to be employed primarily as a civil libertarian device pertaining almost exclusively to the rights of marginal groups with deviant behavioral patterns. The constituency for free exercise protection was thereby weakened. See Angela Carmella, "A Theological Critique of Free Exercise Jurisprudence," *The George Washington Law Review* 60 (March 1992): 782.
7. Another case that has the potential for signalling the direction of Supreme Court decisions is *Church of the Lulumi Babalu Aye v. City of Hialeah*. The City of Hialeah passed a series or ordinances designed to prohibit animal sacrifice for religious purposes that targeted Santeria ritual practices. The ordinances were specifically written to exclude commercial slaughterhouses, exterminators, etc. For a discussion of the implications see Rob Boston, "Blood Feud," *Church and State* May 1992): 7-11.
8. James E. Wood, Jr., "New Religions and the First Amendment," in *Religion and the State*, ed. James E. Wood, Jr. (Waco, Tex.: Baylor University Press, 1985), 185-210. For additional general treatments of legal conflicts involving new religious movements, see Jeffrey Pfeifer and James Ogloff, eds., *New Religious Movements and the Law*, a special issue of *Behavioral Sciences and the Law* 10 (1992); Thomas Robbins, William Shepherd and James McBride, eds., *Cults, Culture and the Law* (Chico, Cal.: Scholars Press, 1985); Thomas Robbins and James Beckford, "Religious Movements and Church-State Issues," in *Handbook of Cults and Sects in America*, ed. David G. Bromley and Jeffrey K. Hadden (Greenwich, Ct.: Association for the Sociology of Religion, Society for the Scientific Study of Religion, and JAI Press, 1993).

9. Nicholas J. Demerath, III and Rhys H. Williams, "A Mythical Past and an Uncertain Future," in *Church-State Relations,* ed. Thomas Robbins and Roland Robertson (New Brunswick, N.J.: Transaction, 1987), 81.

10. See Laycock, "The Remnants of Free Exercise," 65.

11. See Demerath and Williams, "A Mythical Past and an Uncertain Future," 81.

12. Roy Wallis, "Paradoxes of Freedom and Regulation: The Case of New Religious Movements in Britain and America," *Sociological Analysis* 48 (1988): 355-71. According to Wallis, in Britain various controls operate quickly to limit the expansion of religious movements. Such movements may quietly and modestly persist. A more libertarian climate in the U.S., particularly in the 1970s and early 1980s, facilitated the rapid expansion of new movement membership as well as their development of commercial and financial "empires," whose size and visibility as well as associated abuses elicited intense hostility, counter-movement ("anti-cult") mobilization and a more belated but devastating state reaction that imperiled the movements' survival. The rise and fall of Rajneeshpuram in Oregon and the legal conflicts involving the Bhagwan movement of Bhagwan Rajneesh fits Wallis' model. See Lewis Carter, *Charisma and Control in Rajneeshpuram* (Cambridge: Cambridge University Press, 1990).

13. For a discussion of these characteristics, see David Bromley and Anson Shupe, "Organized Opposition to New Religious Movements," in *Handbook of Cults and Sects in America,* ed. David G. Bromley and Jeffrey K. Hadden (Greenwich, Ct.: Association for the Sociology of Religion and JAI Press, 1993).

14. The concepts of settled and unsettled times are borrowed from Ann Swidler, "Culture in Action: Symbols and Strategies," *American Sociological Review* 51 (1986): 273-86.

15. *United States v. Ballard,* 322 U.S. 78 (1944).

16. Many of the cases considered in this chapter are complex and involve both "poison" and "money;" they are categorized here in terms of their primary significance for the argument being developed.

17. *Molko and Leal v. Holy Spirit Association,* 46 Cal. 3d 1092, 252 Cal. Rptr. 122 (1988), cert. denied 109 S.Ct 2110 (1989).

18. Although we focus on proselytization issues in this chapter, clearly there are a number of other "poison" issues as well. Child care and the evaluation of modern medicine are two salient and interrelated points of tension in this connection. These realms become legal minefields for doctrinally distinctive sectarian groups, which become entangled in litigation and criminal prosecution. Faith healing cases tend to involve prosecution of parents (and sometimes their spiritual advisors) for medical

neglect leading to the death of a child. Other kinds of legal actions involve attempts to impose blood transfusions or vaccinations via temporary guardianships or conservatorships granted to the state over children whose parents' religious scruples prohibit such procedures. Recent cases have involved not only marginal or fringe groups such as the Faith Assembly or the Faith Tabernacle but relatively sedate and reputable groups such as the Christian Science Church.

Litigation also has been elicited by the practice of corporal punishment, which is often judged by fundamentalist Christians to be biblically sanctioned. Some communal groups systematically administer such punishment, while other groups counsel parents to employ physical chastisement. Criminal prosecution has arisen when corporal punishment appears to have resulted in the death or serious injury of a minor, although investigations of corporal punishment in groups have transpired in the absence of extreme consequences. Child custody litigation appears to be particularly associated with new and nonconventional spiritual movements. The novelty and unfamiliarity of many groups complicates their situations and deprives them of the legitimacy and legal insulation which is accorded to more familiar nonconformist and close-knit groups, such as the Amish. Religious discrimination in child custody cases may represent a pervasive and decentralized mode of regulation which is less visible than deprogrammings, ex-member suits and criminal prosecutions.

19.   *People v. Angus Murphy and ISKCON, Inc.*, 98 Misc. 2d 235, 413 N.Y. Supp. 2d 540 (1977).

20.   Cited in David Bromley, "The Hare Krishna and the Anti-cult Movement," in *Krishna Consciousness in the West*, ed. David G. Bromley and Larry Shinn (Lewisburg, Pa.: Bucknell University Press, 1989), 281.

21.   Thomas Robbins and Dick Anthony, "Deprogramming," in *The Westminster Dictionary of Christian Ethics*, ed. James F. Childress and John Macquarrie (Philadelphia: Westminster, 1987); Anson Shupe and David G. Bromley, *The New Vigilantes* (Beverly Hills, Calif.: Sage, 1980); David G. Bromley and James T. Richardson, eds., *The Brainwashing-Deprogramming Controversy* (New York: Edwin Mellen Press, 1983).

22.   *Katz v. Superior Court*, 73 Cal. App. 3d 952, 141 Cal. Rptr. 234, modified, 74 Cal. 3d 582 (1977). See also, John LeMoult, "Deprogramming Members of Religious Sects," *Fordham Law Review* 46 (1978): 599-634.

23.   *Katz v. Superior Court*, 73 Cal. App. 3d 952, 989, 141 Cal. Rptr. 234, 256 modified, 74 Cal. 3d 582 (1977).

24.   Ibid.

25. Richard Delgado, "Religious Totalism: Gentle and Ungentle Persuasion Under the First Amendment," *Soutern California Law Review* 51 (1977):1-99. For a critique of Delgado's approach, see Robert Shapiro, "Of Robots, Persons and the Protection of Religious Beliefs," *Southern California Law Review* 56 (1983): 1277-1318.

26. See Delgado, "Religious Totalism," 1-99.

27. Richard Delgado, "When Religious Exercise Is Not Free," *Vanderbilt Law Review* 37 (1984): 1071-1115.

28. For data on the trends in coercive deprogramming, see David Bromley, "Deprogramming as a Form of Exit from New Religious Movements," in *Falling from the Faith: The Causes and Consequences of Religious Apostasy*, ed. David G. Bromley (Newbury Park, Cal.: Sage Publications, 1988).

29. Kit Pierson, "Cults, Deprogrammers, and the Necessity Defense," *Michigan Law Review* 80 (1981): 271-311.

30. *People v. Brandyberry*, District Court, Denver Colo. 87 CR 2056 (1989).

31. XIV Brief Times Rptr. 1534 (Colo. App. 1990).

32. Ibid.

33. *Peterson v. Sorlien*, 299 N.W. 2d 123 (Minn. 1980), cert. denied, 450 U.S. 1031, 101 S.Ct. 1792, 68 L.Ed. 2d 277 (1981).

34. The majority in *Peterson* was clearly influenced by the work of Richard Delgado.

35. *Eilers v. Coy*, 582 F.Supp. 1093 (1984).

36. Thomas Robbins and James McBride, "Eilers v. Coy: A Major Precedent on Deprogramming?" in *Cults, Culture, and the Law*, ed. Thomas Robbins, William Shepherd and James McBride (Chico, Cal.: Scholars Press, 1985), 224-25. The judge allowed the jury to determine punitive and compensatory damages in the case, which were in the amount of $10,000 in compensatory damages and no punitive damages, based on a finding that the deprogrammers had not acted out of animosity toward his religious beliefs.

37. William C. Shepherd, *To Secure the Blessings of Liberty: American Constitutional Law and the New Religious Movements* (New York and Chico, Cal.: Crossroads Publishing Company and Scholars Press, 1985).

38. Ibid., 100.

39. Ibid.

40. Ibid.

41. See Bromley, "Deprogramming as a Mode of Exit from New Religious Movements," 185-204.

42. In one of the most celebrated cases, John Abelseth, a middle-aged member of the Unification Church, was abducted and transported across international and several state boundaries by deprogrammers.

43. An FBI publication did carry three unofficial articles which endorsed the anti-cult position.

44. In the *George* case (see fn. 57) the trial court awarded over $32 million (later reduced to just under $10 million by the trial judge). In the *Wollersheim* case the trial court award was $30 million. See *Wollersheim v. Church of Scientology*, 212 Cal. App. 3d 872, 260 Cal. Rptr. 331 (1989) vacated, 111 S.Ct. 1298 (1991). In both cases the appellate courts reduced awards to $2.5 and $3 million, respectively. Subsequently the *George* award was reduced to $475,000 ($700,000 with interest) by the appellate court. See "Krishna Damages Cut in George Case," *Cult Observer* 9 (1992): 4.

45. Sometimes esoteric concepts (though not necessarily expert testimony) are eschewed in favor of a more conventional label such as "undue influence." See Lawrence Levy, "Prosecuting an Ex-Cult Member's Undue Influence Suit," *The Cultic Studies Journal* 7 (1990): 15-25.

46. See Delgado, "Religious Totalism," 1-99; Richard Delgado, "Cults and Conversion: The Case for Informed Consent," *Georgia Law Review* 16 (1982): 533-64.

47. More generally, it is the cultic rituals (allegedly producing pathological dissociative states), the harsh general regimen, the strong group pressures, and/or elements of alleged deception, which are invoked in support of tort claims, such that the role of beliefs may appear less direct. However, evaluation of the effects of belief (or of rituals which strengthen belief) is arguably inseparable from evaluation of belief itself.

48. See Laycock, "The Remnants of Free Exercise," 45-46.

49. Although not an ex-member suit, the case of *Columbrito v. Kelly* nicely illustrates the tactic of putting group beliefs on trial. In that case, Anthony Columbrito, a member of the Unification Church, brought suit against his deprogrammer. The defense then subpoenaed Rev. Sun Myung Moon to testify in the case concerning, among other matters, conversations with Jesus and Buddha he reported as the impetus for his spiritual mission. Columbrito attempted to discontinue the suit, but the judge ordered testimony to continue before ultimately being overruled by the circuit court of appeals. Thomas Robbins concludes that the trial judge appeared "to have collaborated with the defense strategy of putting the Unification Church on trial." *Columbrito v. Kelly*, 764 F. 2d 122 (2d Cir. 1985). See Thomas Robbins, "'Uncivil Religions' and Religious Deprogramming," *Thought: A Review of Culture and Idea* LVI (1986): 283.

50. See Laycock, "The Remnants of Free Exercise," 65.

51. *Murphy v. ISKCON, Inc.*, 409 Mass. 842 (1991).

52. Ibid., 347.

53. For a detailed discussion of the politics of this case, see James Richardson, "Coercion in Court: Brainwashing Allegations and Religious Proselytizing," unpublished paper, Reno, Nev.: Department of Sociology, University of Nevada.

54. The San Francisco Superior Court issued a summary judgment for the Unification church. The decision was affirmed by a three judge panel of the California Appeal Court. The case was then appealed to the California Supreme Court. The U.S. Supreme Court declined to review the case.

55. *Meroni v. Holy Spirit Association*, 119 App. Div. 2d 200, 506 NYS 2d (1986).

56. Dick Anthony and Thomas Robbins, "Law, Social Science and the 'Brainwashing' Exception to the First Amendment," *Behavioral Sciences and the Law* 10 (1992): 5-30; Dick Anthony, "Religious Movements and Brainwashing Litigation," in *In Gods We Trust*, 2nd ed., Thomas Robbins and Dick Anthony, eds. (New Brunswick, N.J.: Transaction, 1990).

57. *George v. ISKCON, Inc.*, No.D007153 (Cal. App. 4th Dist, 1988), decert. vacated. 109 S.Ct. 1299. (1991).

58. *Frye v. United States*, 293 F (D.C. Circuit, 1923).

59. *U.S. v. Fishman*, 743 F.Supp. (N.D. Cal. 1990). For the key procedural ruling, see Memorandum Opinion of Judge Jensen in *U.S. v. Fishman* (1990), CR-88-01616-DLJ. No. Cal. A related issue involves the question of whether the encapsulation of a defendant in a close-knit or communal group such as a "gang" or "cult" can mitigate the terms of an extreme penalty. See Sandra B. McPherson, "Death Penalty Mitigation and Cult Membership: The Case of the Kirtland Killings," *Behavioral Sciences and the Law* 10 (1992): 65-74.

60. *Green and Ryan v. Maharishi Mahesh Yoga et al*, U.S.D.C. No.87-0015 and 0016 (1991). Additional cases in 1989-1991 in which federal district and circuit courts ruled testimony about psychological coercion inadmissable under the *Frye* standard are discussed in Anthony and Robbins, "Law and Social Science and the 'Brainwashing' Exception to the First Amendment." See also, James Richardson, "Cult/Brainwashing Cases and Freedom of Religion," *Journal of Church and State* 33 (Winter 1991): 55-74; James Richardson, "Coercion in the Courts: Brainwashing Allegations and Religious Proselytizing."

61. Charles Rozenzweig, "High Demand Sects: Disclosure Legislation and the Free Exercise Clause," *New England Law Review* 15 (1979): 128-59.

62. James Beckford, "The Role of the State and Government in the Management of Contemporary Religious Movements," paper presented to the Council on International Affairs, New York, 1986.

63. The bill was introduced as a result of a Senator's twenty-one-year-old daughter becoming involved in Scientology and spending $30,000 within two weeks for courses and loans to friends wanting to take courses. Her father subsequently arranged for her deprogramming. See James T. Richardson, "Consumer Protection and Deviant Religions," *Review of Religious Research* 28 (1986): 168-79.

64. James Beckford, *Cult Controversies* (London: Tavistock, 1985), 290.

65. James T. Richardson, ed., *Money and Power in New Religions* (Lewiston, N.Y.: Edwin Mellen, 1988).

66. Eileen Barker, *New Religious Movements* (London: Her Majesty's Publishers, 1990).

67. James T. Richardson, "The 'Deformation' of New Religions," in *Cults, Culture and the Law*, ed. Thomas Robbins, William Shepherd and James McBride (Chico, Cal.: Scholars Press, 1985).

68. Ibid.

69. Rodney Stark, "How New Religions Succeed," in *The Future of New Religions*, ed. David Bromley and Phillip Hammond (Macon, Ga.: Mercer University Press, 1987).

70. Meade Emory and Lawrence Zelenak, "The Tax-Exempt Status of Communitarian Religious Organizations: An Unnecessary Controversy?" in *Cults, Culture, and the Law: Perspectives on New Religious Movements*, ed. Thomas Robbins, William Shepherd, and James McBride (Chico, Cal.: Scholars Press, 1985), 179.

71. According to the Emory and Zelenak, more recent cases suggest that the IRS may be retreating somewhat from its former position.

72. *Hernandez v. Commissioner of Internal Revenue*, 109 S.Ct. 2136 (1989).

73. Nikos Passos and Manuel Escamilla Castillo, "Scientology and its 'Clear' Business," *Behavioral Sciences and the Law* 10 (1992): 103-16.

74. Ibid., 112.

75. For a summary of this case, see "'The Way' Declared Tax-Exempt," *The Cult Observer* (May/June 1990), 8.

76. Many of the cases classified here as involving solicitation also involve issues of free speech as well and are discussed in this section simply for heuristic purposes.

77. While the Unification Church's appeal was successful, the justices' written opinions contained significant reservations. Justice Byron R. White found differential treatment to be justified by the enhanced probability of fraud in church solicitations from non-members vis-à-vis in-house fundraising. And there were procedural dissents by Justices William H. Rehnquist and Sandra Day O'Connor which questioned the bona fides of the Unification Church and hence the necessity for the court to resolve the constitutional questions. See Richard Regan, "Regulating Cult Activities," *Thought* 61 (1986): 185-96 and James T. Richardson,

"Changing Times: Religion, Economics and the Law in America,"
Sociological Analysis 49 (1988): 14-15s.

78. There is also, of course, the question of selective prosecution. The
authorities seemed far more ready to prosecute Rev. Moon, an
extremely unpopular oriental leader of a very controversial
movement, for tax fraud than to proceed similarly against other
religious groups and leaders. Indeed, the amount of back taxes
claimed by the IRS was under $8,000. Clearly a number of other
religious groups were concerned about the implications of this
decision as over forty organizations filed amicus curiae briefs in
support of the Unification Church's position. Moon's conviction
was upheld, and the Supreme Court declined to review the case.
Moon subsequently served thirteen months (of an eighteen month
sentence) in a federal correctional facility.

79. Sharon Worthing, "The State Takes Over a Church," *The Annals of
the American Academy of Politics and Social Science* 446
(November 1979): 136-48.

80. *Heffron v. ISKCON, Inc.*, 452 U.S. 640 (1981).

81. *Airport Commissioners v. Jews for Jesus, Inc.*, 48 U.S. 569 (1987).

82. Educational institutions, particularly when public, have frequently
provided contexts for litigation and regulatory conflicts. Many
campus administrations are receiving complaints about high
pressure and manipulative proselytizing conducts by cults and
aggressive evangelical Christian groups. Currently debated issues
include whether proselytization is allowable in dormitories,
whether deceptive proselytizing is controllable, and how alleged
"mind controlling" practices by groups proselytizing on campuses
can be curbed. See, for example, Gregory Bliming, "The
Involvement of College Students in Totalist Groups: Courses,
Concerns, Legal Issues and Policy Considerations," *The Cultic
Studies Journal* 7 (1990): 26-40.

83. Dick Lehr, "High Court Allows Ban on Airport Solicitation," *Boston
Globe*, 27 June 1992, 8.

84. This principle is also illustrated in cases regarding religious
employment policies. For an argument that life in "cults" entails a
condition of involuntary servitude, see Richard Delgado,
"Religious Totalism as Slavery," *New York University Review of
Law and Social Change* 9 (1979-80): 51-68. In *Alamo Foundation v.
Donavan*, 470 U.S. 290 (1985) federal minimum wage law was
applied to a religious community in which devotees lived and
worked communally. On the tension between contractual and
covenantal norms in modern society and its bearing on the
regulation of religious groups, see David Bromley and Bruce
Busching, "Understanding the Structure of Contractual and
Covenantal Social Relations," *Sociological Analysis* 49 (Special
Presidential Issue, December 1988): 15s-32s.

A SELECTED BIBLIOGRAPHY

Abelman, Robert, and Steward M. Hoover, eds. *Television: Controversies and Conclusions.* Norwood, N.J.: Ablex Publishing, 1990.

Bau, Alfred. *The Ground Is Holy: Church Sanctuary and Central American Refugees.* Mahwah, N.J.: Press, 1985.

Bau, Ignatius. *This Ground Is Holy.* Mahwah, N.J.: Paulist Press, 1985.

Bellah, Robert N. *The Broken Covenant: American Civil Religion in the Time of Trial.* New York: Seabury Press, 1975.

Bromley, David G., ed. *Falling from the Faith: The Causes and Consequences of Religious Apostasy.* Newbury Park, Calif.: Sage Publications, 1988.

Bromley, David G., and James T. Richardson, eds. *The Brainwashing-Deprogramming Controversy.* New York: The Edwin Mellen Press, 1983.

Browne, Donald R. *Radio Broadcasting: The Limits of the Limitless Medium.* New York: Praeger Publishers, 1982.

Buckman, John W. *The Church in the World of Radio-Television.* New York: Association Press, 1960.

Carter, Lewis. *Charisma and Control in Rajneeshpuram.* Cambridge: Cambridge University Press, 1990.

Crittenden, Ann. *Sanctuary: A Story of American Conscience and Law in Collision.* New York: Weidenfeld and Nicholson, 1968.

Devlin, Patrick. *The Enforcement of Morals.* New York: Oxford University Press, 1970.

Fore, William F. *Television and Religion.* Minneapolis, Minn.: Augsburg Publishing, 1987.

Hadden, Jeffrey K., and Charles E. Swann. *Prime Time Preachers*. Reading, Mass.: Addison-Wesley Publishing, 1981.

Hadden Jeffrey K., and Anson Shupe. *Televangelism: Power and Politics on God's Frontier*. New York: Henry Holt and Company, 1988.

Horsfield, Peter G. *Religious Television: The American Experience*. New York: Longman, 1984.

Kelley, Dean M., ed. *Government Intervention in Religious Affairs*. New York: Pilgrim Press, 1982.

_____, ed. *Government Intervention in Religious Affairs, II*. New York: Pilgrim Press, 1986.

_____. *Why Churches Should Not Pay Taxes*. New York: Harper and Row, 1977.

Mowrer, O. Hobart. *The Crises in Psychiatry and Religion*. Princeton: Van Nostrand Co., 1961.

Nichols, J. Bruce. *The Uneasy Alliance: Religion, Refugee Work, and U.S. Foreign Policy*. New York: Oxford University Press, 1988.

Noonan, John T. *The Believer and the Powers that Are: Cases, History, and Other Data Bearing on the Relationship of Religion and Government*. New York: The Macmillan Co., 1987.

Richardson, Herbert, ed. *Constitutional Issues in Case of Rev. Moon: Amicus Briefs Presented to the United States Supreme Court*. New York: Edwin Mellen Press, 1984.

Robbins, Thomas and Dick Anthony, eds. *In Gods We Trust: New Patterns of Religious Pluralism in America*. New Brunswick, N.J.: Transaction Publishers, 1990.

Robbins, Thomas, William C. Shepherd, and James McBride, eds. *Cults, Culture, and the Law: Perspectives on New Religious Movements*. Chico, Calif.: Scholars Press, 1985.

Robertson, D. B. *Should Churches Be Taxed?* Philadelphia: Westminster Press, 1968.

Schultze, Quentin J. ed. *American Evangelicals and the Mass Media.* Grand Rapids, Mich.: Zondervan, 1990.

Shepherd, William C. *To Secure the Blessings of Liberty: American Constitutional Law and the New Religious Movements.* Chico, Calif.: Scholars Press, 1985.

Sherwood, Carlton. *Inquisition: The Persecution and Prosecution of the Reverend Sun Myung Moon.* Washington, D.C.: Regnery Gateway, Inc., 1991.

Zaretsky, Irving I. and Marc P. Leone, eds. *Religious Movements in Contemporary America.* Princeton, N.J.: Princeton University Press, 1974.

CONTRIBUTORS

DOUGLAS F. ALLEN (A.B., Harvard; M.B.A., Columbia University Graduate School of Business; J.D., Columbia University School of Law) is an associate attorney of Reid and Priest in New York City. Special interests include trusts and estates practice, and exempt organizations.

DAVID G. BROMLEY is Professor of Sociology and Senior Project Director in the Survey Research Laboratory at Virginia Commonwealth University. His primary research interests are in the area of sociology of religion, social movements, and deviant behavior. He is author or editor of twelve books, including *Falling From the Faith: Causes and Consequences of Religious Apostasy; The Future of New Religious Movements; New Christian Politics;* and *The Anti-Cult Movement in America: A Bibliography and Historical Survey.*

ANGELA C. CARMELLA is Associate Professor of Law, Seton Hall Law School. A graduate of Princeton University, Harvard Law School, and Harvard Divinity School, she is a member of the Committee on Religious Liberty of the National Council of Churches and serves on the Editorial Council of *Journal of Church and State.*

DEREK DAVIS is Associate Director of the J.M. Dawson Institute of Church-State Studies and Assistant Professor of Political Science, Baylor University. He is also the Managing Editor of *Journal of Church and State.* An attorney, he is the author of *Original Intent: Chief Justice Rehnquist and the Course of American Church-State Relations* and is co-editor of *The Role of Religion in the Making of Public Policy* and the revised edition of *A Legal Deskbook for Administrators of Independent Colleges and Universities* (forthcoming).

DAVID L. GREGORY is Professor of Law, St. John's University School of Law. Areas of special interest and expertise include labor and employment law, religious discrimination, and civil rights. He is a frequent contributor to numerous law reviews and scholarly journals.

JEFFREY K. HADDEN is Professor of Sociology, University of Virginia. He is the author or editor of more than twenty-five books, including *The Gathering Storm in the Churches; Prime*

Time Preachers: The Rising Power of Televangelism;
Televangelism, Power and Politics on God's Frontier; and *The*
Politics of Religion and Social Changes. He is also a frequent
consultant to various prominent media and research
organizations on a variety of sociological issues.

ROBIN B. JOHANSEN is a partner and trial attorney with the
firm of Remcho, Johansen and Purcell, San Francisco,
California. A graduate of the University of Illinois and
Stanford Law School, she has been active in litigating a broad
range of legal controversies, including church-state and
religious liberty disputes. She is a member of the Editorial
Council of *Journal of Church and State,* a member of the
National Advisory Council of the J.M. Dawson Institute of
Church-State Studies, and, since 1984, a member of the
Committee on Religious Liberty of the National Council of
Churches.

KATHLEEN J. PURCELL is a partner and trial attorney with
the firm of Remcho, Johansen, and Purcell, San Francisco,
California. A graduate of Stanford University and Stanford
Law School, she is a world and Asian history teacher and
assistant campus minister at St. Ignatius College Preparatory.
She is currently responsible for developing a faith and justice
program for high school students at St. Ignatius College
Preparatory.

THOMAS ROBBINS, a research associate for the Santa
Barbara Centre for Humanistic Studies, received his degrees
from Harvard University and the University of North Carolina.
He is author of *Cults, Converts and Charisma* and is co-editor
of *Cults, Culture and the Law, Church-State Relations: Tensions*
and Transitions; and *In Gods We Trust: New Patterns of*
Religious Pluralism in America. Special interests include the
sociology of religion, church-state relations, and social and
religious movements.

SHARON W. VAINO, a New York City attorney, is a member
of the New York and District of Columbia bars. She has
received degrees from Barnard College and Fordham Law
School. She is a member of the Editorial Council of *Journal of*
Church and State, serves on the Committee on Religious
Liberty of the National Council of Churches, and is a member
of the National Advisory Council of Americans United for the
Separation of Church and State. Areas of special interest

include pension trusts, tax-exempt organizations, and government regulation of religious bodies.

STANLEY S. WEITHORN is a practicing attorney in Palo Alto, California, specializing in federal taxation. He has taught law as Special Professor at Hofstra University School of Law and as Adjunct Professor at the University of Miami School of Law. He is author of *Tax Techniques for Foundations and Other Exempt Organizations*, a seven-volume treatise that is widely used by tax professionals. He has been a consultant to Congress and the U.S. Treasury Department on tax legislation and U.S fiscal policy. He is counsel to numerous charitable, humanitarian, and philanthropic organizations, and has received distinguished service awards from the American Jewish Congress and the American Bar Association.

JAMES E. WOOD, JR. is Director of the J.M. Dawson Institute of Church-State Studies and is Ethel and Simon Bunn Professor of Church-State Studies, Baylor University. His publications include *Church and State in Scripture, History, and Constitutional Law* (coauthor); *Nationhood and the Kingdom; Religion and Politics; Religion, the State, and Education; Religion and the State; Readings on Church and State; The First Freedom: Religion and the Bill of Rights* and is coeditor of *The Role of Religion in the Making of Public Policy*. Founding editor of *Journal of Church and State*, he is the author of numerous essays in a variety of books and scholarly journals.

INDEX